THE BOYS ON THE BUS

Timothy Crouse

BALLANTINE BOOKS • NEW YORK

E
859
C76
1974

Grateful acknowledgment is made to the following for per mission to reprint previously published material:

Rowland Evans, Jr., and Robert Novak: For excerpts from five newsletters. Copyright © 1973 by the Evans-Novak Politi cal Report Company, and for excerpts from one column. Copy right © Publishers-Hall Syndicate.

International Famous Agency: For an excerpt from "Wil Ambition Spoil St. George?," by Richard Reeves, from New York magazine, May 8, 1972.

The Sterling Lord Agency, Inc.: For an excerpt from "Nixon," by Nicholas von Hoffman, New American Review #11. Copy right © 1971 by Nicholas von Hoffman.

The New York Times: For excerpts from "The McGovern Image," by James M. Naughton, July 31, 1972, and "Palm Springs Idyll: Agnew and His Pals," by James Wooten, October 10, 1972. Copyright © 1972 by The New York Times Company

Newsweek: For an excerpt from "McGovern's Politics of Righteousness," by Peter Goldman and Richard Stout, News week, November 6, 1972. Copyright Newsweek, Inc. © 1972 Newsweek and Richard Dougherty: For an excerpt from "My Turn: Richard Dougherty 'The Sneaky Bumbler,'" Newsweek January 8, 1973. Copyright Newsweek, Inc. © 1973.

Henry Regnery Company and Sterling Lord Agency: For an excerpt from pages 132-133 of Running A Nixon-McGovern Campaign Journal, by Bob Greene, published by Henry Regnery Company (Chicago). Copyright © 1973 by Bob Greene.

The Washington Post: For an excerpt from "The President's Shield," by David S. Broder, October 1, 1972. For an excerpt from "McGovern's Emotions Are Showing," by William Grei der, September 10, 1972. For an excerpt from "The McGovern Course," by William Greider, August 1, 1972. Copyright © 1972 by the Washington Post.

Photos courtesy of Stuart Bratesman, Owen Franken, Annie Leibovitz, Bob McNeely and Stanley Tretick.

ACKNOWLEDGMENTS

I WOULD LIKE TO ACKNOWLEDGE MY DEBT TO
Hunter Thompson, who talked Jann Wenner into letting me
write the *Rolling Stone* article from which this book grew
and who encouraged me from beginning to end.
I would also like to thank Donald Klopfer for
his encouragement and David Halberstam for his
critical advice. For their help and support I also
owe thanks to Suzanne Beves, Cordelia Jason,
Claire Nivola, Francie Barnard, Drea Rhodin,
Michael Wieloszynski, Mike Thompson, and,
of course, to the members of the press corps
who were generous enough to share their feelings,
thoughts and experiences with me.

I would especially like to acknowledge a debt
to Donald Kaul of the Des Moines *Register* for
his article on Evans and Novak, "The Real
Winners"; and to Stuart Loory for his article
in the Los Angeles *Times* on Clark Mollenhof.

To My Mother

CONTENTS

PART ONE

COVERING THE PRIMARIES AND CONVENTIONS

CHAPTER I

On the Bus

JUNE 1—five days before the California primary. A grey dawn was fighting its way through the orange curtains in the Wilshire Hyatt House Hotel in Los Angeles, where George McGovern was encamped with his wife, his staff, and the press assigned to cover his snowballing campaign.

While reporters still snored like Hessians in a hundred beds throughout the hotel, the McGovern munchkins were at work, plying the halls, slipping the long legal-sized handouts through the cracks under the door of each room. According to one of these handouts, the Baptist Ministers' Union of Oakland had decided after "prayerful and careful deliberation" to endorse Senator McGovern. And there was a detailed profile of Alameda County (". . . agricultural products include sweet corn, cucumbers, and lettuce"), across which the press would be dragged today—or was it tomorrow? Finally, there was the mimeographed schedule, the orders of the day.

At 6:45 the phone on the bed table rang, and a

sweet, chipper voice announced: "Good Morning, M
Crouse. It's six forty-five. The press bus leaves in fort
five minutes from the front of the hotel." She was u
there in Room 819, the Press Suite, calling up the do
ens of names on the press manifest, awaking the agen
of every great newspaper, wire service and network n
only of America but of the world. In response to h
calls, she was getting a shocking series of startled grunt
snarls and obscenities.

The media heavies were rolling over, stumbling to th
bathroom, and tripping over the handouts. Stooping
pick up the schedule, they read: *"8:00—8:15, Arriv
Roger Young Center, Breakfast with Ministers."* Su
denly, desperately, they thought: "Maybe I can pic
McGovern up in Burbank at nine fifty-five and sleep fc
another hour." Then, probably at almost the same i
stant, several score minds flashed the same guil
thought: "But maybe he will get shot at the minister
breakfast," and then each mind branched off into i
own private nightmare recollections of the correspon
ent who was taking a piss at Laurel when they shot Wa
lace, of the ABC cameraman who couldn't get his Bolc
to start as Bremer emptied his revolver. A hundrc
hands groped for the toothbrush.

It was lonely on these early mornings and often e
cruciatingly painful to tear oneself away from a bric
sodden spell of sleep. More painful for some than ot
ers. The press was consuming two hundred dollars
night worth of free cheap booze up there in the Pre
Suite, and some were consuming the lion's share. La
night it had taken six reporters to subdue a promine
radio correspondent who kept upsetting the portab
bar, knocking bottles and ice on the floor. The radioma
had the resiliency of a Rasputin—each time he was p
to bed, he would reappear to cause yet more bedla

And yet, at 7:15 Rasputin was there for the bagga
call, milling in the hall outside the Press Suite with fift
odd reporters. The first glance at all these fellow suffere
was deeply reassuring—they all felt the same pre

sures you felt, their problems were your problems. Together, they seemed to have the cohesiveness of an ant colony, but when you examined the scene more closely, each reporter appeared to be jitterbugging around in quest of the answer that would quell some private anxiety.

They were three deep at the main table in the Press Suite, badgering the McGovern people for a variety of assurances. "Will I have a room in San Francisco tonight?" "Are you sure I'm booked on the whistle-stop train?" "Have you seen my partner?"

The feverish atmosphere was halfway between a high school bus trip to Washington and a gambler's jet junket to Las Vegas, where small-time Mafiosi were lured into betting away their restaurants. There was giddy camaraderie mixed with fear and low-grade hysteria. To file a story late, or to make one glaring factual error, was to chance losing everything—one's job, one's expense account, one's drinking buddies, one's mad-dash existence, and the methedrine buzz that comes from knowing stories that the public would not know for hours and secrets that the public would never know. Therefore reporters channeled their gambling instincts into late-night poker games and private bets on the outcome of the elections. When it came to writing a story, they were as cautious as diamond-cutters.

It being Thursday, many reporters were knotting their stomachs over their Sunday pieces, which had to be filed that afternoon at the latest. They were inhaling their cigarettes with more of a vengeance, and patting themselves more distractedly to make sure they had their pens and notebooks. In the hall, a Secret Service agent was dispensing press tags for the baggage, along with string and scissors to attach them. From time to time, in the best Baden-Powell tradition, he courteously stepped forward to assist a drink-palsied journalist in the process of threading a tag.

The reporters often consulted their watches or asked for the time of departure. Among this crew, there was

one great phobia—the fear of getting left behind. Fres
troops had arrived today from the Humphrey Bu
which was the Russian Front of the California primar
and they had come bearing tales of horror. The Hum
phrey Bus had left half the press corps at the Biltmor
Hotel on Tuesday night; in Santa Barbara, the bus ha
deserted Richard Bergholz of the Los Angeles *Times*
and it had twice stranded George Shelton, the UPI man

"Jesus, am I glad I'm off the Humphrey Bus," sai
one reporter, as he siphoned some coffee out of th
McGovern samovar and helped himself to a McGover
sweet roll. "Shelton asked Humphrey's press office
Hackel, if there was time to file. Hackel said, 'Sure, th
candidate's gonna mingle and shake some hands.' Well
old Hubie couldn't find but six hands to shake, so the
got in the bus and took off and left the poor bastard in
phone booth right in the middle of Watts."

To the men whom duty had called to slog along at th
side of the Hump, the switch to the McGovern Bu
brought miraculous relief. "You gotta go see th
Hump's pressroom, just to see what disaster looks like,"
a reporter urged me. The Humphrey pressroom, a bunk
er-like affair in the bowels of the Beverly Hilton, con
tained three tables covered with white tablecloths, n
typewriters, no chairs, no bar, no food, one phone (wit
outside lines available only to registered guests), and n
reporters. The McGovern press suite, on the other hand
contained twelve typewriters, eight phones, a Xerox Tele
copier, a free bar, free cigarettes, free munchies, and
skeleton crew of three staffers. It was not only Rumo
Central, but also a miniature road version of Thoma
Cook and Son. As the new arrivals to the McGover
Bus quickly found out, the McGovern staff ran the kin
of guided tour that people pay great sums of money t
get carted around on. They booked reservations o
planes, trains and hotels; gave and received messages
and handled Secret Service accreditation with a fierc
Teutonic efficiency. And handed out reams of free infor

mation. On any given day, the table in the middle of the Press Suite was laden with at least a dozen fat piles of handouts, and the door was papered with pool reports.*

IT WAS JUST THESE WOMBLIKE CONDITIONS that gave rise to the notorious phenomenon called "pack journalism" (also known as "herd journalism" and "fuselage journalism"). A group of reporters were assigned to follow a single candidate for weeks or months at a time, like a pack of hounds sicked on a fox. Trapped on the same bus or plane, they ate, drank, gambled, and compared notes with the same bunch of colleagues week after week.

Actually, this group was as hierarchical as a chess set. The pack was divided into cliques—the national political reporters, who were constantly coming and going; the campaign reporters from the big, prestige papers and the ones from the small papers; the wire-service men; the network correspondents; and other configurations that formed according to age and old Washington friendships. The most experienced national political reporters, wire men, and big-paper reporters, who were at the top of the pecking order, often did not know the names of the men from the smaller papers, who were at

* Every day, a "pool" of one or two reporters was delegated to stay close to the candidate at those times (i.e., during motorcades, small dinners, fund-raising parties) when the entire press corps could not follow him. The regular reporters on the bus took turns filling the pool assignments. After each event, the pool wrote a report which was posted in the pressroom, and was usually also Xeroxed by the candidate's press staff and distributed on the bus. According to the rules, the pool reporters were not supposed to include in their own articles any information which they had not put in the pool report. The reports usually dealt in trivia—what the candidate ate, what he said, whose hands he had shaken. Pool reports varied in length. Jim Naughton of the *Times,* the most meticulous pooler on the bus, once turned in a report that went on for eight double-spaced pages. Dick Stout of *Newsweek* wrote the year's shortest report: "Oct. 30, 1972. 5 P.M. to bed. Nothing happened untoward. Details on request."

the bottom. But they all fed off the same pool report, the same daily handout, the same speech by the candidate; the whole pack was isolated in the same mobile village. After a while, they began to believe the same rumors, subscribe to the same theories, and write the same stories.

Everybody denounces pack journalism, including the men who form the pack. Any self-respecting journalist would sooner endorse incest than come out in favor of pack journalism. It is the classic villain of every campaign year. Many reporters and journalism professors blame it for everything that is shallow, obvious, meretricious, misleading, or dull in American campaign coverage.

On a muggy afternoon during the California primary campaign, I went to consult with Karl Fleming, a former political reporter and Los Angeles bureau chief for *Newsweek,* who was rumored to be a formidable critic of pack journalism. Fleming was beginning a whole new gig as editor of a fledgling semi-underground paper called *LA;* I found him in dungarees and shirtsleeves, sitting behind a desk that was covered with the makings of *LA*'s pilot issue.* He was a ruggedly built North Carolinian with the looks and accent to play Davy Crockett in a Disney remake. He was very busy putting his magazine together, taking phone calls, and giving instructions to one long-haired writer after another, but he seemed to enjoy letting off steam about political journalism. One of the reasons he quit *Newsweek* was that he got fed up riding around on campaign extravaganzas.

"I got so frustrated during the Nixon campaign in 1968," he grinned, "that I went to Ron Ziegler one day —we were flying some-goddam-where—and said, 'Ron, I come to you as a representative of the press corps to ask you this question.' I said, 'The question is, What does Nixon do upon the occasion of his semiannual erection?' Ziegler never cracked a goddam smile. Then I

---

* *LA* folded several months later.

said, 'The consensus is that he smuggles it to Tijuana.' "

Fleming leaned back in his chair and laughed hard.

"Gee," I said, "you must have been fucked after that."

"It doesn't make any difference if you're fucked or you're not fucked," said Fleming. "You delude yourself into thinking, 'Well, if I get on the bad side of these guys, then I'm not gonna get all that good stuff.' But pretty soon the realization hits that there *isn't* any good stuff, and there isn't gonna *be* any good stuff. Nobody's getting anything that you're not getting, and if they are it's just more of the same bullshit."

I told Fleming that I was puzzled as to why so many newspapers felt they needed to have correspondents aboard the press bus; a couple of wire-service guys and a camera crew should be able to cover a candidate's comings, goings, and official statements more than thoroughly.

"Papers that have enough money are not content to have merely the AP reports," said Fleming. "They want to have their own person in Washington because it means prestige for the paper and because in a curious way, it gives the editors a feeling of belonging to the club, too. I'll guarantee you that three fourths of the goddam stuff—the good stuff—that the Washington press corps reporters turn up never gets into print at all. The reason it's collected is because it's transmitted back to the editor, to the publisher, to the 'in' executive cliques on these newspapers and networks and newsmagazines. It's sent in confidential FYI memos or just over the phone. You give the publisher information that his business associates or his friends at the country club don't have; you're performing a very valuable function for him, and that, by God, is why you get paid.

"But while these papers want to have a guy there getting all the inside stuff, they don't want reporters who are ballsy enough and different enough to make any kind of trouble. It would worry the shit out of them if their Washington reporter happened to come up with a page-one story that was different from what the other guys were getting. And the first goddam thing that happens is they pick up the phone and call this guy and say, 'Hey, if this is such a hot story, how come AP or the Washington *Post* doesn't have it?' And the reporter's in big fuckin' trouble. The editors don't want scoops. Their abiding interest is making sure that nobody else has got anything that they don't have, not getting something that nobody else has.

"So eventually a very subtle kind of thing takes over and the reporter says to himself, 'All I gotta do to satisfy my editor and publisher is just get what the other guys are getting, so why should I bust my ass?' And over a period of a few years he joins the club. Now, most of these guys are honest, decent reporters who do the best job they can in this kind of atmosphere. The best reporters are the ones who sit around and talk about what assholes their editors and publishers are, and that still happens, thank God, with a great amount of frequency, even at the high levels of the Washington press corps.

"All the same, any troublemaking reporter who walks into a press conference and asks a really mean snotty question which is going to make the candidate and his people really angry is going to be treated like a goddam pariah. 'Cause these guys in this club, they don't want any troublemakers stirring up the waters, which means they might have to dig for something that's not coming down out of the daily handout, or coming in from the daily pool report about what went on. They'd rather sit around the pressroom at the hotel every night, drinking booze and playing poker."

Fleming said that in June, and as I followed the press through the next five months of the campaign, I discovered that some of his accusations checked out, but others did not. Almost everything he said held true for the White House press corps,* but his charges did not al-

---

* It applied best to the White House reporters in the Johnson years, many of whom knew all about Johnson's growing isolation and loosening grip on reality, but wrote nothing about it. In 1967,

ways apply to the men who covered the Democratic candidates in 1972. It was true that some editors were still reluctant to run a story by their own man until the wire services had confirmed it. It was true that newsmagazine reporters and network correspondents occasionally leaked part of a hot story to *The New York Times* or *The Wall Street Journal;* after the story had gained respectability by appearing in one of these major establishment organs, the correspondent would write the whole story for his own organization. And it was impossible to tell how often the reporters censored themselves in anticipation of some imaginary showdown with a cautious editor, preferring to play it safe and go along with whatever the rest of the pack was writing.

But things had also begun to change since Fleming's campaign stories in 1968. The men on the bus had more authority and independence than ever before, and many of them were searching for new ways to report on the freakish, insular existence of the press bus, and for ways to break away from the pack. Very few of them filed any confidential memos to their superiors, or phoned in any inside information, except to suggest that such information might be worked up into a story.

Take, for example, the case of Curtis Wilkie, a young reporter for the Wilmington, Delaware *News-Journal* whom I met for the first time on the morning of June 1. I walked out of the lobby of the Wilshire Hyatt House, past all the black Nauga-hide furniture, and stepped into

David Halberstam met a China expert in Hong Kong who recounted several fascinating anecdotes about Johnson's increasing lack of control. When Halberstam asked about the source of the stories, the China expert said that he had heard the anecdotes from three top White House correspondents who had recently been in Hong Kong during one of Johnson's trips to Asia. "The White House guys were talking about these things and they were concerned, but they weren't writing about them," says Halberstam. "Because that's a hell of a story to have to write, saying the President of the United States is isolated from reality. They'd have a goddam crazy, angry President the next day."

They were, however, passing on these anecdotes to the executives on their papers.

the first of the two silver buses that were waiting at the curb. It was the kind of bus to which most bus-fanciers would give three stars—the windows were tinted and there was a toilet in the rear, but the seats did not recline. The time was 7:30 A.M. and two-thirds of the seats were already filled with silent and bleary-eyed reporters who looked as cheerful as a Georgia chain gang on its way to a new roadbed. Most of them were sending out powerful "No Trespassing" vibes. My company was in no great demand, word having gotten around that I was researching an article on the press. Reporters snapped their notebooks shut when I drew near. The night before, Harry Kelly, a tall, hard-eyed Irishman from the Hearst papers, had looked at me over his shoulder and muttered, "Goddam gossip columnist."

I finally sat down next to a thirtyish dark-haired reporter wearing a Palm Beach suit and a drooping moustache, who looked too hungover to object to my presence. After a long silence, he spoke up in a twangy Southern accent and introduced himself as Curtis Wilkie. He was from Mississippi and had been a senior at Ole Miss in 1964 when General Walker led his famous charge on the administration building. After graduating, Wilkie had put in seven years as a reporter on the Clarksdale, Mississippi *Register* (circ. 7,000), and, as I later found out, had won a slew of journalism prizes. In 1968, he had gone to the Chicago Convention as a member of the "loyalist" Mississippi delegation and had cast his vote for Eugene McCarthy. Soon after that, he won a Congressional fellowship and worked for Walter Mondale in the Senate and John Brademas in the House. In 1971, the Wilmington paper hired him as its main political writer; they got their money's worth, for he wrote two separate 750-word articles every day, a "hard" news story for the morning *News* and a "soft" feature story for the afternoon *Journal*.

"Last night, I filed a story unconditionally predicting that the Hump's gonna get rubbed out in the primary," he said. Now he was worried that his editors might ob-

ject to so firm a stand, or that Humphrey, through som
terrible accident, might win. As if to reassure himsel
Wilkie kept telling funny, mordant stories about th
last-ditch hysterics of the Humphrey campaign.

Wilkie had experienced a few bad moments over
Humphrey story once before. During the Pennsylvani
primary, Humphrey unwisely decided to hold a studen
rally at the University of Pennsylvania. The studen
booed and heckled, calling Humphrey "America's Num
ber 2 War Criminal," until Humphrey, close to tear
was forced to retreat from the stage. Wilkie filed a lon
story describing the incident and concluding that Hum
phrey was so unpopular with students that he could n
longer speak on a college campus.

There were no TV cameramen at the rally, and of th
fifteen reporters who covered the speech, only one be
side Wilkie filed a detailed account of the heckling. Th
next day, when Wilkie went into the office, the manag
ing editor was laughing about the story. "We've kind
started wondering," he teased Wilkie. "Several peopl
have called and said that they didn't see anything abou
Humphrey on Channel Six, and they seem to think yo
made it up. And we're beginning to wonder ourselve
because none of the wire services mentioned it." Wilki
began to sweat; he nearly convinced himself that he ha
grossly exaggerated the incident. Late that afternoor
Wilkie came across a piece by Phil Potter, a veteran re
porter for the Baltimore *Sun*. Potter's version of the ir
cident agreed with Wilkie's. With great relief, Cu
clipped the article and showed it to the managing edito

For months afterward, Wilkie felt slightly qualmis
whenever he thought about the Humphrey story. "The
sort of put me on notice that somebody was carefull
reading my stuff, that time," he said after the electio
"It may have inhibited me, I don't know." But it didn
drive him back to the safety of the pack. He continue
to trust his own judgment and write about whatever h
himself thought was important. In October, when he wa
one of the few reporters to file a full account of an ug

Nixon rally where the President smiled at the sight of demonstrators being beaten up, the paper printed his articles without questioning them. "After a while," he said, "the guys on my desk began to have enough faith in me that they would accept anything I gave them regardless of what their wire services were telling them. They may have wondered a couple of times, but that didn't prevent them from running it."

What made this all the more remarkable was that the *News-Journal* was owned by the arch-conservative Du-Pont family,* and had long been famous for resisting news stories that gave any comfort to liberals. Ben Bagdikian, in his book *The Effete Conspiracy,* had used the *News-Journal* as a case study in biased journalism. According to Bagdikian, one of the owners had once even "complained bitterly to the editors that the paper's reporter had written a conventional news account of a Democratic rally when he should have turned it into a pro-Republican essay."† In the late sixties, however, stronger editors had taken over, and in the fall of 1972 they decided not to endorse either Nixon or McGovern, much to the displeasure of the DuPonts. The DuPonts' dissenting editorial, which exhorted readers to vote for every Republican on the ballot, was relegated to the letters column under the coy heading "A View from the Top." Wilkie was assigned to write a story about the rift. Interviewing the DuPonts, he asked whether a proposed merger pending before the SEC had anything to do with their endorsement of Nixon. Only a few years before, such impertinence would have been unthinkable.**

---

* Most American newspapers—at least 85 percent—are owned by conservative Republicans and regularly endorse Republican candidates. The greatest cross that these owners have to bear is that most reporters are Democrats.

† *The Effete Conspiracy* by Ben H. Bagdikian (New York, Harper & Row, 1972) p. 75.

** On the other hand, take the case of Hamilton Davis, the political reporter and Washington Bureau chief of the Providence *Journal,* who was also on the McGovern bus that day. In January 1972, Davis was given a weekly column. As the year went on the column got increasingly ballsy. Davis took well-aimed shots at both

But one should not make too much of Curt Wilkie
d the *News-Journal*. There were still lazy men on the
s, and men with large families to feed or powerful
ibitions to nurture, who feared losing their jobs and
us played it safe by sticking with the pack. And there
re still editors whose suspicions of any unusual story
ade pack journalism look cozy and inviting to their re-
rters. Campaign journalism is, by definition, pack
urnalism; to follow a candidate, you must join a pack
other reporters; even the most independent journalist
nnot completely escape the pressures of the pack.

OUND 8:15 A.M. ON JUNE 1 the buses rolled past the
cco housefronts of lower-middle-class Los Angeles
d pulled up in front of a plain brick building that
ked like a school. The press trooped down a little al-
 and into the back of the Grand Ballroom of the Rog-
Young Center. The scene resembled Bingo Night in a
uth Dakota parish hall—hundreds of middle-aged
ople sitting at long rectangular tables. They were
tching George McGovern, who was speaking from
 stage. The press, at the back of the room, started fill-
 up on free Danish pastry, orange juice and coffee.
tomatically, they pulled out their notebooks and
ote something down, even though McGovern was say-
 nothing new. They leaned sloppily against the wall
 slumped in folding chairs.

McGovern ended his speech and the Secret Service
n began to wedge him through the crush of ministers
d old ladies who wanted to shake his hand. By the
ie he had made it to the little alley which was the only
ute of escape from the building, three cameras had set

national candidates and the Rhode Island candidates. He was
ally critical of both of Rhode Island's Senatorial candidates, Sen.
iborne Pell and the Republican challenger, John H. Chafee.
ly one problem. The Chafee family owned a hunk of the paper.
vis was abruptly informed that the paper's policy was that no
orter should write a column. Davis thought it very strange that
owners had taken eleven months to remember this policy.

up an ambush. This was the only "photo opportunit
as it is called, that the TV people would have all mo
ing. Except in dire emergencies, all TV film has to
taken before noon, so that it can be processed and tra
mitted to New York. Consequently, the TV people
the only reporters who are not asleep on their feet in
morning. Few TV correspondents ever join the w
hour poker games or drinking. Connie Chung, the pr
Chinese CBS correspondent, occupied the room next
mine at the Hyatt House and she was always back
midnight, reciting a final sixty-second radio spot into
Sony or absorbing one last press release before gettin
good night's sleep. So here she was this morning, bri
and alert, sticking a mike into McGovern's face and a
ing him something about black ministers. The pr
reporters stood around and watched, just in case M
Govern should say something interesting. Finally M
Govern excused himself and everybody ran for the b

8:20–8:50 A.M.	En Route/Motorcade
8:50–9:30 A.M.	Taping—"Newsmakers"
	CBS-TV 6121 Sunset Boulevare
	Hollywood
9:30–9:55 A.M.	En Route/Motorcade
9:55–10:30 A.M.	Taping—"News Conference"
	NBC-TV 3000 West Alameda A
	Burbank
10:30–10:50 A.M.	Press filing
10:50–Noon	En Route/Motorcade
Noon–1:00 P.M.	Senior Citizens Lunch and Ra
	Bixby Park—Band Shell
	Long Beach
1:00–1:15 P.M.	Press filing

The reporters began to wake up as they walked i
the chilly Studio 22 at CBS. There was a bank of t
phones, hastily hooked up on a large worktable in
middle of the studio, and six or seven reporters m
credit card calls to bureau chiefs and home offices. D

tout of *Newsweek* found out he had to file a long story
nd couldn't go to San Francisco later in the day. Steve
erstel phoned in his day's schedule to UPI. Connie
hung dictated a few salient quotes from McGovern's
reakfast speech to CBS Radio.

A loudspeaker announced that the interview was
bout to begin, so the reporters sat down on the folding
hairs that were clustered around a monitor. They didn't
ke having to get their news secondhand from TV, but
ey did enjoy being able to talk back to McGovern
ithout his hearing them. As the program started, sever-
l reporters turned on cassette recorders. A local news-
aster led off by accusing McGovern of using a slick
edia campaign.

"Well, I think the documentary on my life is very well
one," McGovern answered ingenuously. The press
ared with laughter. Suddenly the screen of the monitor
ent blank—the video tape had broken. The press start-
d to grumble.

"Are they gonna change that first question and make
a toughie?" asked Martin Nolan, the Boston *Globe*'s
ational political reporter. "If not, I'm gonna wait on
e bus." Nolan, a witty man in his middle thirties, had
e unshaven, slack-jawed, nuts-to-you-too look of a
artender in a sailors' café. He grew up in Dorchester, a
oor section of Boston, and he asked his first tough po-
tical question at the age of twelve. "Sister, how do you
now Dean Acheson's a Communist?" he had chal-
enged a reactionary nun in his parochial school, and the
eprimand he received hadn't daunted him from asking
viseacre questions ever since.

The video tape was repaired and the program began
gain. The interviewer asked McGovern the same first
uestion, but Nolan stayed anyway. Like the others, No-
n had sat through hundreds of press conferences hold-
g in an irrepressible desire to heckle. Now was the big
hance and everyone took it.

"Who are your heroes?" the newscaster asked Mc-
overn.

"General Patton!" shouted Jim Naughton of t
Times.

"Thomas Jefferson and Abraham Lincoln," sa
McGovern.

"What do you think of the death penalty?" asked t
newscaster.

"I'm against the death penalty." There was a lo
pause. "That is my judgment," McGovern said, a
lapsed into a heavy, terminal silence. The press laughe
at McGovern's discomfiture.

By the time the interview was over, the press was in
good mood. As they filed back onto the buses, the no
mal configurations began to form: wire service reporte
and TV cameramen in the front, where they could g
out fast; small-town daily and big-city daily reporters
the middle seats, hard at work; McGovern staffers
the rear seats, going over plans and chatting. Dick Sto
and Jim Naughton held their tape recorders to the
ears, like transistor junkies, and culled the best quot
from the TV interview to write in their notebooks. L
Dombrowski of the Chicago *Tribune,* who looked like
hulking Maf padrone, typed his Sunday story on t
portable Olympia in his lap. The reporters working f
morning newspapers would have to begin to write soo
and they were looking over the handouts and their not
for something to write about.

So it went. They went on to another interview in a
other chilly studio, at NBC. This time the reporters s
in the same studio as McGovern and the interviewer,
there was no laughter, only silent note-taking. After t
interview there were phones and typewriters in anoth
room, courtesy of the network. Only a few men us
them. Then to Bixby Park for a dull speech to old pe
ple and a McGovern-provided box lunch of tiny, ru
bery chicken parts. Another filing facility, this one in
dank little dressing room in back of the Bixby Pa
band shell. While McGovern droned on about senior c
izens, about fifteen reporters used the bank of twel

phones that the McGovern press people had ordered Pacific Telephone to install.

At every stop there was a phone bank, but the reporters never rushed for the phones and fought over them as they do in the movies. Most of them worked for morning papers and didn't have to worry about dictating their stories over the phone until around 6 P.M. (Eastern Standard Time).* Earlier in the day they just called their editors to map out a story, or called a source to check a fact, or sometimes they called in part of a story, with the first paragraph (the "lead") to follow at the last moment. There was only one type of reporter who dashed for the phones at almost every stop and called in bulletins about almost everything that happened on the schedule. That was the wire service reporter.

IF YOU LIVE IN NEW YORK OR LOS ANGELES, you have probably never heard of Walter Mears and Carl Leubsdorf, who were covering McGovern for the Associated Press, or Steve Gerstel, who covered him for the United Press International. But if your home is Sheboygan or Aspen, and you read the local papers, they are probably the only political journalists you know. There are about 1,700 newspapers in the U.S., and every one of them has an AP machine or UPI machine or both whirling and clattering and ringing in some corner of the city room, coughing up stories all through the day. Most of these papers do not have their own political reporters,

---

* The reporters who worked for afternoon papers, such as the Washington *Star*, the Philadelphia *Bulletin*, or the Boston *Evening Globe*, had a much rougher schedule. Their deadline was between six and eight in the morning, and they usually wrote their stories late at night, when everyone else was having supper or drinking. Having gone to bed late, they then had to be up to inspect the first handouts and to cover the first event, just in case there was something important to file in the last few minutes before their papers went to bed. If a reporter from a morning paper missed an early morning event, he had the rest of the day to catch up on it.

and they depend on the wire-service men for all of the national political coverage. Even at newspapers tha have large political staffs, the wire-service story almos always arrives first.

So the wire services are influential beyond calcula tion. Even at the best newspapers, the editor alway gauges his own reporters' stories against the expectation that the wire stories have aroused. The only trouble i that wire stories are usually bland, dry, and overly cau tious. There is an inverse proportion between the num ber of persons a reporter reaches and the amount he ca say. The larger the audience, the more inoffensive an inconclusive the article must be. Many of the wire me are repositories of information they can never convey Pye Chamberlyne, a young UPI radio reporter with a untamable wiry moustache, emerged over drinks as a expert on the Dark Side of Congress. He could tell yo about a prominent Senator's battle to overcome his add iction to speed, or about Humphrey's habit of poppin twenty-five One-A-Day Vitamins with a shot of bourbo when he needed some fast energy. But Pye couldn't te his audience.

In 1972, the Dean of the political wire-service report ers was Walter Mears of the AP, a youngish man wit sharp pale green eyes who smoked cigarillos and had nervous habit of picking his teeth with a matchboo cover. With his clean-cut brown hair and his conserva tive sports clothes he could pass for a successful go pro, or maybe a baseball player. He started his caree with the AP in 1955 covering auto accidents in Bostor and he worked his way up the hard way, by getting hi stories in fast and his facts straight every time. He didn go in for the New Journalism. "The problem with a lo of the new guys is they don't get the formula stu drilled into them," he told me as he scanned the morn ing paper in Miami Beach. "I'm an old fart. If you don learn how to write an eight-car fatal on Route 128 you're gonna be in big trouble."

About ten years ago, Mears' house in Washingto

burned down. His wife and children died in the fire. As therapy, Mears began to put in slavish eighteen-hour days for the AP. In a job where sheer industry counts above all else, Mears worked harder than any other two reporters, and he got to the top.

"At what he does, Mears is the best in the goddam world," said a colleague who writes very non-AP features. "He can get out a coherent story with the right point on top in a minute and thirty seconds, left-handed. It's like a parlor trick, but that's what he wants to do and he does it. In the end, Walter Mears can only be tested on one thing, and that is whether he has the right lead. He almost always does. He watches some goddam event for a half hour and he understands the most important thing that happened—that happened in public, I mean. He's just like a TV camera, he doesn't see things any special way. But he's probably one of the most influential political reporters in the world, just because his stuff reaches more people than anyone else's."

Mears' way with a lead made him a leader of the pack. Covering the second California debate between McGovern and Humphrey on May 30, Mears worked with about thirty other reporters in a large, warehouse-like press room that NBC had furnished with tables, typewriters, paper and phones. The debate was broadcast live from an adjacent studio, where most of the press watched it. For the reporters who didn't have to file immediately, it was something of a social event. But Mears sat tensely in the front of the press room, puffing at a Tiparillo and staring up at a gigantic monitor like a man waiting for a horse race to begin. As soon as the program started, he began typing like a madman, "taking transcript" in shorthand form and inserting descriptive phrases every four or five lines: HUMPHREY STARTED IN A LOW KEY, or MCGOV LOOKS A BIT STRAINED.

The entire room was erupting with clattering typewriters, but Mears stood out as the resident dervish. His cigar slowed him down, so he threw it away. It was hot, but he had no time to take off his blue jacket. After the

first three minutes, he turned to the phone at his elbow
and called the AP bureau in L.A. "He's phoning in
lead based on the first statements so they can send out a
bulletin," explained Carl Leubsdorf, the No. 2 AP man
who was sitting behind Mears and taking back-up notes.
After a minute on the phone Mears went back to typing
and didn't stop for a solid hour. At the end of the debate he jumped up, picked up the phone, looked hard at
Leubsdorf, and mumbled, "How can they stop? They
didn't come to a lead yet."

Two other reporters, one from New York, another
from Chicago, headed toward Mears shouting, "Lead?
Lead?" Marty Nolan came at him from another direction. "Walter, Walter, what's our lead?" he said.

Mears was wildly scanning his transcript. "I did a
Wallace lead the first time," he said. (McGovern and
Humphrey had agreed near the start of the show that
neither of them would accept George Wallace as a Vice
President.) "I'll have to do it again." There were solid
technical reasons for Mears' computer-speed decision to
go with the Wallace lead: it meant he could get both
Humphrey and McGovern into the first paragraph, both
stating a position that they hadn't flatly declared before
then. But nobody asked for explanations.

"Yeah," said Nolan, turning back to his Royal. "Wallace. I guess that's it."

Meanwhile, in an adjacent building, *The New York
Times* team had been working around a long oak desk
in an NBC conference room. The *Times* had an editor
from the Washington Bureau, Robert Phelps, and three
rotating reporters watching the debate in the conference
room and writing the story; a secretary phoned it in
from an office down the hall. The *Times* team filed a
lead saying that Humphrey had apologized for having
called McGovern a "fool" earlier in the campaign. Soon
after they filed the story, an editor phoned from New
York. The AP had gone with a Wallace lead, he said.
Why hadn't they?

Marty Nolan eventually decided against the Wallace

lead, but NBC and CBS went with it on their news shows. So did many of the men in the room. They wanted to avoid "call-backs"—phone calls from their editors asking them why they had deviated from the AP or UPI. If the editors were going to run a story that differed from the story in the nation's 1,700 other newspapers, they wanted a good reason for it. Most reporters dreaded call-backs. Thus the pack followed the wire-service men whenever possible. Nobody made a secret of running with the wires; it was an accepted practice. At an event later in the campaign, a New York *Daily News* reporter looked over the shoulder of Norm Kempster, a UPI man, and read his copy.

"Stick with that lead, Norm," said the man from the *News.* "You'll save us a lot of trouble."

"Don't worry," said Norm. "I don't think you'll have any trouble from mine."

2:00–2:45 P.M.	*Fullerton Junior College*
	321 East Chapman, Fullerton
2:45–3:00 P.M.	*Press filing*
3:00–3:30 P.M.	*En Route/Motorcade*
3:30–340 P.M.	*Load Aircraft*
3:40 P.M.	*Depart Orange County Community Airport*
4:45 P.M.	*Arrive Oakland, California*
5:00–5:40 P.M.	*En Route/Motorcade*
5:40–6:45 P.M.	*Private dinner*
6:45–7:30 P.M.	*Rest—San Francisco Hilton*
7:30–8:30 P.M.	*En Route/Motorcade*
8:30–9:15 P.M.	*McGovern for President Rally St. James Park, San Jose*
9:15–10:00 P.M.	*En Route/Motorcade*
10:00–10:45 P.M.	*Private meeting*
10:45–11:15 P.M.	*En Route/Motorcade*
11:15 P.M.	*Arrive San Francisco Hilton*

At Bixby Park, Walter Cronkite showed up and rode on the press bus to Fullerton Junior College. Most of the reporters were quite dazzled and wanted to know why Cronkite was around. "He wants to be one of the guys and to get a feel for something outside Moscow," Connie Chung explained. Fred Dutton, Gary Hart and Bill Dougherty of the McGovern staff had joined the bus too. They were singing football songs and hymns in the back seats. In fact, things were getting chummy as hell. Shirley MacLaine was sitting in Marty Nolan's lap. Gary Hart was cracking up with the men from *The New York Times* and *Newsweek*. Bill Dougherty was chatting with David Schoumacher of CBS.

"I'd like to lock up the candidate," Dougherty confided.

"Like to take the vote right now, huh?" said Schoumacher.

Fullerton Junior College looked like a large complex of parking garages. The sweltering gym was packed with kids who treated McGovern as if he were Bobby Kennedy. The cameramen surrounded McGovern as he fought his way to the platform and the kids tried to push through the cameramen. The heat and commotion energized reporters as they squatted around the platform. When McGovern began to speak, they made frantic notes, although he said nothing new. Gradually they wound down.

"If there is one lesson it is . . ." said McGovern.

Carl Leubsdorf put up his finger. "I know what it is," he said to Elizabeth Drew of PBS. "Never again."

"It is that never again . . ." said George.

By the end of the speech no one was taking notes. As deadlines began to loom for the big-city daily reporters, the early afternoon euphoria began to give way to grumpy sobriety. Walter Cronkite went back to Los Angeles because his back was bothering him and he needed to rest. The rest of the press flew to Oakland.

The schedule began to go to hell. Instead of going to San Francisco, the bus took the press to an airport hotel called the Oakland Inn, where McGovern was going to have a hastily scheduled press conference with some black ministers. The press went to a small function room in the motel that had phony wood paneling on the walls and gold vinyl chairs. While reporters began to munch at the Danish lying on a small table at the rear, or worked at the five typewriters on a large table pushed up against a side wall, the cameramen set up in the front. Soon there was an outcry from the print press. "Do *you* want to go to a press conference where we stand behind the cameras?" James Doyle of the Washington *Star* asked Adam Clymer of the Baltimore *Sun*.

Doyle found Kirby Jones, McGovern's press secretary, and chewed him out. Jones made some excuses.

"Yeah," said Doyle, "but you're *never* organized at these press conferences."

Jones shrugged and walked away.

The press had to sit behind the cameras for the press conference, which was short and dull. As the reporters were getting up to stretch, Kirby Jones and Gordon Weil, another McGovern aide, began to pass the word that the Field Poll results were out: McGovern was twenty points ahead.

It was the only hard news of the day. Harry Kelly of Hearst, Steve Gerstel of UPI, and James Doyle all headed for the typewriters and began to hunt-and-peck. Pye Chamberlyne, Curt Wilkie, and about twenty other reporters headed for the four pay phones in the hall outside the function room. People were getting testy. Carl Leubsdorf of the AP leaned over Jim Doyle's shoulder, took a good look at Doyle's lead and then asked, "Hey, can I see?"

Doyle looked up and registered what was happening. "Jesus, no!" he exploded. "Fuck you! Get outa here!"

A few moments later Steve Gerstel sauntered over to Doyle and said, "Let me see your lead, Jim."

"You might as well," Doyle said unhappily. "The AP just catched it."

Leubsdorf walked by again on his way to the phones and patted Doyle on the back. "I like it," he said, and chuckled.

An hour went by, and everybody got a chance to file on the Field Poll. The scene began to look like a bad cocktail party. Haynes Johnson of the Washington *Post,* Elizabeth Drew of PBS, and Jules Witcover of the Los Angeles *Times* were doing Humphrey imitations. Kirby Jones was trying to get nine people to go in the helicopter to San Jose as "pool" reporters—that is, to write a report for all the reporters who could not fit in the chopper. The San Jose rally promised to be McGovern's major lunge for the Bobby Kennedy Chicano constituency, but no one wanted to go. San Francisco lay ahead, and it was a great restaurant town. Finally Jim Naughton, Marty Nolan, and a couple of camera crews signed up.

At 7:00, Kirby Jones announced another press conference—McGovern would read a statement on Nixon's Moscow trip. At 7:30, Jones announced that *he* would read the statement. There was a general groan. Kirby launched into a predictable text. "Stop the presses," said Haynes Johnson, shutting his notebook.

The campaign day was drawing to a dreary close. Had all the events taken place in a single room, the reporters would have been climbing the walls with boredom by mid-afternoon. It was the bus rides and plane flights, the sense that a small army was being efficiently deployed, that had given the day its pace, variety, and excitement. Yet the reporters seldom wrote about this traveling around, which was so important in forming their gut feelings about the campaign. The day had yielded its one easy story: McGovern was leading Humphrey by twenty points in the Field Poll. This statistic sounded somehow *right* to the reporters, for it jibed with their half-digested notion that the McGovern campaign was a juggernaut about to flatten Hubert Humphrey. And where had this notion come from? "They partly got it from the slickness of the McGovern press operation," said a reporter who was covering Humphrey in California. "When a reporter got to his room at night his bag was there. When he called the pressroom, he didn't get a yo-yo saying there was nobody there. He got handouts telling him where the candidate was going to be the next morning and who he could interview at 2 A.M. if he needed to get a fast quote. And so pretty soon the reporter started saying to himself, half-consciously, 'If the press operation is this good, they must have a helluva voter registration operation!' The press didn't create the McGovern juggernaut, but they sure as hell *helped* create it."

On June 1, a normal campaign day, the reporters had gained no fresh insights into George McGovern; they had not gone out of their way to look for any. They had not tried to find out whether the large sums of money that were suddenly pouring into the campaign coffers had changed the candidate; or whether the prospect of the nomination, now so close at hand, was tempting him to bend on some of his more controversial stands; whether, as some of his detractors charged, he had a ruthless streak to match Bobby Kennedy's. "We spent tons of ink on that guy," one of the reporters later lamented, "and I'd be willing to bet that on the night he got the nomination we hadn't told anybody in the United States who the hell we were talking about, what kind of man he was."

CHAPTER II
Coming to Power

FOR THE men following the primary campaigns in 1972, and later the general election campaigns, such as they were, campaigning was no longer the easy ride it had once been. Campaign coverage began to settle into a neat and comfortable science around the time of Theodore Roosevelt, the first big-time American politician to rationalize the handing out of news. Stepping into the White House over McKinley's dead body, Roosevelt had given the Washington correspondents a White House pressroom for the first time; installed phones for them; held occasional news conferences in the Oval Office while his barber gave him a late afternoon shave; frequently leaked items to his favorite reporters; and had given out what were the first primitive campaign press schedules.

"He made our work tons lighter," wrote a beholden reporter aboard Teddy's campaign train in 1904. "Whenever he returned to the car after a speech he would round us up and say, 'Now, the next stop will be

Bankville. You don't have to bother about that; I'm going to get off the usual thing.' Or, 'At Dashtown, where we stop next, you'd better be on the job. I'll have some new stuff there.' Sometimes he would even tell us in the rough what the new stuff was to be . . . In this way he not only saved us useless physical and mental work, but economized our time and systematized our schedules. It also aided the editors at home to plan out their work without uncertainty . . ."

From Teddy Roosevelt's time until 1956, when Stevenson began taking large jumps around the country by airplane, candidates campaigned by train. For fifty years, the routine hardly changed. In the post-Depression era, the thirty or forty reporters would pile out at each whistle stop, wearing fedoras, carrying notebooks and pencils, and when the high school band had blared its last sour note, and the candidate had stepped out onto the rear platform, they would stand on the tracks making notes and counting the crowd. When the speech was done, the train's whistle would blow, and the reporters would clamber back into their fetid press car—the aroma was a compound of cigar smoke, whiskey and the stench of men who had not bathed for five or six days. The smell sometimes became so rank that porters burned incense in the Pullmans.

The press car was a Pullman car whose seats had been ripped out and replaced with two boards which ran the length of the car on either side. The men sat at these long tables, looking out at the passing countryside, and wrote their stories on bulky typewriters. The stories contained three simple elements: what the candidate had said, the size of the crowd, and the weather. (In their Sunday stories, the men would usually try to assess the candidate's chances, or report what hastily interviewed local politicians thought of the candidate's chances.) Then they would give the stories to the Western Union man. He would tie the stories up in a bundle and toss them off at the next small station, whence the telegrapher would transmit them to the reporters' home offices.

There is a story, perhaps apocryphal, that Merriman Smith of the UPI, anxious to file a story before coming to the next station, tied pillows around his number-two man and tossed him off a moving train.

After filing, they would repair to the dining car for lunch or dinner—Rocky Ford melon and fresh mountain trout if they had just passed through Denver, and Dungeness crab if they had made a stop in San Francisco. Traveling on Presidential trains, they ate with the Secret Service men, and since these Secret Service men were husky fellows and had a food allowance of only six dollars a day, the reporters would often treat them to sirloin steak.

As for the candidate, he was usually accessible for news conferences or informal chats throughout the trip. Truman even played poker with the boys; one of them, Joe Short of the Baltimore *Sun,* lost four hundred dollars to the President in one afternoon and had to make it up by padding his expense account for the next few months. "We liked Harry Truman very much," an old timer, Edward T. Folliard, recalled, twenty-four years later. "Of course we felt sorry for him. Poor son of a bitch. We knew he was going to lose."

"It was all very friendly and romantic," said Folliard. Once the Washington *Post*'s chief campaign reporter, he was now seventy-four and lived in retirement in suburban Washington. A tall, skinny man with black hair and the face of a Norman Rockwell farmer, he covered his first campaign when he was twenty-eight—the Herbert Hoover–Al Smith contest of 1928.

Folliard remembered his colleagues as hard-working men who wrote objective, unbiased stories. "I think 95 percent of the men wrote what they heard and saw and damn little what they thought," he said. "They left that to the editorial writers." Folliard was proud of that objectivity. Yet other observers had a different view of that era of campaign reporting. They saw the reporters of the thirties, forties and fifties as poorly educated men, drawn from the ranks of police reporters and sportswrit-

ers, who had neither the intellectual curiosity nor equip
ment to dig below the shimmering surface of the cam
paign.

In 1937, Leo C. Rosten did a scholarly survey of th
127 main Washington correspondents and found tha
only half of them had finished college. Eight did no
have a high school diploma and two had no high schoo
education at all. Rosten concluded that "men without
'frame of reference' and with an uncontrolled impres
sionistic (rather than analytic) approach to issues ar
driven to a surface interpretation of events."

They are oriented [Rosten continued] with reference t
normative words of ambiguous content: "liberty," "Ameri
canism," "justice," "democracy," "socialism," "commu
nism," . . . Newspaper men evidence a marked insecurit
in the presence of social theories or political conceptuali
zation. In this light the caustic reportorial reaction t
"New Deal professors," "crackpot theories," "the Brai
Trust," "Frankfurter's bright young men" soon suggests th
projection of doubts of personal adequacy upon men wh
have unwittingly increased personal and professional inse
curities.*

But most of these men were not overly worried by th
fact that they lacked a diploma. Some simply sent hom
the kind of news which they knew would please thei
publishers. The rest were secure in the knowledge tha
they were not paid to think, analyze, or judge. With fev
exceptions, these reporters were interchangeable drone
who wrote the same simple formula stories day afte
day.

When these men began to retire, in the fifties, the
were replaced by a new generation of young reporter
who had gone to college and were asking different kind
of questions. In those days the younger men wrote th
same formulaic stories, but at the same time, they wer
more comfortable with theories and concepts, and mor

* Leo C. Rosten, *Journalism Quarterly*, June 1937.

anxious to analyze the political process and report on how it worked.

Their dominance of the profession was sealed with the rise and election of John F. Kennedy. Kennedy played on the values he shared with these young reporters in order to engage their loyalty. He knew many of them socially, and he was careful to treat them with respect and affection. His Harvard-trained advisers spoke in an academic, sophisticated idiom that excluded many of the older reporters but appealed to the new generation. Because they were so obviously in tune with the youthful, "intellectual" atmosphere of the New Frontier, the young reporters who had covered Kennedy's campaign in 1960, and now covered him in office, found their stock soaring. It was no coincidence that many of them—reporters like David Broder, Ben Bradlee, Bob Novak, Rowland Evans, Mary McGrory, and Russell Baker—would become leading journalists in the sixties and seventies, and would help to change the techniques of campaign reporting.

But in 1960, campaign coverage had changed very little from what it had been in the 1920's. Planes replaced trains, and the networks made their first all-out attempt to cover an election, but most of the reporting remained superficial, formulaic, and dull. Newspapers approached campaign coverage as a civic duty, like reporting sermons and testimonials to retiring fire chiefs.

The most devastating comment on the political coverage of the time was the reception that greeted Theodore White's book, *The Making of the President 1960*. The book struck most readers as a total revelation—it was as if they had never before read anything, anywhere, that told them what a political campaign was about. They had some idea that a campaign consisted of a series of arcane deals and dull speeches, and suddenly White came along with a book that laid out the campaign as a wide-screen thriller with full-blooded heroes and white-knuckle suspense on every page. The book hit the number-one spot on the best-seller lists six weeks after publication and stayed there for exactly a year.

White had started covering American politics in 1953 for *The Reporter,* after fifteen years in Europe and Asia as a *Time* correspondent. Two years later, he signed on with *Collier's* as the magazine's national political correspondent and began covering his first Presidential campaign. The press entourage in the first primary consisted of White and an AP man riding around New Hampshire with Estes Kevauver. There were occasional interloping visits from a *Times*man or a CBS crew out on a day trip, but in 1956 primaries were considered minor, local events, too inconsequential to rate extensive national coverage. All spring, White had the candidates almost entirely to himself, and he took advantage of the opportunity to build up good relationships with Kefauver, Harriman, and Stevenson as they passed through the primaries and the convention.

He was flying high on the greatest assignment of his life. The only trouble was that *Collier's* was going down for the third time. In September, just as the campaign was gearing up, the management called him back with instructions to supervise a total reorganization of the editorial department in a last-ditch move to save the magazine. Four months later, in spite of White's best efforts, *Collier's* was dead.

What upset White as much as anything was that he had not had the chance to finish the campaign. "It was a classic case of coitus interruptus," said White as he sat in the living room of his Manhattan town house, taking a break from writing the fourth *Making of the President* volume. "There I was, stiff cock, ready to go for the massive summary of the 1956 campaign, and here I am out of a job and no place to write it." Instead, he dined out for the next couple of years on campaign anecdotes, stories about what had *really* happened as opposed to the newspaper accounts, and he found that these stories intrigued a lot of people. He also wrote two novels, the second of which he sold to Hollywood for $85,000.

With his financial future secure for at least two years, he decided to indulge himself in his great love, political reporting, and write a book about the 1960 Presidential campaign. He had to go to several publishers before he found one who was enthusiastic about the project, and he assumed that the book would make very little money.

If it was hard to imagine in 1972 that only thirteen years before, a proven novelist had a difficult time selling the idea of a popular book about Presidential politics, it was just as hard to imagine the absolute virginity of much of the territory White set out to explore. "It was like walking through a field playing a brass tuba the day it rained gold," said White. "Everything was sitting around waiting to be reported."

The Republicans were not overly helpful; being somehow convinced that White was writing a work of fiction, they kept assigning him to the Zoo Plane with the television technicians and foreign reporters, listing him on the manifest as "Theodore White, novelist." Fortunately, they lost. White had all of his best contacts among the Democrats anyway, and the Kennedy people were especially cooperative, perhaps sensing that they could use White to help them promote the New Frontier. White got to know all the staffers well, and had little trouble seeing Kennedy himself. Flying back from the Montana convention early in 1960, for instance, White had only one CBS correspondent, Blair Clark, for competition. "Blair and I sat around with John F. Kennedy all the way from Montana back to the East Coast, just shooting the breeze," he remembered. "You can't do that any more. Because now there are 27 million correspondents squeezing in."

The reason that 27 million reporters now show up for every kaffee klatsch in New Hampshire has a lot to do with White's first book. "When that book came out," said White, "it was like Columbus telling about America at the court of Ferdinand and Isabella. Goddam thing was an unbelievable success." White is not the world's humblest journalist, but he is not far off the mark about the book's success—the number of imitations and spin-offs testify to that. The first rival, published by *The New York Times,* came out in 1964. By 1968, White was competing against seventeen other campaign books. The London *Sunday Express* and *Sunday Times* both sent teams of writers; White began to see himself as a small independent businessman fighting off giant corporations which had swooped down to cash in on his success. Most of the books adopted White's magic formula: present politics in novelistic terms, as the struggle of great personalities, with generous helpings of colorful detail to sugar the political analysis.

The book competition was bad enough, but White also had to contend with the newspapers jumping his claim. In 1972, the AP told its men: "When Teddy White's book comes out, there shouldn't be one single story in that book that we haven't reported ourselves." Abe Rosenthal, the managing editor of *The New York Times,* told his reporters and editors: "We aren't going to wait until a year after the election to read in Teddy White's book what we should have reported ourselves." It took from eight to twelve years for the newspapers to accept White as an institution, but by 1972 most editors were sending off their men with rabid pep talks about the importance of sniffing out inside dope, getting background into the story, finding out what makes the campaign tick, and generally going beyond the old style of campaign reporting.

Of course, reporters had been doing many of these things as early as the 1968 campaign, causing George Romney to howl that he had been a victim of "the Teddy White syndrome." By that, Romney meant that flocks of reporters had started looking into the embryonic stages of Presidential campaigns, scrutinizing aspirants even before the primaries, killing candidacies with untimely exposure.

If this premature mass coverage upset politicians, it nearly drove Teddy White to distraction. After the *succès fou* of the 1960 book, he had looked to make a living from the *Making of the President* series for the next twenty years. Now, with the market glutted, he was no longer sure that he could. "People have read so much of what I have to say in *Newsweek,* in *Time,* in *The New York Times* and the Washington *Post,*" he lamented that afternoon in New York, as he started on his third or fourth pack of cigarettes.

But his uneasiness stemmed from more than a fear that the 1972 book might not sell as well as the earlier ones. He sometimes felt that the methods he had pioneered had gotten out of control, had turned into a Frankenstein's monster. Thinking back to the early spring of 1960, he remembered watching a relaxed John Kennedy receiving the Wisconsin primary returns in a Milwaukee hotel room. White had been the only journalist present, except for a young film maker working on a documentary, and he had blended in with the Kennedy Mafia as unobtrusively as a distant in-law.

Then he recalled the July night, only a few months before, when George McGovern had won the Democratic nomination in Miami. White had been in McGovern's suite at the Doral Hotel:

"It's appalling what we've done to these guys. McGovern was like a fish in a goldfish bowl. There were three different network crews at different times. The still photographers kept coming in in groups of five. And there were at least six writers sitting in the corner—I don't even know their names. We're all sitting there watching him work on his acceptance speech, poor bastard. He tries to go into the bedroom with Fred Dutton to go over the list of Vice Presidents, which would later turn out to be the fuck-up of the century of course, and all of us are observing him, taking notes like mad, getting all the little details. Which I think I invented as a method of reporting and which I now sincerely regret. If you write about this, say that I sincerely regret it. Who gives a fuck if the guy had milk and Total for breakfast?"

"There's a conflict here—the absolute need of the

public to know versus the candidate's need for privacy, which is an equivalent and absolute need. I don't know how you resolve it. McGovern was so sweet, so kind to everybody, but he must have been crying out for privacy. And I felt, finally, that our being there was a total imposition."

The reporters who followed the Presidential hopefuls in 1972 would probably have been surprised to hear White say these things. They were arriving in Washington, or were first beginning to make their reputations, around the time that the first *Making of the President* books hit the stores. Now they took White and his techniques for granted; it made sense to them to treat a political campaign as a growing, organic drama and to examine the psychological and sociological causes of political decisions. Many of the new generation of campaign reporters looked down on White as a pathetic, written-out hack. They saw him as a political groupie who wrote flattering, mawkish descriptions of major politicians in order to keep them primed as sources for future books. His 1968 volume, with its penitently overkind description of Richard Nixon, had taken a beating from reviewers. A lot of reporters laughed out loud when they read sentences like: "In 1968, Nixon conspicuously, conscientiously, calculatedly denied himself all racist votes, yielding them to Wallace." It was left for three of White's British competitors, in a book called *An American Melodrama,* to give a decent account of Nixon's wholly opportunistic Southern Strategy.

By 1972, the traveling press openly resented White. They felt that he was a snob, that he placed himself above the rank and file of the press. White would suddenly appear in some pressroom, embracing old friends on the campaign staff, and would immediately be ushered off to the candidate's suite or the forward compartment of the plane for an exclusive interview. And the reporters would grumble about Teddy White getting the royal treatment.

These same reporters forgot that Teddy White's first

books had radically altered the function of the campaign press. Because of him, the press now began to cover political campaigns two years before the election.* Unlike White, the reporters were not collecting tidbits for use at some remote future date, in case one of the primary candidates went on to win the Big One. They were using the information immediately, exposing flaws and inconsistencies in the candidate that could ruin his chances before he even reached the primaries. As recently as 1960, or even 1964, a coalition of party heavies, state conventions, and big-city bosses had chosen the candidate in relatively unviolated privacy, and then presented him to the press to report on.

Now the press screened the candidates, usurping the party's old function. By reporting a man's political strengths, they made him a front runner; by mentioning his weaknesses and liabilities, they cut him down. Teddy White, even in his wildest flights of megalomania, had never allowed himself this kind of power. The press was no longer simply guessing who might run and who might win; the press was in some way determining these things. The classic example was George Romney. Romney had opened his campaign almost a year before the first primary, expecting a press contingent of two or three reporters. Instead, twenty or thirty showed up for Romney's first exploratory trips around the country, and they all reported Romney's embarrassing inability to give coherent answers to their questions about Vietnam, thus dooming his candidacy. But Romney was the perfect, textbook example. The process was usually more subtle, and more difficult to describe.

* White's emphasis on the vital importance of John F. Kennedy's early start was the main reason for all this early coverage. There was also another factor. In 1961, a political amateur named Clifton White started assembling the political machine which eventually won the 1964 Republican nomination for Barry Goldwater. The press did not find out about Clifton White's activities until early 1963. Many reporters later felt chagrin that they had taken so long to catch on to the Goldwater movement, and resolved not to let it happen again.

The journalists involved in this selection process were a very small group, consisting mostly of the national political correspondents, and they formed what David Broder called "the screening committee." Of the two-hundred-odd men and women who followed the candidates in 1972, fewer than thirty were full-time national political correspondents. Most of the campaign reporters came from other beats around Washington—the Justice Department, the Pentagon, the Hill, or the White House. After the campaign, they would go back to these beats, and if they did well, they would rise to a management position at their newspaper, magazine or network. But the national political correspondents had covered the whole political scene for five, ten or fifteen years and were likely to continue doing so until they died in harness; and if the actuarial tables were correct, their jobs would kill them at a relatively early age. Many of the members of this group belonged to an organization called Political Writers for a Democratic Society, an organization whose evoution requires some explaining.

In 1966, a stolid, slightly pompous *Christian Science Monitor* reporter named Godfrey Sperling started organizing breakfasts where he and some of his friends could meet with leading politicians and government officials. He would have the Monitor's secretaries call up Warren Weaver of the *Times,* David Broder of the *Post,* Phil Potter of the Baltimore *Sun,* Bob Donovan of the Los Angeles *Times,* Peter Lisagor of the Chicago *Daily News* and nine or ten other political writers, to invite them to breakfast at the National Press Club, where for five dollars a head they would get scrambled eggs and hash-browns and a chance to further their acquaintance with some politician. The breakfasts were also "background" sessions—any news that came out of them was not for attribution but had to be treated as coming from "a highly placed Democrat" or a "Republican strategist." A great deal of useful information was served up with the orange juice at these sessions. Romney first stumbled over Vietnam at one of Sperling's breakfasts, and Agnew made his debut as a buffoon by declaring that Humphrey was "soft on communism." At another breakfast, shortly before the 1968 Republican Convention, the reporters kept suggesting to Nelson Rockefeller that his chances were nil. "Gee," Rockefeller finally said, "if I thought I was as bad off as you guys say I am, I'd drop out." The most memorable breakfast took place in January 1968, when Robert Kennedy anguished out loud for an hour as to whether or not he should run. The reporters there recalled the scene in the stories they wrote when Kennedy finally decided to enter the race.

By 1970, Sperling's breakfast club began to go to hell; almost anybody who wanted to could come, and the guests often spoke on the record, which meant that they said nothing of importance. But in the early days, Sperling restricted the breakfasts to his friends, which caused great bitterness among the writers who were not invited. Jack Germond, the chief political writer for the Gannett chain, was furious. He had eighteen papers in New York State and he was tired of getting scooped by *The New York Times* whenever John Lindsay, Nelson Rockefeller or Robert Kennedy appeared at Sperling's breakfasts. So in 1969 he and Jules Witcover, who was working for the Newhouse chain and was also shut out, organized a rival group. Witcover christened it, with tongue in cheek, Political Writers for a Democratic Society.

The main purpose of PWDS was to get to know politicians in easy, informal surroundings. The meetings were usually held at Germond's three-story row house in southwest Washington. The fourteen members would assemble once a month, have a couple of drinks with the guest, eat a catered supper downstairs in a big family room, and then go back upstairs to the long, rectangular living room. The guest sat in a large armchair in the middle of the room, taking questions from the reporters, who sat around him on sofas and other easy chairs. More drinks were served. Finally, after the guest had

left, the men would pull out their notebooks and reconstruct the main points of the evening, trying to decide
what the guest may or may not have meant in certain
statements and generally sizing him up.

The most interesting thing about PWDS was its com-
position, which had been determined largely by Germond and Witcover. I cornered Germond one August
night in the McGovern pressroom at the Biltmore Hotel
in New York to ask him about the group. He was sitting
all alone at one of the long typewriter tables, waiting in
vain for a poker game to materialize and slowly getting
drunk. He was a little cannonball of a man, forty-four
years old, with a fresh, leprechaunish face, a fringe of
white hair around his bald head, and a pugnacious,
hands-on-hip manner of talking. He was not simply
drawn to journalism as a profession; like Hildy Johnson
in *Front Page,* he was addicted to it as a way of life.

Although he himself sometimes described his chain as
a "bunch of shitkicker papers," he was proud of his position as a national political writer and the dues he had
paid to win it.* Nothing made him angrier than small-
town newspapermen—"homers"—who came up to him
during campaigns and told him that he was ignoring "local factors." "God," he said, "I remember this one homer in Columbus. I've worked in these jobs, you know,
as a homer. I've been a city-side reporter, a statehouse
reporter, I've done the whole bit—and I've worked for a
bunch of obscure newspapers. Christ Almighty, they
were obscure. And for some guy from Ohio who works
for this goddam shitty newspaper to come up and tell
me that I don't understand the whole thing—I've been
covering this campaign for about sixteen months—and
this asshole comes up and tells me this after two weeks'
exposure—ooh, I was outraged. Got pretty testy in the
saloon, I must say. Told him what I'd do with his fucking newspaper."

---

* He was also the Washington Bureau chief for Gannett, which
meant that he was as powerful within the organization and as
well-paid as many of the publishers of the chain's newspapers.

So PWDS was not for homers or tyros. It was for the professionals' professionals. More specifically, said Germond, sipping a Scotch and soda, the standard was this: Who are the men who cover an obscure Western governors' conference in an off political year? "Everyone covers the national governors' conferences," said Germond, "that's easy. You go out there and they just drop stories in your goddam lap. But you go out there and cover the Western governors, or the Southern governors in a year like '67 or '69, and if you can make a story out of that—if you can even convince your office they ought to pay your fare home—you're a goddam genius." Germond and Witcover had found fourteen men who passed this test. Not counting themselves, there were:

David Broder of the Washington *Post*

Paul Hope of the Washington *Star*

Robert Novak of the Chicago *Sun Times Syndicate*

Warren Weaver of *The New York Times*

Ted Knapp of Scripps-Howard

Bruce Biossat of the Newspaper Enterprise Association

Jim Dickenson of the *National Observer*

Loye Miller of Knight Newspapers

Tom Ottenad of the *St. Louis Post-Dispatch*

Marty Nolan of the Boston *Globe* (Who replaced James Doyle in the group when Doyle moved from the *Globe* to the Washington *Star*)

Pat Furgurson of the Baltimore *Sun*

Jim Large of *The Wall Street Journal*

These people, said Germond, rated membership because of what they did, not because of the organizations they represented. The rule was that no member could send a substitute to a dinner. It was an elite group of men who, by their own consensus, were the flame-keepers of political journalism—the heavies. "We took a couple of guys who we thought were pretty dumb," said Germond, "but we brought 'em in because they were entitled by what they did." No doubt there were some serious omissions—reporters like Johnny Apple of *The New York Times,* Alan Otten of *The Wall Street Journal,* Peter Lisagor, Jim Doyle, Harry Kelly of Hearst, and Jim Perry of the *National Observer*—who either were not congenial to the group or worked for papers already represented. But by and large this group was the elite's idea of the elite. They did not consider the network correspondents to be serious political reporters, nor did they hold a high opinion of the wire-service men (except for Walter Mears) or of newsmagazine reporters (except for John Lindsay of *Newsweek*). But Lindsay could not be admitted because he would have got more out of the dinners than the rest—little pieces of color that the daily journalists couldn't use. And Mears had to be excluded because, on the rare occasions when a not-for-attribution story emerged from one of the dinners, he would have put it on the wire and beaten everybody else. "Most of the wire-service reports generally reflect nothing about what is going on," said Germond, "but Walter's good enough so that he would *whip our ass off.* Walter and I are good friends and he was pissed and kept asking me why he couldn't get in the group. And I said, 'Jeez, Walter, I brought it up and you had eight co-sponsors, but the vote was 13 to 1 against you.' "

The members of PWDS did not constitute a pack. They were too confident, competitive, proud, and self-sufficient for that. They also differed ideologically. Germond for instance was a political agnostic, leaning toward liberalism;* Novak was increasingly embracing the ideological tenets of the Sun King; and Nolan stood, on many matters, to the left of George McGovern.

But they did form a sort of club, with a certain code and certain rituals. If you shared a cab with members of

---

* Germond often talked like a hardhat and made a point of being equally cynical about all the candidates. However, when Washington liberals decided to help rehabilitate the poor black southwest section of town by buying homes there, Germond had been one of the first people to move in. He was one of the last to leave the area after it became clear that the project was a failure.

PWDS, for instance, they would invariably dive for the back seat, leaving you to ride with the driver. At the end of the ride, one of them would say, "I think we'd better invoke the Germond rule."

"What's that?" you would say.

"The Germond rule states that the person who rides up front has to pay."

It was an established rule, widely accepted throughout the world of political journalism, and most people paid.

But PWDS was primarily a dinner group, and their main goal was to set themselves up for the 1972 campaign. They did the drudge work of political journalism, therefore they were entitled to an advantage, a closer relationship with the candidates. They saw the dinners as a new tool of the trade. The alternative was to go around, individually, and formally interview each new cabinet member or potential candidate—which would teach them next to nothing about the man's personality. "What we were trying to do," said Germond, "was to sit down with the guy without having to file any shit about his program or something. Have a couple of pops and dinner, talk, and decide 'What kind of a guy is this, has he got any class?' You don't hand down arbitrary, ex cathedra judgments—get to know the man. And this was true of cabinet members, Presidential candidates— you learn—the people are nice, a lot of them anyway. Or sometimes you don't learn anything. Our great nonlearning session was George McGovern. Jeez, we were the dumbest bastards in the world about George McGovern."

McGovern actually came twice, and the second time, in 1971, he carefully spelled out his entire strategy for winning the nomination. "To show you how strange it was," says Warren Weaver, "I do not even remember it. I just didn't believe the man. I thought it was a pipe dream." That was the consensus of the whole group that night. "We thought he was a nice guy, even a savvy guy," says Germond. "But we didn't believe him. We figured he was a total loss." So George McGovern slipped right through the screening process. The incredulity of the press failed to stop him.

In fact, the dinners yielded very few tangible results. Mel Laird, Bob Finch, Teddy Kennedy provided nothing more than a few minor stories. From dining with George Wallace, the group was surprised to discover that he was consistently witty and genuinely puritanical, but they found out little else. The dinners provided only one solid insight—that Ed Muskie had a bad temper. At his first guest shot, in 1970, the members gave him the old George Romney treatment, boring in with question after question about Vietnam. Muskie kept giving equivocal answers and finally he blew up, attacking the group for trying to trap him. They *were* trying to trap him, but Presidential candidates were supposed to stay cool in the face of such questioning. Some of the members knew about Muskie's temper from covering his vice-presidential campaign in 1968, but most of them were stunned.

Muskie appeared again in December 1971, accompanied by his press secretary, a former Boston *Globe* editor named Dick Stewart. Every time Muskie began to lose control, Stewart would say, "Now, Ed, don't get testy!" They began to wonder a little about Muskie's stability, but most of them decided that it was just a minor flaw and wouldn't make any difference.

Nevertheless, when the national political correspondents—PWDS members and a few others—checked their scratch sheets at the end of 1971, Muskie looked like the only man who really had a chance. Johnny Apple had written a series of exclusive articles in the *Times* about various big Democratic politicians endorsing Muskie, and these articles helped to build up an impression that Muskie had it made. If he took New Hampshire he would be hard to stop, but because he looked like the one and only contender, he could not afford to do poorly in that first primary.

On January 9, 1972, David Broder, the most influential political writer in Washington, wrote from Manches-

ter, New Hampshire: "As the acknowledged front runner and a resident of the neighboring state, Muskie will
have to win the support of at least half the New Hampshire Democrats in order to claim a victory." At the beginning of the campaign, that was the wisdom of the
screening committee of national political journalists.
And when Muskie's big Scenicruiser bus rolled out of
Manchester in January, most of them were on it—writing down every fact that might prove useful six months
later when they did the big piece about how Muskie had
won the nomination. Thanks to the screening committee, no other candidate in sight had half the press entourage that Muskie had.

The screening committee had never held a meeting to
appoint Muskie the front runner. They had never even
discussed it at great length. If there was a consensus, it
was simply because all the national political reporters
lived in Washington, saw the same people, used the
same sources, belonged to the same background groups,
and swore by the same omens. They arrived at their answers just as independently as a class of honest seventh
graders using the same geometry text—they did not
have to cheat off each other to come up with the same
answer. All signs pointed to Ed Muskie as the easy winner, and as the wisdom of the national political men began to filter down through the campaign reporters and
the networks to the people, victory began to seem assured for the Senator from Maine.

Of course, Muskie made no such predictions for himself. All he wanted to do was win, he said, and with all
the time he had to spend shuttling back and forth between Florida and New Hampshire, he'd consider himself *lucky* to get fifty percent. Nobody listened to him.
And when the returns came in on the night of March 7,
leaving Muskie with only 46 percent of the vote, the
press started muttering about a Muskie set back.

The next morning Muskie held a press conference in
the dingy ballroom of the Sheraton Carpenter Hotel in
Manchester, and several members of the screening com-

mittee turned out for it. David Broder and Tom Ottenad kept asking him about the percentage of his victory. Why hadn't he done as well as predicted? What had happened? Suddenly Muskie's temper exploded and he launched into a tirade, lashing out at Broder and Ottenad, who were two of the gentlest and most soft-spoken men in the business. The percentage, said Muskie, had nothing to do with anything. The press was misinterpreting it because the press was out to get him.

Nothing daunted, Broder asked him how, specifically, the New Hampshire results would affect his chances in Florida and in the other primaries. "I can't tell you that," Muskie snapped. "You'll tell me and you'll tell the rest of the country because you interpret this victory. This press conference today is my only chance to interpret it, but you'll probably even misinterpret that."

Broder just shrugged, but Marty Nolan, who was sitting directly behind him, raised his hand and said sternly, "Senator, will you answer the question?" Muskie simply looked at him and went on to some other subject. Nolan asked him again, and got the same response.

After the press conference, Nolan stalked over to Dick Stewart and some Muskie aides who were talking in a corner.

"Calm down, Marty, calm down," said Stewart.

"Look," said Nolan. "I've taken three and a half years of this kind of shit from Nixon and those people, and I'm not gonna take it from you pricks."

Muskie, who had known Nolan for many years, came over and put his hand on Nolan's shoulder. "What's the problem, Marty?" he asked in his gravest tones.

Nolan turned around and looked at him. "The bullshit you've been handing out—that's the problem, Senator."

Nolan then repeated to Muskie that he was tired of taking bullshit from Nixon and Agnew. "I expect much more of you and I intend to hold you to it," he said sharply.

"Well, Marty," said the Senator. "I guess you're

right." For the next five minutes, he apologized for his outburst.

If the press had ever been more powerful than in 1972, nobody could remember when.

CHAPTER III

The Muskie Three and Other Campaign Reporters

THE JOURNALISTS on any campaign plane or bus were divided into two distinct types: the national political reporters, who were aboard for only a few days at a time and were free to go off and cover another candidate whenever they wished; and the campaign reporters, who were on board for the duration. The campaign reporters had been assigned to live with a single candidate for as long as he was in the race, or until further notice. They followed the candidate everywhere, heard his standard speech so many dozens of times they could recite it with him, watched his moods go up and down, speculated constantly on his chances, wrote songs about him, told jokes at his expense, traded gossip about him, and were lucky if they did not dream about him into the bargain. They ate and drank with his staff and, in some cases, slept with his lady staffers. At their best, they were his short order biographers, experts on his positions, habits and character. At their worst—and the deadly fatigue of the campaign trail guaranteed that all but the hardiest of them were occasionally at their worst—they were like the foreign service officer who is sent abroad and goes native; they identified with the candidate and became his apologists.

In 1971, long before the primaries began, Jim Naughton of *The New York Times* and Dick Stout of *Newsweek* were assigned to cover Edmund Muskie. Later they were joined by Bruce Morton of CBS,* and together these three men made up the nucleus of the campaign reporters on the Muskie bus; they had been around the longest and had the best knowledge of the workings of the campaign. It was a great compliment to their abilities that they had been put on the front runner's campaign, but with the decline of Muskie, which was accelerated when he placed fourth in the Florida primary in March, they found themselves further and further from the center of the action. By the time the Wisconsin primary rolled around, in April, they had begun to look like characters in a Solzhenitsyn novel—forgotten men, and for no reason but fate's perverse amusement.

* Morton's first assignment of the campaign year, starting in December 1971, had been to cover the seemingly quixotic campaign of George McGovern. While Morton did not appear overly disappointed with this job, his camera crew referred to the McGovern Bus as the "Morgue Patrol" and were convinced that they had been assigned to McGovern as a belated punishment for having botched CBS's coverage of the Tet Offensive. Six weeks later, however, Morton was rotated to the Muskie Bus. The networks tended to favor such rotations, on the theory that a change of pace prevented the reporters from getting stale or from growing too attached to a single candidate.

Apparently, however, CBS had not informed its correspondents of the rotation scheme, for David Schoumacher was shocked and angered when he learned, in mid-January, that Morton was to replace him on the Muskie Bus. Several weeks earlier than most of his colleagues, Schoumacher had realized that Muskie could be beaten; he thought that Muskie's demise would make a great story and wanted badly to stay with the Senator from Maine. He was so unhappy at being transferred to the Humphrey campaign that he began quietly negotiating with ABC, which was a land of opportunity for reporters who felt that their careers were being blocked at CBS or NBC. In recent years, Herb Kaplow (NBC), Bill Matney (NBC), and Harry Reasoner (CBS), had moved to ABC. Late in 1972, Schoumacher also made the move.

The member of the trio who had spent the longest time with Muskie was Stout. Stout had covered the Man from Maine in the '68 and '70 elections, had traveled to Moscow and Israel with him, and had come to know him more intimately than any other writer. Stout looked like an overgrown schoolboy—tall, hulking, overweight, his suit always rumpled, and his blond forelock constantly falling down over his perspiring forehead and his glasses. A native of Indianapolis, he had gone to De Pauw University and worked for papers in Dayton and Chicago. In the early sixties, he contracted "Potomac Fever" by reading *Advise and Consent,* and landed a job in *Newsweek*'s Washington Bureau as a general assignment reporter. He was capable of writing well, witness his book on Eugene McCarthy *(People)* or the campaign piece he did for the *Atlantic Monthly* in March 1972; but little of his prose survived the blades of the *Newsweek* blender.

Stout was a man of startling moods. When he was depressed, his gloom could drown the good mood of a room. But when he was feeling happy, he often displayed a terrifying sense of humor that hovered somewhere between Jack Benny Deadpan and Jonathan Winters Bizarre. He had an alarmingly strong sense of the absurd.

In August 1971, for instance, Stout was sent to Zanesville, Ohio, to interview a sample of twenty-five people for a segment in an ongoing mood-of-the-country series, which *Newsweek* had announced with much fanfare several months earlier. Stout did his twenty-five interviews, and he was on his way out of Zanesville when he came upon an encampment of Jesus freaks. Joining their prayer circle, he fell to his knees, threw up his arms and cried, "Oh, Jesus, I am a sinner! Dear Jesus, come and help this poor sinner!" The Jesus freaks were thoroughly convinced by Stout's performance. Later that evening, they insisted that he come to a formal church service, where they proudly pointed him out as their prize convert.

The day after Stout filed his Zanesville article, President Nixon announced his wage-price controls. Stout's editors decided that the announcement made the article dated and irrelevant, so it was killed. A week later, Stout was put back on the Muskie watch and the whole mood-of-the-country series was forgotten.

One of Stout's first moves was to refresh his acquaintanceship with the Muskie family. In the late summer of 1971, he had supper with them at their home in Maine. After dinner, he rushed back to the Naragansett Bar in Kennebunkport and scribbled in his notebook for an hour. The dinner had been full of just the kind of material that most appealed to Stout, and he could not resist writing it up as an FYI memo for his editors—one of the few such memos he filed all year. In the memo, Stout detailed Muskie's swearing at table in front of his kids, his pride in property, his observations on his golf game, and his arguments with his wife, Jane. At one point, Muskie had realized that he needed his tuxedo the next night, and that it was too late to send it to the cleaners. Muskie and his wife had locked horns in an argument over who was going to iron the tux. "You iron it," she said finally. "You're the tailor's son." Muskie had exploded in a rage.

HALF A YEAR LATER, during the Wisconsin primary, Dick Stout played a star role on the night when Muskie and the press had what was probably their most intimate get-together. After a long day, the Muskie Bus had finally pulled in at the Northland Hotel in Green Bay, one of those huge, ancient salesman's hotels that are forever burning down on the front pages of tabloids. The press gave off an aura of cheerfulness as they came out of the wretched snowy night into the relative snugness of the seedy hotel lobby, and then hunkered down for the first drinking of the evening. There was a party in the offing, a celebration of Ed Muskie's fifty-eighth birthday.

Around 9:30, reporters began to filter down a long

corridor on the second floor, past a gauntlet of mean-looking Secret Service men, and into a small meeting room where a makeshift bar had been set up in the far corner. Just behind the bar sat an old-fashioned red Coca-Cola tub filled with ice.

Most of the fifty reporters gathered in the room had trudged after Muskie through the long, depressing days of his decline in Florida, Illinois and Wisconsin. They were ravenous for a good time. The entire stock of liquor at the bar was gone within fifteen minutes. The Senator himself was there, slowly sipping a bourbon and stiffly joking with reporters.

Soon after the liquor ran out, Dick Stout went to the Coke tub, placed on it a stand-up ashtray to use as a lectern, and took out his notebook, in which he had made some hasty notes that afternoon. The room fell silent as Stout began a laborious and sometimes deadly accurate parody of a Muskie speech. The main point of the speech was that, like any Muskie oration, it went on forever. But the reporters roared at anything that faintly resembled a punch line; they laughed until they cried. Stout was making wooden, Muskie-like gestures and laughing at his own jokes; he seemed to be having a wonderful time.

Muskie and Jane sat behind the table, a few feet away from Stout. Whenever he had to, Muskie gave a harrowing grin, as if he had just received a shock through alligator clips attached to his genitals. Jane smiled indiscriminately at everything, just to be on the safe side.

When Stout finished the speech, he and Naughton and Morton presented Muskie with gifts they had purchased the day before. The Senator winced as they handed him a Polish Power sweatshirt and other joke-shop fare. A large rectangular birthday cake was brought in, and Muskie rose to cut it. The cake was decorated to look like the White House. As he summoned each reporter by name to claim a piece of the cake, the party suddenly turned somber and formal. It looked like the Last Supper, with fifty Judases present. Several reporters gathered around Stout to compliment him on his wit, but Stout seemed distracted and uneasy. He was skating on thin social ice with the Muskies. In December, *Newsweek* had cribbed a *Women's Wear Daily* account of Jane's mild swearing; William Loeb, the curmudgeon publisher of the reactionary Manchester *Union Leader*, New Hampshire's only statewide paper, used the *Newsweek* item in a vicious anti-Muskie editorial. Muskie had been defending his wife's honor outside of the *Union Leader* office when he broke down and started to cry. So it was safe to bet that somewhere in the back of Muskie's mind, *Newsweek* was mixed up with the fatal "crying incident" and Stout was mixed up with them both.

Now Stout had treated the Senator to a good roasting, which had been designed to burst the tension that had built up between Muskie, ever secretive and suspicious, and his journalistic adversaries. But the speech had left a curious malaise in the room. The party was meant to let off steam, but Muskie's safety valve was jammed.

As the Senator continued to cut the cake, he was approached by Jack English, his campaign coordinator. Jack English's hair was dyed jet black, and he had one of the last crew cuts to be given in New York State. He looked like a washed-up pug and was normally aloof, but tonight he was gregarious and almost pixyish. Prancing over to the Senator, he whispered something in his ear. Muskie peered over at Stout, grinned his first heart felt grin of the evening, and said, "No, Jack, I don't think a Presidential candidate should stoop to slapstick comedy."

"What?" asked Jane Muskie, looking confused. "What are you talking about?"

Muskie ignored her and went back to dissecting the cake. But Jane puzzled out the exchange and suddenly a light bulb went on; she smiled a victorious smile. Picking up a piece of cake—marble cake with thick white icing—she marched over to Stout, who was standing alone, lost in meditation.

"Dick?" she cooed.

"Yes," said Dick, and turned around.

"Here," said Jane, and pushed the cake into his face. She smeared the cake around, as if it were a mudpack. The icing got into Stout's nostrils, all over his cheek and into his left ear. He had the surprised expression of a poleaxed sheep.

"One good turn deserves another," said Jane, doubling up with laughter. Muskie looked as if he wanted to crawl out of the room. He chuckled good-naturedly for lack of anything to say. Some reporters laughed and others looked horrified. Stout looked humiliated and sad as he pulled out his blower and began to wipe off the goo. The party was over.

IT IS DOUBTFUL whether the press ever came closer to making contact with the Man from Maine than at that bizarre and manic party. At the start of the primary races, the press had by and large been disposed to like the Senator, but it took Muskie only a few short weeks to poison that good will. He whipsawed between begging the press and bullying them. On a flight from Los Angeles to Washington in August '71, he interrupted the reporters' cribbage game to tell them that his fate was in their hands. "You can make me or break me," he said. At other times he would turn on reporters, as he did at his post-election press conference in New Hampshire, and treat them to a stream of arrogance and abuse, blaming them for his setbacks.

Ironically, Muskie's campaign was a reporter's dream, for if the Senator treated the press badly, he treated his staff worse. He intimidated them, made scapegoats of them, and often ignored their advice. There was nearly always some wounded staffer who didn't mind telling you what was going on up in the Candidate's Suite. Surprisingly, very few reporters availed themselves of these willing sources, and several interesting developments in the Muskie campaign went largely unchronicled.

There was, for instance, the incident on election night in Florida when Muskie went into a rage over the poor returns and tried to resign. "All his major advisers were up there in his hotel room," recalled an eyewitness, "and Muskie just had a fit. He screamed and ranted like something out of *Marat/Sade*. He kept shouting, 'You guys made me commit political suicide! You made me come out against the Space Shuttle!' "

When Muskie had calmed down, he and his advisers left the room and crowded into an elevator to go down to the doomed election night party where he was to deliver his concession statement.

The dialogue in the elevator, according to the same eyewitness, went like this:

"What are you going to say, Senator?" asked Berl Bernhard, Muskie's campaign manager.

Muskie stared at him. "You'd like to know, wouldn't you?" he growled.

"Yes, Senator, we certainly would," Bernhard said nervously.

Muskie just stood and glared. Jane put her head on his shoulder. "Oh, Ed," she said. "If you go back to Maine we can have another baby."

And Muskie, said the eyewitness, suddenly seemed to change his mind. One thought of another kid in Kennebunkport, and he walked right out to the microphones and told the crowd he was still in the race. "I swear to God," said the eyewitness. "That's what did it."

Now, if the protagonist of this incident had been George McGovern, and the incident had taken place in the fall, it would have got into print without a doubt—though perhaps in sketchy, abbreviated form. The rumors of Muskie's attempt to withdraw were in the air within a few days after the Florida election. A little guileful prodding should have unearthed the whole story. But not even a hint of the story showed up in the press, except in a *Rolling Stone* column written by Hunter Thompson several weeks later.

A month and a half later, in a front page *New York Times* story that appeared the day after Muskie withdrew from the primaries, Jim Naughton finally revealed that the Senator had wanted to pull out after the Florida election. But why didn't the reporters trace down the full story at the time it happened? All of the ones I asked said that they had not heard the rumors. I believed them, but I thought another factor might have been operating. I thought that they *didn't want* to hear the rumors—not because they necessarily supported Muskie's candidacy, but because they wanted to be on the Winner's Bus.

There is nothing drearier than following a loser all the way to his grave. The candidate is exhausted, the staff is crabby, the hotels are bad and get worse, and the campaign generates less and less news. Off in the distance is the Winner's campaign—a cornucopia of big stories, excitement, power, money, and a burgeoning sense of promise. Everybody in the business is suddenly talking about the Winner's campaign. The best reporters seem to be there. It grows like a fad, you have to be there, at the center of the action.

But it goes beyond that. A campaign reporter's career is linked to the fortunes of his candidate. If he is writing about the front runner, he is guaranteed front-page play for his articles, and, as Walter Mears once told me, "Everything is measured by play in this business." If he can hang on to a winner through the primaries, he will probably be assigned to follow him through the fall election—perhaps all the way to the White House.

A campaign reporter who covers one of the two major candidates is usually headed for bigger things. "The Presidential politics beat is one or two steps down from being a junior or senior executive on the paper," David Broder said after the election. "Most of the guys who covered the first campaign that I was on in 1960 are now editors of the editorial pages of their papers, or managing editors, or bureau chiefs who spend most of their time doing stuff around Washington." Ben Bradlee, for example, who covered the Kennedy campaign for *Newsweek,* rose within two years to become chief of the magazine's Washington bureau, and soon thereafter became the managing editor of the Washington *Post.*

Even if the reporter does not immediately receive an editorial job, he may be assigned to the White House, which is also a springboard to executive positions. Robert Semple was a good example. In 1966, he had been covering urban affairs for *The New York Times.* His articles usually appeared at the bottom of page 63. In 1967, he was assigned to cover Richard Nixon, and he followed him all through the primaries and fall campaign, and then served as the *Times'* White House correspondent for four years. At the end of 1972, he was sent to New York as an assistant editor on the national desk, and many *Times*men assumed that Semple was being groomed for the prestigious position of Washington Bureau chief.

At the very least, a reporter who latches on to the Winner in the primaries can always write a book about a losing Presidential nominee. But nobody wants to read a book about a losing Presidential hopeful.

So the correspondents did not like to dwell on signs that their Winner was losing, any more than a soup manufacturer likes to admit that there is botulism in the vichyssoise. If the Winner turned into a clear-cut loser, the campaign reporter might get assigned to the new Winner. Or he might not. There was always that nagging fear that the editor might have forgotten him, that he might be destined to spend the rest of the year in some dull secondary assignment. Besides, he had spent months making a close, monomaniacal study of the candidate. He had become a very narrow specialist. He could tell you everything about the candidate from his favorite dish to the political opinions of his war buddies.

If there was any justice in the world, the reporter thought, the candidate would come through and justify this fantastic expenditure of time. Otherwise, what a tragic, absurd, depressing waste . . .

For these reasons, I thought that the men on the Winner's Bus subconsciously pulled for their man to come through.

When Muskie's campaign began to go down the tubes, it didn't do much for the morale of Messrs. Stout, Morton, and Naughton. "It didn't matter six beans to me whether Muskie was or was not the nominee," Naughton told me months later. But after Florida, Naughton began to have trouble getting his stories in the *Times*. Half the time, he had to contribute his information to some other *Times* reporter who was writing a more general story about the campaign. "We all have large egos or we wouldn't be in this business," said Naughton. "It made it a bit harder to go through those twenty-hour days when you didn't see any personal involvement in print."

After Muskie's birthday party in Green Bay, I walked into the dark cryptlike hotel bar and spotted Naughton, Stout, and Morton at a table behind a blue-mirrored column in the middle of the room. They were exuding gloom like three guys who had just dropped their life savings at the track. Five rounds of Scotch-on-the-rocks came to the table before closing time.

Stout was slumped in his chair with his collar open. Having abandoned all hope that he was riding on the Winner's Bus, he had found some degree of peace. Or perhaps the absurdist in him had already accepted the whole campaign as a bad joke. He was trying to bet everyone that McGovern would win in Wisconsin. No one wanted to bet against him.

Morton, who had weathered six months in the CBS Saigon Bureau and Nixon's 1968 campaign, was smoking nervously. He had been the No. 2 man on the Hill when CBS sent him to cover Muskie. He was forty-two, but his neat blond hair, his smooth features, and his eyeglasses made him look like an Eton boy. There was a weird contrast between his deep, confident voice and his frightened eyes.

At the third side of the table was Naughton. If Dickens' Tiny Tim had reached the age of thirty-four, he would look like Naughton—small, frail, with badly cut short blond hair, red-rimmed eyes, a small puckered mouth, and a bargain basement suit. He was a soft-spoken, meticulously polite graduate of Notre Dame who had learned to get what he wanted by quiet, subtle means. Whenever a petition was circulated or a prank was played, Naughton was almost always the invisible instigator. He would plant an idea in the minds of the other men and then quietly fade into the background. It was he who had organized the entertainment and gift-buying for Muskie's birthday party, for instance, although Stout had ended up in the spotlight.

Naughton was a natural leader, and the others followed him almost unconsciously. He was always in the middle of the excitement, and when he left a place, the others would slowly filter away. An ambitious reporter, he had an almost feminine knack for seeming to hold a casual conversation while really sucking out information like a bilge pump. It was no coincidence that he was the big winner in the running poker game—when he wanted to, he could draw another man out and never hint at what was in his own hand. He had a pleasant sense of humor which sometimes emerged in his lighter pieces. His black typewriter case was decorated with a "Dingbat for President" sticker.

The son of a dispatcher for a shipping company on the Great Lakes, he was the first writer in his family, and his greatest ambition was someday to take over Russell Baker's humor column in the *Times*. He had come to the *Times'* Washington Bureau from the Cleveland *Plain Dealer* in 1969, and had served as the back-up man at the White House. In the summer of 1971, he had put in for a campaign assignment, expecting to be given a minor candidate like Harold Hughes. To his complete surprise, he was told that he would cover Muskie. It was extraordinary for a rookie in the bureau to receive such a weighty assignment, and Naughton was fully aware of the importance of the job.*

Naughton was still covering the White House, but he immediately began, as an extracurricular duty, to familiarize himself with the candidate, his staff, and the financial situation of the Muskie campaign. In trying to find out about the sources of Muskie's campaign money, he ran up against a roadblock—he learned that staffers and contributors had been told not to discuss the subject. So in August of 1971, he set up an informal, get-acquainted dinner with Muskie and some of his staffers at a Washington restaurant. "During the course of the dinner," Naughton remembered later, "I mentioned to Muskie that it seemed to me that if he really meant what he was saying about deserving the trust of the voters, he had to do business in a different way on finances. I told him how I had had this difficulty getting this information, and told him that it ought to be made public." Muskie blew up. He launched into a twenty-minute tirade, pounding the table and shaking his fist. Every time Naughton tried to say something, Muskie cut him off with "Don't give me any of those lawyer's tactics! Don't give me any of your weasel's words!" Naughton persisted in his argument and finally Muskie looked at him and said, "You're nothing but a goddam purist!"

---

* While it was extraordinary for a reporter so new to the *Times* to rise so quickly on the paper, it was not unusual for a young reporter, inexperienced in Presidential politics, to be assigned to a candidate. Many of the 1972 crop of campaign reporters, perhaps a majority, were covering a Presidential campaign for the first time. Dick Stout, who had covered his first Presidential contest in 1964, said he supposed he was "as old a pro as there was" among the campaign reporters. "It scares me when I think about it," he said. "I have more experience at this thing than most of them, and I don't know *anything* about it." Stout later said that he thought campaign coverage was "pretty bad," but he couldn't think how to improve it. "I don't think very many publications or TV stations go at it with any sense of a pattern," he added. "They don't profit by experience, mainly because the turnover of editors and reporters is so rapid."

"I only hope you think I'm a goddam purist after the campaign," said Naughton. Muskie laughed, and from that time on, the two enjoyed an amicable relationship. The only thing Naughton regretted about the go-around was that it had been off the record.

Sometimes Naughton seemed to be divided into two separate personalities, the questioner and the writer. As a questioner, he could often be as blunt and fearless as he had been at that dinner with Muskie—prodding, needling, playing a ferocious devil's advocate. But as a writer he tended to be prudent to a fault. It was as if he felt the entire grey-goddess tradition of *The New York Times* weighing down on him. "The *Times* is after all a record of history," he once told me. "I wouldn't want to vilify Richard Nixon if he doesn't deserve vilification— even though *I* may feel he deserves it."

His articles on Muskie, at any rate, were extremely cautious. "Naughton didn't have the confidence in himself to buck conventional wisdom," said an older, more experienced journalist. "I think his major problem was that he didn't understand the internal politics of the *Times*. When he got a job as good as he got, he should have known he had clout to write it the way he saw it.

"But never did Jim say anything first. He was filing AP shit. Every time he talked about this problem or that flaw, it had already been headlined in the Washington *Post* or a national magazine. I think he knew what was happening, but he just wasn't sure of his instincts."

There were several examples of Naughton's pulling his punches with Muskie, but one stood out—the "crying incident" article. In his story of February 27, which was buried inside the *Times,* Naughton did not mention that Muskie "broke into tears" until the sixth paragraph. David Broder, the chief political writer for the Washington *Post,* played the incident in his lead, thereby producing a piece that had a devastating effect on the Muskie campaign. Naughton, constantly on the Muskie Bus, saw the incident as a minor feature in a generally bizarre day of campaigning. Broder, who had just flown into New Hampshire for the weekend, saw it as a major news story.

SINCE THE NEW HAMPSHIRE PRIMARY, I had formed my theory about the Winner's Bus, and I wanted to try it out on Naughton, Stout, and Morton. For some reason, even in the general emotional sag that followed the birthday party, I didn't feel reticent about inviting myself to join them in the Northland bar, or about bugging them with my theory.

"I think that you're going kind of easy on Muskie," I said after my first drink. "I don't mean that you're fudging things for him consciously, I just think that you give him the benefit of the doubt because you've put in a lot of time with him and you'd like to see him get the nomination to justify that time. I mean, life is short, and four or five months is a pretty big investment of time."

"Well," said Morton gravely and politely, "Stout has been with him on and off for three years, for that matter. But I don't think we've favored him."

"No," said Naughton, "I think we've been hard on him, if anything. We took him to task for not disclosing finances, just among other things."

Stout leaned back in his chair and pointed at me. "Listen to the kid," he said. "He's got something to say."

That took me by surprise, and I didn't know quite what to say.

I began to attack Muskie in vague terms. "He's a whore like Humphrey," I said. "He'll sell out to anybody who will give him the Job." The interesting thing was that they responded to my attack on Muskie by taking up his defense.

"I'd rather see the nomination go to Muskie than to Humphrey, who *is* a complete whore," said Naughton. "I'm a pragmatist, and I think Muskie may be the best we can get. Coming off the White House beat, almost any Democrat looks attractive. Muskie has impressed me as being honest and candid. He's not just a politician."

"He wants to be President so bad he can taste it," I said.

"No," said Naughton. "The man is really a fatalist. He's been pushed into this race and he's accepted his role, but he'd be happier being a Senator from Maine for the rest of his life."

Morton nodded. "I'll grant you that he's petulant, that he's ill-at-ease with the press, and that he doesn't know what to say sometimes, but that doesn't mean he's all bad."

"You've got to remember that he's a state politician, and that he's being advised by people who have run state campaigns," Naughton said earnestly. "But he's learning. He's educable. That's why we told him about the importance of having an open administration during that bull session in Portsmouth, New Hampshire. We can educate him before it's too late."

Just before closing time, Naughton and I made a trip to the bar to collect the last round of drinks. As we stood at the rail, I realized for the first time that we were both quite drunk. Not pig drunk, but unnaturally loose-tongued. Naughton was talking to me intensely, but it was hard for me to concentrate on his words because Dick Stewart, Muskie's press secretary, was sitting only a few feet away and singing "On the Street Where You Live" at the top of his lungs. But I remember the gist of what Naughton said, and he has since repeated the rest for me.

"When I was in Cleveland and I was a young political reporter—fairly naive, fairly idealistic, fairly liberal— there was a state representative named Carl Stokes who came along. Black. A man of immense charm. Seemed to me to represent what was right, what was the future. I thought he would make one helluva mayor. And my news stories may have reflected that, and I'm sure my columns did. And that may or may not have helped get him elected.

"And as soon as he got elected, he turned around and shat on all the people who had worked their asses off for him. He was just a bastard. He had terminal ego. And that convinced me you should never place your trust in a politician. And I think that was a very valuable object lesson."

Four weeks after the night at the Northland, Muskie withdrew from the primaries. Naughton took several days off to write an obituary of the Muskie campaign for *The New York Times Sunday Magazine.* "I never really had a chance to stop and decide whether I was distressed about Muskie's withdrawal or whether I regarded Muskie as the most capable candidate," Naughton said later. "But I felt like the guy who had invested his life's savings constructing a building, only to see it collapse. I mean, I had spent hours and months getting to know the intricate details of the Muskie campaign and how it functioned, to the point where I was finally confident that I knew where to go and who to talk to and could put my fingers on the developments as they occurred. From that standpoint it was a great disappointment, because here was something I had gotten to know intimately and suddenly it wasn't there any more."

Muskie's demise threw the campaign reporters into a limbo of uncertainty. Naughton, for instance, had no idea what his next assignment would be, and at first his editors also seemed unsure. He was sent to Columbus to help analyze the returns in the Ohio primary. That done, he was told to fly to Detroit to coordinate coverage of the Michigan primary. No sooner had he arrived in Detroit, however, than he got a call from the Washington Bureau, telling him to pick up McGovern in Nebraska. At first, Naughton thought that this was a temporary assignment, but after a couple of weeks he realized that he was on the Winner's Bus again. Within a few weeks after the collapse of the Muskie campaign,

Stout and most of the other Muskie campaign reporters also ended up with McGovern.

This massive influx of new reporters onto the Mc-Govern Bus meant that most of the reporters who had followed McGovern since January had to be transferred to other, less glamorous assignments. For at the beginning of the year, the McGovern campaign, seemingly so hopeless, had been regarded as an ideal training ground for promising reporters who needed seasoning. "I don't have the vaguest idea what I'm doing," Michelle Clark, a young, extremely beautiful black reporter from CBS's Chicago Bureau had said during the New Hampshire primary. "I think they're just letting me get my feet wet."*

Like all campaign reporters, the small crew of early McGovern regulars had soon begun to identify with the candidate they were covering, and they spent much of their time trying to insure that their newspapers and networks would treat McGovern as a serious contestant. For instance, Christopher Lydon, a thirty-three-year-old *New York Times* reporter covering his first Presidential campaign, began to feel as early as January that Mc-Govern had a chance to make a strong showing. Lydon rapidly became so enthusiastic about McGovern that Robert Phelps, the *Times'* political editor, felt obliged to remind him not to "write from the heart." Later, when McGovern surged in Wisconsin, Lydon began to pontificate in private, becoming a self-appointed expert on the McGovern phenomenon, and he was deeply disappointed at being bumped from the McGovern Bus and transferred to the Humphrey campaign in mid-May.*

Quite naturally, this first batch of McGovern report-

---

* Clark, who covered McGovern through Wisconsin and later covered Humphrey, proved herself to be an excellent correspondent. On December 8, 1972, she was killed in a plane crash at Chicago's Midway Airport.

* As it turned out, Lydon did such a good job covering Humphrey and carrying out other assignments that he was chosen to succeed Johnny Apple as the *Times'* national political correspondent when Apple moved to the White House beat in early 1973.

ers had not written in great detail about McGovern's proposals; they were lucky to get enough space to describe the day-to-day progress of McGovern's campaign. The band of ex-Muskie regulars who took over in May had a different problem. Coming in late, they had to learn about the workings of the McGovern campaign as quickly as possible. They had no time to study his more complicated proposals. Thus, neither group of reporters was able to give McGovern the careful scrutiny he deserved, and which might have saved him from making disastrous mistakes later on.

The people who saw this problem most clearly were the reporters on the Humphrey Bus, who felt that their candidate, a two-time loser in whom the public had lost interest, was being slighted, while McGovern, a bright and unknown new face, was fussed over. The most outspoken Humphrey reporter was *Newsweek*'s John J. Lindsay, a cynical, witty, melancholic old pro with a penchant for challenging political clichés.*

"We were captivated by a goddam hula hoop," Lindsay said in August of the press's attitude toward McGovern. By *we,* Lindsay really meant *they*—the editors who doled out space and the reporters who covered McGovern. He felt that the McGovern reporters had failed to look hard at the fact that McGovern would have done poorly in several primaries if not for the votes of Republicans and of Wallace voters who did not have Wallace on the ballot. Lindsay also thought that the McGovern press corps had failed to quiz the Senator rigorously on his defense budget and income redistribution plan.

"At least," said Lindsay, "Humphrey managed to turn a very dull primary season into something fairly in-

* Lindsay had covered Humphrey off and on since 1971 and followed him full-time from March through the Democratic Convention. Both he and Hayes Gorey, the Humphrey reporter for *Time,* had to live with the fact that their magazines gave less space to Humphrey than to McGovern. They also had to live with Humphrey's exhausting eighteen-hour days and his incompetent press secretary, who never learned that reporters needed time to file.

teresting, and in the end became the only thing that stood between George McGovern and a free ride.

"Humphrey cut McGovern up a little bit in California, which the process is supposed to do. Cut him up on the issues. It disclosed to me for the first time that McGovern had gotten where he was by some alchemist's formula, but he sure as hell didn't get there on the basis of what he really stood for. He didn't know what the hell he really stood for. He didn't know what the hell his stands really implied. So Humphrey served a good purpose. And the opportunity was given to him on a silver platter by the press, because the press had never done it.

"From Wisconsin on, we should have been all over McGovern's *ass,* backing him up against the wall on the issues. The fact of the matter is that we're doing a helluva lot more damage to George McGovern right now, in August, by simply reporting what's happening to his campaign than if we'd done it last spring when it really didn't matter."

Lindsay was quite correct. In fact, only one reporter really probed George McGovern's stands in the spring of 1972—Richard Reeves, the political reporter for *New York* magazine. Reeves was a seasoned journalist in his late thirties who had recently cut the umbilical cord to what he called the "Mother *Times*" to do free-lance magazine work. Free at last to write with a sweeping authoritativeness that the *Times* had never allowed, Reeves was out on a shooting spree, turning his personal, sometimes opinionated style on every politician in sight. "If there's anything good about the guy, fuck it, his press officer will get it out," Reeves once told me. "So why should I waste my time, for McGovern or anybody else. I don't tend to think in terms of their problems."

Reeves regarded George McGovern as a garden variety pol with an unwarranted reputation for saintliness. "George would rather be President than be right," he wrote in a *New York* piece which came out in early May. In the same article, Reeves pointed out that Mc-

Govern was fudging on busing (saying one thing in Florida, another in Massachusetts); that McGovern's accusation that forty percent of American corporations were paying no income tax was "ridiculous"; that McGovern gave little indication of caring much about the plight of the poverty-stricken Indians in his own South Dakota backyard; and that McGovern's ADA rating had plummeted from 94 to 43 in 1968, the year he ran for reelection to the Senate.

"Politicians are different from you and me," Reeves went on, apropos of McGovern. "The business of reaching for power does something to a man—it closes him off from other men until, day by day, he reaches the point where he instinctively calculates each new situation and each other man with the simplest question: what can this do for me?" Reeves saw that McGovern was a politician, and he predicted the compromises that McGovern would make with party regulars later in the year.

The article had little impact, and few of the reporters on the McGovern Bus seemed to share Reeves' perception of the Senator. Which was not to say that they wrote glowing, laudatory stories about the candidate. During the California primary campaign, in late May and early June, they gave thorough coverage to McGovern's inability to put a price tag on his welfare plan and to his growing defensiveness in the face of Humphrey's shrill attacks. At the same time, however, the phenomenon of the Muskie Bus seemed to be recurring; the McGovern reporters did not seem anxious to probe for McGovern's flaws, to examine the ruthless, pragmatic side of his personality. True, a few of the national political reporters, notably Jules Witcover and Marty Nolan, wrote a satirical song poking fun at McGovern for his political alliance with Meade Esposito, the old-guard Democratic party boss of Brooklyn, New York. But many of the reporters seemed content to take McGovern at face value, accepting him as the anti-politician he claimed to be. In California, there was sometimes a feeling of general giddiness on the McGovern Bus. Mc-Govern was so close to victory, and if he won the nomination it would be perhaps the most sensational political story since Lyndon Johnson took himself out of the running in 1968. No one wanted to spoil a story that good.

It would have been far better for McGovern if the reporters had regarded him as a common politician from the outset. For when, in the course of the Eagleton mess, they finally discovered that he could resort to expediency as quickly as the next pol, many of them acted as though they had been deceived and betrayed. Jim Naughton, for instance, sounded shocked and outraged in the "New Analysis" which he wrote on July 31. Naughton described the less-than-straightforward way in which McGovern had disposed of Eagleton and argued that it might have shattered McGovern's idealistic image. "The biggest political casualty in the Eagleton affair may prove to be not Senator Thomas F. Eagleton but the man who chose him to seek the vice-presidency," he wrote. "Mr. McGovern appeared, even to disillusioned members of his campaign staff, to be saying one thing and doing another—which was the charge he had been preparing to make against President Nixon. It all seemed to illustrate, as have other events since Mr. McGovern won the Democratic nomination, that he is, after all, a politician."

Naughton did not sound like the same man who had written about Ed Muskie. His on-the-one-hand-on-the-other-hand equivocations had been replaced by a tough, certain tone. But then Naughton's circumstances had changed. He was no longer covering a shaky primary candidate, wondering what the future held in store. He had made it through the eliminations and was one of the two anointed *Times* correspondents who had been assigned to cover the one and only Democratic candidate. As a result, he had a new confidence in himself, a self-assurance which allowed him to operate by the principle he had learned years before in Cleveland: "You should never place your trust in a politician."

CHAPTER IV

The Heavies

ONE AFTERNOON after the election, I asked Dick Stout what he thought of a certain campaign reporter. Stout was in one of his darker moods. "He's as good as any," he grumbled.

I waited for Stout to elaborate.

"Hell, political reporters," Stout said disgustedly. "Shit, they're like sportswriters. The job's a lot the same. It's fun to do. And the quality isn't very high. Anybody can be a political reporter or a sportswriter. Even though publications and networks put some of their best people on the candidates in an election year, they really don't have to. Because anybody really can do it. But you have to be exceptional to do it well. It really takes something to be a good one."

There were only a handful of reporters who everyone in the business agreed were exceptional. In any discussion or straw poll, the names that always came up were Johnny Apple, David Broder, Jules Witcover, Bob Novak, and Haynes Johnson.* Nobody could quite define what made these reporters exceptional. It was not just their wide knowledge of politics. Nor the fact that they worked for big papers. Nor that they were right all the time, because they weren't. When you asked around, the consensus was that they were a lot like other reporters except that they somehow had more energy, they were more monomaniacal about their work.

Here then are portraits of some of the Heavies:

Johnny Apple of *The New York Times*

"Take a look at Johnny Apple over there," said a celebrity-watching politico on the closing night of the Democratic Convention. "He practically goes around with a T-shirt saying, 'I work for the *Times:* I'm Number One!' "

R. W. "Johnny" Apple, Jr., *The New York Times'* national political correspondent, was standing in a shadowy area at the south end of the blue wooden stands of the Press Gallery. A chubby mid-thirtyish man with a pug nose and narrow eyes, he was wearing a polo shirt and slacks and looked like a country-club golfer. All of a sudden Ted Kennedy, who had just finished his speech nominating George McGovern for President, came around a corner a few feet away from Apple, walking briskly and followed by his entourage.

"Hey, Ted," shouted Apple, and waved him over. They chatted for about a minute.

"You know," said the politico as Ted left Apple, "Johnny thinks he's better than the pols he writes about. He thinks they need him. He seems to forget it's *The New York Times* they need, not him. If Johnny worked

---

* Other names frequently mentioned were Al Otten of *The Wall Street Journal*, Peter Lisagor of the *Chicago Daily News*, Walter Mears of the AP, Jim Perry of the *National Observer*, and Jack Germond of Gannett.

for the Denver *Post* and he said, 'Hey, Ted,' Teddy would have kept on walking."

Johnny Apple never hesitated to let you know that he was important. He once described to me the elaborate twenty-man "grid system" that the *Times* had developed to cover the primaries. "And then, floating above all that," he concluded, "is me. Nobody has as much authority as I do. I can do virtually any story I want to, and I can help shape what other people do."

In the eyes of many of his colleagues, Apple was a compulsive bullshit artist, the kind of man who could not resist adding $5,000-a-year when he told you his salary. Returning to New York from the *Times'* Saigon Bureau, Apple announced that he had killed several Vietcong, which prompted one *Times*man to mutter: "Women and children, I presume." At least a few journalists saw Apple as a ruthlessly ambitious hustler who had stabbed and flattered his way up through the ranks of the *Times*. Not many people had ever accused Apple of dishonest reporting; it was Apple's personality that turned them off—his braggadocio, his grandstanding, his mammoth ego. In a business populated largely by *shy* egomaniacs, he stuck out like a drunk at a funeral.

I first met Apple around noon on the Sunday before the California primary. Along with a dozen other very heavy media people, he had passed up the tacky Wilshire Hyatt House in favor of the posh Beverly Wilshire, in Beverly Hills. Most of his fellow journalists were lounging by the pool, but Apple had been pounding on his Olivetti since eight, finishing up his story for Monday's paper. He was phoning the last paragraphs to New York as I arrived. In a room as elegant as a Design Research store window, with bronze foil wallpaper and mod furniture, he was sitting in white BVD's taking a last hurried look through the mess of yellow legal paper on the desk.

"Hi," he thrust out his hand, "John Apple." As he slathered soap on his face to shave, he enthusiastically outlined the *Times'* campaign coverage. Talking nonstop, he pulled on some sports clothes, led me through the lobby and commandeered a good table on the shaded patio of the hotel restaurant. Having ordered a bullshot and a pack of Salems, he started attacking the basket of sweet rolls on the table. We were talking about the piece he had written for that morning's paper, in which he flatly predicted that a pack of Southern governors trying to stop McGovern would get nowhere.

"Believe it or not, they gave me an unlimited travel budget at the *Times*," he said, buttering a roll. "So when I get into a situation like that piece this morning, I *know* fifteen people in Georgia who I can get on the phone and will level with me, and I know another ten in Kentucky, because I've been all these places three and four times. That piece took about sixty-five phone calls—two whole days and part of a third. I'm a great string-saver —while I'm doing one story like that I'll duck into a phone booth and make half a dozen phone calls for another story.

"My all-time record"—he reached for a second roll and urged one on me—"my all-time record is a hundred calls in one day. That was on a story I did about five state conventions and a couple of territorial conventions or something. But I sat down at my desk at nine o'clock in the morning and got up at ten after seven. And I made about twenty-five of those calls trying to find out what happened in the Canal Zone. 'Cause I was determined I wasn't gonna have to write: 'A convention was also held in the Canal Zone, but we don't know what happened.' That's just a little matter of pride."

The waiter brought the poached eggs and caviar we had ordered. "The important thing is the amount of money a publisher is willing to contribute to travel," Apple went on. "Because travel is the soul of this business. You've gotta be there, you can't do it all on the telephone.

"Tell you a little story. When Tunney [Sen. John Tunney, D.-Cal.] and Moretti [Robert Moretti, Speaker of the California Assembly] made their announcement for Muskie, which I had a couple of days early, a rather bitter California reporter said to Moretti, 'How come we have to read what you're going to do in national politics in *The New York Times,* when *we* cover California?' And Moretti looked at the guy and said, 'If you'd been in my office four times in the last year drinking Scotch the way Johnny Apple was, maybe you wouldn't have to read about it in *The New York Times.*'"

Which implies that Apple got the story from his well-primed source, Moretti. That is not exactly what happened, according to a Tunney aide. The Tunney aide claims to have fed the story to Apple via a couple of intermediaries and for his own purposes. In other words, Apple was being used.

The Tunney endorsement was a big story, the first of a string of front-page scoops that Apple got on major political figures endorsing Muskie. Tunney was a bosom pal, law school roommate and fellow Senator of Ted Kennedy; if Tunney came out for Muskie, it was probably with Ted's consent and meant that Ted wasn't going to run.

Late in November '71, Muskie approached Tunney to ask for an endorsement. Tunney checked it out with Kennedy and got the green light. So Tunney's aide went ahead to make a deal: Tunney would endorse the Man from Maine if Muskie would promise to make him chairman of the California delegation at the Convention. Muskie agreed, and Tunney scheduled the press conference for a week later—Wednesday, December 7.

Meanwhile, Alan Cranston, the other Senator from California, got wind of Tunney's plans. Cranston decided he'd better endorse Muskie, too. So he called up Muskie and offered his endorsement in return for a promise that he would be chairman of the California delegation at the Convention. Muskie said yes. When Tunney's people found out that Muskie had promised the chairmanship to both Tunney and Cranston, they were furious. They called Muskie and raised hell. As usual, Muskie couldn't make up his mind what to do.

So, late on Monday, December 5, two days before the scheduled announcement, Tunney's aide decided to pull the rug out from under Cranston by leaking the Tunney endorsement to *The New York Times*. He found out that Johnny Apple was in Columbus, Ohio, seeing an old friend, John Gilligan, the governor of Ohio. The aide phoned Mark Shields, a Gilligan aide; Shields relayed the information to Gilligan; and Gilligan leaked the story to Apple. A three-cushion shot with Apple as the eight ball—it was hard for anyone to trace the story back to Tunney's aide and accuse him of screwing Cranston. On December 7, Johnny Apple's story—"Tunney Endorsement of Muskie in 1972 Race Is Reported Near"—appeared on the front page of the *Times*. It was almost an exclusive, but not quite. Just for insurance, Tunney's aide had also leaked the story to Sam Roberts of the New York *Daily News*.

In the next month, Mark Shields, the Gilligan aide, became a national coordinator of the Muskie campaign and proceeded to leak several Muskie endorsement stories exclusively to Apple, including the news that Leonard Woodcock of the UAW was going to come out for Muskie. Several high-level members of Muskie's staff were outraged that Shields was favoring one reporter and felt that Shields ought to be punished. But Shields, one of the shrewdest men on Muskie's staff, was sure he had done the right thing. By giving the stories exclusively to *The New York Times*, he had guaranteed: a) that *The Times* would give them front-page play and b) that every other paper in America would give them prominent coverage. Once a story hits page one of the *Times*, it is certified news and can't be ignored.*

---

* Apple had played this game at least twice before. When Robert Kennedy was about to enter the Senate race in New York in 1964, said a colleague of Apple's, "the Kennedy people played him like a yo-yo. His needs and their needs absolutely coincided. They wanted

"You build up confidence in people," Apple was saying as he sipped his bull-shot. "They tell you things." No small part of Apple's success was that he had been, for as long as anyone could remember, a red-hot, gung-ho overachiever. He was editor-in-chief of the yearbook at his Ohio prep school, Western Reserve Academy. At Princeton, he ran the newspaper, got elected vice chairman of the student council, and was thrown out for bad grades. He worked for *The Wall Street Journal*, did a hitch in the Army (moonlighting for a newspaper in Virginia), and finally graduated *magna cum laude* from Columbia in 1961. He was editor of the newspaper there, too. After a couple of years as a writer for Huntley-Brinkley at NBC, he joined the *Times* and became a protégé of Abe Rosenthal, who was then the metropolitan editor.

". . . he never stopped running. . . ," Gay Talese wrote of Apple in his book on the *Times*. "The result was that he got more good stories into the paper than anyone on Rosenthal's staff. This is not what bothered his older colleagues so much, for they soon recognized his ability to get a story and write it; what really bothered them was Apple's incredible enthusiasm for everything he had been assigned to cover—a Board of Estimate hearing, a talk by the tax commissioner, a repetition of political speeches—and Apple's insistence, once he had returned, on telling everybody in the newsroom what he had seen and heard."*

Apple practically *ran* up the ladder of good reportorial jobs—Bobby Kennedy's 1964 Senate campaign, the Albany Statehouse, Vietnam, Nelson Rockefeller's '68 Presidential campaign, Africa, and then the whole na-

to be in the paper every day and he wanted to be in the paper every day. They just leaked him stuff and he put it right in. And of course, the *Times* wanted a story on Bobby Kennedy every day. Same thing when Rockefeller was trying to decide whether or not to go in before the 1968 Convention. Again, the Rockefeller people played him like a yo-yo."

* *The Kingdom and the Power* by Gay Talese (New York, World, 1969).

tional political scene. He was a golden boy. Someone once asked Abe Rosenthal what was the best decision he had ever made. "Hiring Johnny Apple," Rosenthal shot back immediately.

The lowlier employees of the *Times* were not so enamored of Apple. Among his fellow reporters, Apple had the reputation of an ass-kisser. He not only flattered Rosenthal, it was said, but also took pains to ingratiate himself with the Sulzberger family, who owned and published the *Times*. He had, for instance, gone out and written an enthusiastic feature about a radio show that was run by Ellen Sulzberger Straus (cousin of Punch Sulzberger, the publisher). It was around this time, in 1964, that David Halberstam returned to the *Times'* New York office after having reported on Vietnam for several years, for which coverage he had won a Pulitzer Prize. One afternoon, as he sat at his desk, Halberstam spotted a round-faced young man walking around the city room as if he owned it. Halberstam realized that this must be Abe Rosenthal's current pet, Johnny Apple. Apple sauntered over to Halberstam's desk and announced with studied nonchalance: "Say, I was over at Peter and Ellen Straus's—you know, Punch's favorite cousin—last night, and Harding Bancroft [vice president of the *Times*] was there, and your name came up and I thought you'd be pleased—it was very favorably commented upon."

Halberstam said his first words to Johnny Apple: "Fuck off, kid!"

What constantly amazed people, as the years passed, was that Apple remained the same eager, egregiously ambitious kid he had been when he first arrived at the *Times*. He still had a restless, stir-crazy desire to get every story first—a commendable trait in a reporter. But some of his colleagues thought that he was less interested in covering the election than in seeking out small pieces of information that some of his more eminent rivals, like David Broder, did not have in their stories. He did not seem to develop the depth, reflectiveness, and moral courage necessary to become a great journalist. He never stopped running for long enough to form any ideas; one could not imagine him writing a thoughtful magazine piece or a book review. "Johnny has not grown up in one way," said a reporter who had known him for years. "And that is that he literally believes that newspapermen are judged on how many by-lines they get, not what they say. We all used to think that way when we were kids—'Gee, I got six by-lines this week' —but Johnny still talks that way. He travels all over and spreads himself thin. He should write one or two pieces a week and give people some insight into what the fuck's going on, but instead he tells people how many delegates McGovern had on Thursday as opposed to Tuesday. Scoreboard journalism, and the *Times* has a hundred good reporters who can do that.

"In April," the reporter continued, "Apple wrote one of the best stories of the campaign—that interview with John Gilligan where Gilligan talked about all the things that were going wrong with Muskie's campaign. Apple has worked Gilligan as a source for a long time and he got Gilligan to say things that politicians never say. It was funny, it was sad, it was insightful. And he blew it. He could have taken a week and made that interview the centerpiece for a long front-page article on what it's like to run a campaign and how Muskie's failed. But as it was he got that interview in two hours and got on a plane and the fucking thing ran way inside the paper with a one-column head and only professionals saw it. He just never bothered to develop it."

Some reporters, when they have passed thirty and have achieved some success, begin to nurture healthy doubts about their work, about the use of the power they have attained, about the difference between the reality they witness and what they report as news. Apple never seemed to feel a twinge of doubt. As long as he was getting exclusives, writing big stories, breaking news earlier than other reporters, he was happy. He was not anxious to analyze, to explore the meaning of events. He liked to write prediction stories, to be the first reporter to say that a certain candidate was going to win. I once asked Edward Folliard, the Washington *Post's* emeritus political reporter, why so many reporters want to write prediction stories. "They do it because it's fun," said Folliard. A few reporters were gradually coming to realize that it did the public little good to know who was going to win or which way a certain state was going to vote—they would find that out on election day anyway. But it was a game with reporters to predict these things, and Apple liked to win the game.

Apple had a mania for being "one jump ahead." Over lunch at the Beverly Wilshire, he mentioned the story he had written three days before the New Hampshire primary, saying that Muskie was in trouble in three of the first four primary states. "We had men traveling with the candidates and men assessing the situation in New Hampshire, and that enabled me to stay one jump ahead," he said. "So in New Hampshire, I had talked to a lot of candidates, managers and local people I knew and I got this idea Muskie was slipping. I thought, 'Shit, if this is happening here, it must be happening elsewhere.' So I went to Florida and Wisconsin in the three weeks before the election, and it was as obvious as the nose on your face."

Apple always stayed ahead of the pack on day-to-day events, but he was seldom ahead of public opinion on major social issues. In 1966, when he first arrived in Saigon, he had aspired to be "Combat Johnny," wearing a German brush cut, talking tough, and bragging about the number of VC he had killed. By 1967, however, he perceived a general feeling that the war was not admirable; suddenly he began to write that the war was a stalemate—even though it had already been stalemated for at least a year.

"He is classically the reporter that the *Times* would have invented," says a fellow reporter. "He asks just the questions that they want asked and not one more; he doesn't probe too deeply; and if he ever started to doubt what he was doing, he would tell them about those doubts. He's not like that deliberately to please the *Times*. It's just the way he is."

For all Apple's energy, ambition, and haste to get to the top, he was not an overreacher. Although he thrived on leaks and plants, he never pretended to get information from a high authority when he had got it from a lowly source, and he was careful not to lie in print. The closest he ever came was in a dispatch from Saigon, in which he claimed that a bullet had split the seat of his pants while he was under enemy fire. When skeptical colleagues asked to inspect the evidence, Apple said that he had thrown the trousers away. "Threw them away!" one of the skeptics later exclaimed. "He's so full of it. I mean, you better believe that if a bullet *did* go through your pants you'd save the goddam things and frame them!"

The tale of the pants is among the most famous stories about Apple, but there are hundreds of others. Apple is probably the leading character in contemporary American journalistic folklore. Other reporters are fascinated by him and love to tell stories about him. Even back in the early sixties, when Apple was covering the Statehouse in Albany, his fellow reporters constantly traded anecdotes about his boastfulness and incredible aggressiveness. Apple stories so completely dominated the conversation of a group of Statehouse reporters who dined every night in the same restaurant that anyone who mentioned Apple had to pay a fine of fifty cents. One night one of the reporters angrily stalked into the restaurant and threw a ten-dollar bill onto the table. "That fucking Apple. . . ," he began, and went on to complain about ten dollars' worth of outrages.

There was a reason why reporters told stories about Apple: they recognized many of their own traits in him, grotesquely magnified. The shock of recognition frightened them. Apple was like them, only more blatant. He openly displayed the faults they tried to hide: the insecurity, the ambitiousness, the name-dropping, the ass-kissing, and the weakness for powerful men. So, like prep school boys tormenting the class goat, they shifted the spotlight off themselves by making fun of Johnny Apple. When they talked about him, they were really saying: "I hope it doesn't show so much in me. I hope I'm not that bad. I'm really much better than that."

At the same time, the reporters admired Apple. (The class goat happens to be a genius at Math and becomes popular at exam time). He knew more about the fine, mundane details of national party politics than almost anyone in the business. "During the primaries," said Jim Doyle, "Johnny did it best. Johnny became a source for many, many guys who weren't getting around as much as he was. He became a source for me."

Not only did other reporters read Apple's articles for unique information, they also looked to him for guidance whenever they had to cover a story where there were no handouts, no speeches, and no easy answers. Such a situation arose in late January, when the Democratic precincts of Iowa held caucuses to vote for delegates to the Convention. The Iowa precinct caucuses were the first test of Muskie's strength, and thirty or forty reporters—national political reporters, campaign reporters, and men from small papers—descended on Des Moines to report and interpret the results. When they crowded into the tiny, steamy Democratic headquarters on the night of January 24 to hear a local Democratic official announce the hour-by-hour returns, none of them could make much sense of the figures. Except for Apple.

A McGovern worker who was present recalled the scene. It was the first time he had ever seen the national press in operation. "It really amazed me," he said, "because what happened was that Johnny Apple of *The New York Times* sat in a corner and everyone peered over his shoulder to find out what he was writing. The AP guy was looking over one shoulder, the UPI guy over the other and CBS, NBC, ABC and the Baltimore *Sun* were all crowding in behind. See, it wasn't like a primary. No one knew how to interpret these figures, nobody knew what was good and what was bad, so they were all taking it off Apple. He would sit down and write a lead, and they would go write leads. Then he'd change his lead when more results came in, and they'd all change theirs accordingly. When he wanted quiet to hear the guy announce the latest returns, he'd shout for quiet and they'd all shut up. Finally, at midnight, the guy announced that Muskie had 32 percent and Mc-Govern had 26 percent, and Apple sat down to write his final story. He called it something like 'a surprisingly strong showing for George McGovern.' Everyone peered over his shoulder again and picked it up. It was on the front page of every major newspaper the next day."

Because of Apple's enormous power, politicians were sensitive to anything he wrote and often had gripes with him. During the early primaries, Lindsay and Mc-Govern people complained that Apple was favoring Muskie. Although Apple claimed that he had tried to insure from the beginning that the *Times* would give serious coverage to McGovern's campaign, the fact remains that he relied heavily on party regulars as sources. This constantly irritated the more liberal, reform-minded Democrats.

On the last night of the Democratic Convention, I was waiting for a floor pass with a young lady journalist, who had taken time off in the spring to serve as Sissy Farenthold's press officer during Farenthold's bid for the Democratic gubernatorial nomination in Texas. Suddenly Apple came charging out of the Press Gallery, beaming and heading straight for us.

"Wasn't I right?" he demanded as he reached us. "Didn't I tell you back in California that McGoo was going to get the nomination!"

"Yeah, you sure did," I said. Apple always referred to McGovern as "McGoo." Apple was a *Times*man to the core, so to speak, but he often seemed anxious to prove that he was not a running dog of the establishment, especially when he was around young people. So

he did naughty little things to assert his independence
—like calling the candidate "McGoo," or wearing his
hair long, or refusing to wear a jacket and tie—things
that made him stand out from the stuffy grey image of
the *Times*. He was one of the few men on the *Times*
with aspirations to hipness.

I had a vague recollection of Apple telling me in June
that McGoo had the nomination sewed up. "You were
right about that," I shouted at Apple over the blare of
the band and the clamor of the delegates.

He smiled again and launched into another sentence,
but the young lady cut him off. "Boy," she said, "I've
been meaning to talk to you. You completely misrepre-
sented Sissy Farenthold. You were inaccurate."

"No I wasn't," said Apple. His smile crumpled and he
began to hedge away like a criminal who had just spotted the one witness he thought was dead.

"You said Sissy's issues were gun control, abortion,
and the Texas Rangers, but they weren't . . ." the
young lady fired away, but Apple had given a little
wave, backed off fast, and disappeared into the crowd.

"My God," said the young lady. "Sissy's main issue
was tax reform, and he never said anything about that.
David Broder of the *Post* rode around with us, but we
never saw Apple on the campaign plane. Instead, he got
most of his information from some of Ben Barnes' people—the powerful oil-interest Democrats who were running against Sissy. I guess he saw a few of *our* staffers in
Dallas. But Dallas is the home of Texas radical chic. He
never saw the Chicanos and blacks and poor whites who
were working for Sissy in Houston. He missed the whole
point of the campaign. I always believed that the *Times*
was accurate, but I'll never trust it again after reading
that story."

Johnny Apple's confidence wasn't shaken like that
very often. One of his virtues as a journalist was that he
took confident stands in many of his stories. He didn't
hedge a lot of bets. "Part of that is because I have the

strong backing of a strong newspaper," he said at the Wilshire. "I'm never questioned on what I write. Never! Occasionally there will be a small hassle about phraseology—but as to my overall judgment of what a situation is, they don't argue."

So it shook him like an earthquake when the *Times* killed his major Democratic Convention story—his on-the-money analysis of the South Carolina vote. On Monday night, when the McGovern forces purposely "lost" the South Carolina challenge rather than risk a narrow "Twilight Zone" victory that would have brought up sticky parliamentary questions, Walter Cronkite announced that it was a serious setback for the McGovern people, and NBC acted momentarily confused. But Apple filed five-hundred words explaining the whole Byzantine mess, and showing that it was really a victory for McGovern's crack troops.*

Apple knew it was coming. The week before, he had written about the parliamentary skirmishing that was likely to break out at the Convention. That morning, in Monday's *Times,* he had a piece outlining the parliamentary game plans that the McGovern generals might put into effect. At one o'clock that afternoon, he got a memo from Jim Naughton predicting the McGovern tactic. And when the vote actually came up, he was sit-

---

* The South Carolina credentials challenge was not overly complicated in itself; the question was whether more women should be put on the South Carolina delegation in order to comply with the equality guidelines that McGovern's own party reform commission had handed down. What made this challenge a crucial battle was the fact that if the vote fell in the "Twilight Zone" between 1,496 and 1,509 votes, the Stop McGovern forces (led by Humphrey) would have been able to raise certain procedural questions that might have caused McGovern to lose 151 California delegates in a later credentials challenge. If that happened, McGovern might have lost the nomination. So the McGovern forces had either to win decisively or lose decisively, but they could not afford to get caught in the "Twilight Zone." Seeing that they could not win big, the McGovern command ordered their delegates to throw votes to Humphrey's side and deliberately lose the challenge. This move effectively blocked the Humphrey forces' last chance at sinking McGovern.

ting on a folding chair at the *Times* counter in the press bleachers, keeping a tally for Max Frankel, the Washington Bureau chief.

"When the two states switched—I knew people in the delegations—I turned to Max and said, 'Throw something in the story about how they're switching votes to put off the main showdown until the California vote'," Apple recalled later. "Then I wrote a new top for my 'Convention Notes' column, explaining the whole thing. We sent it off and heard not a single word. We presumed it was in the paper, everybody was happy, and we went off to bed."

Around noon the next day, Apple sauntered into the *Times* office to look at his story in the late edition, which was flown to Miami every morning. The *Times* had the biggest office of any newspaper at the Convention; it occupied half of the vast East Riviera Room of the Fontainbleau Hotel. The far wall of the office contained plate-glass windows that looked out on the pea-green Atlantic. The near wall was a tall aluminum partition that had been erected to make the *Times* office a little fortress within the gilded and thickly carpeted ballroom.

When Apple walked in and picked up the *Times,* a UPI machine was softly sputtering away, a couple of operators were typing on the big Western Union machines, and several *Times*men were working behind an array of steel desks. Apple carefully scanned the first section of the paper for his story. He couldn't find it. It didn't take him long to realize he couldn't find it because it wasn't there. The editors in the "bullpen" in New York had axed it. His face turned crimson, he wheeled, and then he lashed the *Times* against the aluminum partition. It made a sound like a locomotive hitting a Mayflower moving van. Several writers jumped in their seats. "Those motherfucking cocksuckers ought to be fired!" he screamed. "They are a goiter on the body of journalism!"

At least, that's what he said he screamed. Some witnesses claimed that he quit on the spot, but Apple denied it. "I had a cow, to say the least," he chuckled over Long Distance when I called to ask about the incident. "But I didn't resign. I only said I was going to resign. The whole incident was over within an hour because I had to get the hell to work on the next day's story. Gene Roberts, the national editor, got on the phone to New York. He was extremely angry and felt that we had been ahead on the parliamentary story; we had far more on the maneuvering than anyone else, and then, when the denouement arrived, they cut us off. They had no reason for doing it, no matter what the reason was."

It was rumored that the New York editors had killed Apple's story when they saw Walter Cronkite saying that the South Carolina vote marked a defeat for McGovern, that they had chosen to believe Cronkite over Apple. Everyone at the *Times* denied this, including Apple. "No," he said, "somehow one of the editors decided we didn't need any additional information to that in Max's story. Or that it didn't fit with what I had written before. He took one or two paragraphs out of mine and slapped them way down in Max's story."

In the end, the editors retooled Apple's story and ran it a day late, but it is difficult to measure the long-range effect of the whole explosion. Apple had reached the higher echelons of the *Times,* where politics is practiced almost as much as journalism, and the South Carolina incident occurred just as he was jockeying for the position of Washington Bureau chief. Max Frankel was getting a promotion, and the job was up for grabs. During June and July, Apple's hair was short and neat. He had got a haircut, it was said, to show the Powers in New York that he was just as clean-cut as Anthony Lewis (London Bureau chief and columnist), Robert Semple (White House correspondent), and Hedrick Smith (Moscow Bureau chief), who were also supposed to be contenders for the prize.

But when Apple showed up in August for the Republican Convention, his prematurely grey hair again flopped over his ears and crawled down the back of his neck. The night before the Convention, he was hopping around the Poodle Room in the Fontainbleau, a dark and noisy bar where middle-aged hookers hustled over-weight Babbitts from Midwestern delegations.

"You're going hip," I said. "You've turned into a goddam longhair."

"Come on," he said, genuinely insulted. "You know my hair's always been long."

A young *Times*man wandered up and began to make in-jokes about internal politics on the paper. All *Times*-like propriety had dissolved many drinks ago.

"Hey," the young *Times*man needled Apple, "too bad about the Washington Bureau. What are you gonna do now?"

Everybody thought at this time that the fix was in for Anthony Lewis to be the new chief. The job actually went to Clifton Daniel in a surprise move several weeks later.

"Same thing I've been doing all along—I'm just a re-porter," Apple said with his best country-boy smile.

"Come on."

"Naw," said Apple, "I never expected them to con-sider me seriously for the job."

"You know you wanted it."

Apple shrugged the way Rocky used to shrug when pressed about his Presidential aspirations. "Do I *look* like a Washington Bureau chief of *The New York Times?*" he asked rhetorically. And he flashed a big What-Me-Worry? smile. He had not watched a hundred concession speeches without learning a few tricks of the trade.

David Broder of the Washington *Post*

The high priest of political journalism, the most power-ful and respected man in the trade, was David Broder. He was Johnny Apple's counterpart—national political correspondent—on the Washington *Post,* a paper which vies with the *Times* to give the best political coverage in the country. Since the *Post* is located in a city which has an almost insatiable hunger for political news, it devotes an enormous amount of space to politics, and its coverage is often more thorough and colorful than that of the *Times.* The *Post's* only competition in the Capital is the Washington *Star-News*—a decidedly parochial paper that often ends up losing its best political writers to the *Post.* The *Post* is a great national newspaper, and a permanent berth on its national staff is enough to give clout to any reporter. But Broder's reputation transcends even the prestige of the *Post.* If he were to quit tomorrow and begin publishing a mimeographed tip sheet in his basement, Broder would still probably wield the kind of influence that can change campaigns in their course and other reporters in their opinions. "Broder's the mark," said another reporter. "You have to measure your own stuff against what he writes. He's also the target, and you always find things in his articles to tear apart. But at the end of a year, when you look at his total output, he's always given the best picture of what happened."

Many of the reporters on the press bus believed that in 1968 Broder divined, through some dark kind of journalistic voodoo, that Nixon would choose Spiro T. Agnew as his running mate. As a result they saw Broder, and sometimes venerated him, as a certified oracle. The Agnew story hardly ever failed to come up when Broder was introduced, and it had probably done more than anything else to enhance his reputation. Broder enjoyed exploding the myth.

"That story of mine was a plant," he said with a laugh when I asked him about it.

"A plant?" I said incredulously. "From whom?"

"From Nixon!" said Broder, as if he still couldn't believe it himself. "We were on a plane flying from Pendleton to Portland, Oregon, and Nixon sent somebody back to the press section to get me to come up and talk to him, and in about two minutes' time he had gone

from the fact that he was confident of Oregon, to the
fact that Oregon would cinch him the nomination, to the
fact that he was now thinking seriously about what kind
of person should be his Vice Presidential running mate.
He threw out a couple of obvious names that you would
have to think about, and then he said, 'What would be
the reaction to Ted Agnew, what kind of a reputation
does he have among the reporters?'

"And so we talked about Agnew, and Nixon said,
'You know, he's quite an urban expert, he was a county
executive, he's a lawyer,' and I said, 'OK. I'm beginning
to get the message.' "

High up in his subsequent story, Broder mentioned
the Agnew possibility, wrapping it in many qualifica-
tions. "I wrote it in May, and promptly forgot about it.
It never crossed my mind again that it was a serious
prospect, and I was as astonished as everyone in that
Convention when it came to pass. But out of that, I've
become 'a great confidant of Richard Nixon's' and 'the
only reporter who knew he was going to pick Agnew.' "

With his short, greying hair, his horn-rims, and his
unhurried, straight-necked, dignified walk, Broder has
the look of the youngest full professor on the faculty of
M.I.T. Indeed, the columns which he frequently writes
for the *Post*'s Op-Ed page often have a slightly profes-
sorial tone, as if he were giving a civics lecture. Unlike
most political journalists, Broder has a philosophy, even
a passion; he believes that the two-party system will save
America. He admits that the two parties have shattered
and rotted, but he wants to see them repaired. He believes in the system as it is outlined in the civics books
and he wants to see it work. The alternative, he fears, is
"the rule of the streets" and "confrontation politics, with
its constant threat of violence and repression."

The son of a dentist, Broder grew up in Chicago
Heights, Illinois, in a family that supported Roosevelt
and constantly talked politics at the dinner table. He
broke into journalism at the age of ten, when a friend
got a hectograph machine for Christmas, and they began

publishing a weekly sheet and peddling it around the neighborhood. After that, Broder never wanted to be anything but a journalist.

Broder acquired most of his political theory from a couple of left-leaning professors at the University of Chicago, who impressed on him the role of the state in creating the good life for individuals. But his first practical lessons in politics came from running the campus newspaper. Broder had entered college a couple of years after World War II, at a time when the Communist party was trying to take over student organizations. He was a leader of the liberal faction of student journalists that eventually beat out the Communist faction in a bloodless political battle for control of the paper. "Both sides used the classic tactics," he said. "Come early, stay late, vote often, pack the staff with your people, and always find an acceptable stooge to front for you. We had some incredible goddam fights. You even had to worry about the political affiliation of the guy who was taking the paper down to the print shop on any given night, because if he was on the other side he damn well might rewrite a lead or a headline to get the party line into the paper." Broder carried away from college both a fascination for the nuts and bolts of political organization and a strong distaste for political groups which tried to subvert the system.

After serving in the Army, he made a rapid rise as a political reporter, working first for the Bloomington (Ill.) *Pantograph,* then moving to Washington in 1955 to write for the *Congressional Quarterly,* then going to the Washington *Star.* In 1965, when Johnny Apple was still a Statehouse reporter, *The New York Times* hired Broder as its national political reporter; he resigned a year and a half later, having run into irreconcilable differences with the national desk. The *Post* immediately grabbed him as its national political man.

As he rose from job to job, Broder kept adding to his list of contacts; by the early sixties, he seemed to know every politician, county chairman, and legislative aide in

America. His fascination with the machinery of politics
continued to grow as he came to know it more intimately. For instance, no story intrigued him more than the
way in which Richard Nixon set out to rebuild the frac-
tured Republican party, and his own political career, in
1966. Broder's coverage reflected his awe for Nixon's
impeccable professionalism.

In 1967, Broder flatly stated that Eugene McCarthy
could not topple an incumbent President. As the antiwar
movement grew, Broder first underrated its strength and
then attacked it as a threat to the system. In the fall of
1969, while he was a Fellow at Harvard's Kennedy
School of Government, Broder filed his now-famous
"Breaking of the President" column. Broder accused the
Vietnam Moratorium Committee of trying to destroy
Nixon just to prove that it could. "There is no great
trick in using the Vietnam issue to break another President," he wrote. "But when you have broken the President, you have broken the one man who can negotiate
the peace." There was an immediate uproar. While the
Republicans happily distributed copies of the article,
protests poured in from antiwar leaders, and the graduate students in Broder's seminar insisted on hotly dis-
cussing the article for the whole first half of the semes-
ter.

At these discussions, Broder realized that he still really believed that "our party system was an exquisitely
tuned mechanism, designed to deal with the regional,
economic and political differences in a continent-sized
democracy." He didn't wish to see that system damaged.
He admitted that his was "essentially a very status quo
view." And he began to see, for the first time, that there
was a widespread disaffection with conventional politics
throughout the country. But when he finished his year at
Harvard, Broder wrote a book, *The Party's Over,* in
which he argued that the cure for this massive disaffection was to reform and revive the two parties so that the
system would work well again.

Most of Broder's colleagues felt that his hope for a revival of two well-disciplined parties, each with leaders committed to clearly delineated programs, was a pipe dream. Some felt that Broder's understanding of politics was narrow and mechanical, and that his fear of change, conflict and disorder continued to blind him to the broad political upheavals that were taking place outside of Washington. Saul Friedman, a political writer for Knight Newspapers who had covered the civil rights and antiwar movements through much of the sixties, had even written a rebuttal to Broder's "Breaking of the President" piece back in 1969. "Like many who are close to the people and processes of the American political system," wrote Friedman, "Broder knows and loves it best when it operates with undisturbed beauty. He is really concerned, I think, not only that the process is now being disturbed but that the disturbance comes from outsiders who do not practice politics for its own sake." Friedman felt that this still held true in 1972.

Of course, in his tendency to focus on old-fashioned party politics instead of new movements, Broder was no different from 95 percent of the political reporters in Washington. The difference was that he had more contacts than the rest and often had a quicker sense of what was happening in the arena. He was also one of the few reporters in town with a clearly defined philosophy, which, if it limited his view, also gave his columns a coherency and helped him to put the crazy happenings of an election year into clear perspective.

Above all, Broder was a man who knew what he wanted. He wanted freedom to write about what he felt were the important stories and to supply the background and analysis necessary for understanding these stories. Broder had left the *Times* in 1966 partly because the editors in New York restricted his turf, not allowing him to cover stories in the New York area. But, as Gay Talese wrote in *The Kingdom and the Power*, Broder also "chafed repeatedly at the . . . general tendency in

New York to overplay news stories with big names and to underplay trend stories or stories of a more analytical character." In a memo Broder sent to the managing editor after resigning, he complained that the editors favored political stories about extremists, about political action by Southern Negroes, and about the Kennedys. "These may be the grist of political talk at New York cocktail parties," he added, "but, as you know, they do not begin to embrace the variety of concerns that really animates national politics." Time and again, Broder's beloved analysis stories had been tampered with, killed, or held until they were stale, usually because of bureaucratic snafus. At the *Post*, Broder was largely free of these frustrations, free to travel where he wanted, write as he pleased, and to suggest and carry out innovations in the paper's political coverage.

Broder did not like anyone telling him what to write, including politicians. He was fully aware of the "mutual manipulation process that goes on constantly" between reporters and politicians, but while he accepted this as a fact of life, he himself was extremely wary of being used.

A professional political hustler, a man whose livelihood often depended on his success at "planting" stories, said: "You can't feed a story to Broder. If you call him up with a tout, he's insulted, he usually won't use it. He likes to find things out for himself. And he doesn't like to just *break* a story, he likes to look at the story and see what it means." Even when Nixon handed him the Agnew plant, Broder treated it as if it were a package that ticked and refused to make much out of it.

OF COURSE, Broder was far from infallible. In fact, it was Broder's fallibility that led Hunter Thompson, the iconoclastic *Rolling Stone* reporter, and myself to visit him at the *Post* on one tropical afternoon in June 1972. Thompson wanted to collect on a couple of bets. In Wisconsin, Broder had bet him a hundred dollars that McGovern would do better than 30 percent in the primary and another hundred that Wallace would get under 10 percent. He lost on both counts. McGovern did exactly 30 percent, not a hair better; and Wallace came in at 22 percent. Thompson immediately announced in his column that he meant to "hunt the bastard down and rip his teeth out if he tries to welsh," which may have accounted for the long silence from Broder.

Then Broder suddenly came out of his cave and offered to go for double or nothing. Humphrey, he said, would win in California. That scared the hell out of Thompson, but he took the bet. Thompson kept the bet a secret, though. He was afraid that if the rest of the press found out that Super-Wizard David Broder had money on Humphrey, they might start predicting a Humphrey victory and thereby give his failing campaign a last-minute lift.

After June 6, Thompson started looking for Broder and his four hundred dollars. Two weeks later, Thompson finally ran into Broder at a McGovern Victory Party in New York, at which time Broder hastily offered to make out on IOU on a napkin. But Thompson had a head full of mescaline and was in no condition to conduct serious business, so he put it off. By the time we showed up at the *Post*, Thompson was beginning to be troubled by guilt feelings about taking Broder's money.

Broder was standing in his shirt-sleeves by his grey metal desk in the *Post*'s brand new, flourescent-lit, morgue-like city room. "Here come the *Rolling Stone* boys," he said with a big grin. He immediately proposed a new, astounding, double-or-nothing offer: Jules Witcover would run a foot-race with Jack Germond in the sand of Miami Beach. Broder was backing Germond.

Since Witcover's legs were twice as long as Germond's, Thompson agreed to the bet—on the condition that he could run a urinalysis on Germond. Broder accepted.* They shook hands on it. Then, like a couple of sports in a Canadian Club ad, we asked Broder out for drinks. He looked skeptical. It was three in the afternoon. But he straightened his tie, got his suit jacket, and we set off for the dining room of the Pick Lee Hotel, a few doors up from the *Post*. The dining room was closed, so we headed up the street to the next bar in sight, the New York Lounge. It was greatly to Broder's credit that he didn't flinch as we entered the place, which I later found out had been taken over by the *Post*'s linotypists. The reporters had their five o'clock beers a couple of doors up, at the more respectable Post Bar. The New York Lounge was a grimy one-room affair, dark enough to suggest that no light bulbs had been changed since the fifties. There was a jukebox at the back, playing Smokey Robinson tunes, and a woman bartender named Lou behind the bar. We sat down in a rear booth, avoiding the part of the seat where the spring was coming through. Thompson put in a complicated order of Margaritas and beer, I ordered Scotch, and Broder asked for a Coke. An extremely disciplined man, he never smoked and hardly ever took a hard drink; his only vice was chewing his fingernails. I switched on the Sony, and Thompson and I began to probe the sensitive subject of fallibility in political journalism.

"I will now be an old fart for one minute," Broder said cheerfully, "and tell you that the most distressing thing about covering politics is that the guy who was absolutely right, whose wisdom was almost breathtaking one election year—you go back to that same man for wisdom some other year and he'll be as dumb as dogshit. That's why it's not a science. You can say, 'In

---

* Jim Naughton was later substituted for Witcover. In Miami, Germond "won" the race "by default," using the expedient of posting announcements all over the Fontainebleau Hotel to the effect that he was sorry to hear that Naughton had a "personal problem" and could not race. Although Naughton was in perfect health and willing to race, he gave in to Germond's ruse, and thus Broder was spared having to pay off the bet.

1968, I learned the following key lessons, which I'm
going to write down in the front of my notebook and
look at them twice a day all through 1972'—and you'll
get absolutely deceived by doing that."

Which was true; anyone who tried to apply old lessons to 1972 would have looked hopelessly bad. Broder
had tried to avoid the trap of fighting the last war, but
he had gone astray nonetheless in 1971 and early '72.
He had devoted a lot of space to Muskie (always with
the caveat that it was nonsense to consider the contest
locked up), he had spent no less than ten days researching and writing an exhaustive article on the Birch Bayh
machine, and he had generally slighted the candidacy of
George McGovern. We kept asking Broder where he
had gone wrong, and whether it had been possible for
even the wisest of men to foresee the situation this year.

"The one thing I'll say in my defense," said Broder,
"is that I repeatedly wrote, 'Front runner is a meaningless term.' There's a lawyer named Milt Gwirtzman who
works for McGovern, and I keep cribbing his laws of
politics, and his first law of Presidential politics is that
nothing that happens before the first Presidential primary really has any relevance at all. So those three years
are a very artificial environment.

"They're campaigning for us and putting on parades
for us in the press, they're putting on shows for other
politicians; it has very little to do with the voters. A
good case could be made that we shouldn't say anything
about them at all, except that's an impossible rule to follow in this town because the appetite for politics is con-
tinuous. Also you want some sense of the evolution of
these guys as personalities. But no matter how you play
it, you're going to end up with a rather low yield of significant information in an odd-numbered year.

"I was very proud of that piece I did on how Birch
Bayh, who seemed to have no following at all in the
country, had nonetheless assembled this marvelous machine. Turns out I should have been looking at Mc-
Govern—bad judgment on my part. But I'm damned if

I can tell you even in retrospect how I should have known at that point."

We nodded and asked Broder how any of us was supposed to know a year ahead that, for instance, a twenty-six-year-old kid named Gene Pokorny was already nailing down Wisconsin for McGovern. Did the press miss the McGovern story, or was it even there to get?

"Oh, yeah," said Broder, "I knew that Pokorny was there and I knew he was making lists, but he was one of twelve guys in twelve different Presidential camps who was busy, busy, busy making lists. As it turned out, *his* lists were made up of people who honest-to-god when the time came were ready to go to work, and the others weren't.

"That's why this all may be unknowable in advance. I went back over my notes from New Hampshire, and I had all this stuff about the Muskie organization in the fall of 1971. They had this very clear organization: they would have two thousand volunteers signed up by December 15, and they would do a sample run-through on this date and so on, and all of it was beautiful on paper. It was not until you came to the first of February and it was evident by even the most simple kind of check that *no* canvassing had been done for Muskie, that you began to be able to say, 'This is a facade.' "

Which was pretty nearly what Broder had said in a piece in late February. Broder and several other *Post* reporters had gone from door to door in several New Hampshire precincts, conducting a private canvass. They found far fewer Muskie voters than they had expected. The resulting article was the first to question Muskie's strength, and it had an enormous impact on the other reporters in New Hampshire, who immediately began to doubt the myth of the Muskie juggernaut. The article also infuriated the Muskie people, who were not yet admitting to themselves that their organization was a paper tiger. On the morning the piece hit the stands, Broder received three irate phone calls from Muskie people in Washington before he even got out of bed.

"I think," said Broder, "that it would have been useful for me to get out of Washington more. The Pokorny thing for instance. I ran into Pokorny at a picnic with a bunch of liberal friends of mine in Austin, Texas—I was there with Harold Hughes on one of his exploratory swings. And there was this strange Gene Pokorny in May of 1971, and he had flown in that day, and he and some of these crazy Travis County liberals were busy plotting about precinct caucuses a year from then. But what never crossed my mind was that their people really had a commitment to do some work and that George McGovern had a potential of developing a constituency beyond those five or ten thousand people who were obviously involved."

Misjudging McGovern was one mistake that Broder continued to make, which was why he was willing to put big money on Humphrey in California. He still hadn't adjusted to the new political situation. He figured that Humphrey would have his first big Jewish vote in California, his first big black vote there, plus a big last-ditch effort by labor. And he was right about all that (with the possible exception of labor). "Now, where I was wrong," he said ruefully, as he continued to nurse his Coke, "and where I have been consistently wrong all year, was in sort of underestimating the ability of the McGovern people to maximize McGovern's assets."

His wrong-headedness on this point often smacked of righteousness. He repeatedly indicated in his writing that he was afraid the McGovern delegates wouldn't be housebroken. It was the "Breaking of the President" piece all over again. In his column of June 20, he cited several examples of McGovern delegates misbehaving at state caucuses. (Except for pushing through a resolution sanctioning homosexual "marriage," the delegates didn't do anything Richard Daley hadn't been doing for forty years.) Broder wrote:

"As word of these and similar incidents in recent weeks has filtered back to Washington, a shudder of apprehension has gone through Democratic ranks. For the

first time, there is beginning to be widespread concern
that the Miami Beach convention hall may prove to be
the disaster for the Democrats that the San Francisco
Cow Palace was for the GOP in 1964." Of course, it
turned out to be the best-behaved Convention in history.

Broder was looking at his watch more and more frequently in the dim barroom light. Thompson was trying
to catch the waitress's eye to order two more beers for
himself. Our clothes were beginning to stick to the vinyl
upholstery in the heat. So, while Thompson finally tore
out of his seat to head off the waitress, I finished up the
interview by asking Broder what changes he would like
to see made in political journalism.

First, he said, the press was still using very primitive
means to "gauge and describe the dynamics of public
opinion." He liked the fact that the *Times* and the *Post*
had both hired pollsters to help them out in 1972. Later
in that year, he and Haynes Johnson, another *Post* reporter, would travel across America interviewing voters
to see how they felt about the candidates and the major
issues.

At the same time, Broder was not going out into the
field simply to "make a special effort to understand
Middle America," as Joe Kraft had advised the press to
do in a famous article in 1968. "I disagreed strongly
with that piece of Kraft's and do so now," he said. "I
think what he did in that piece was to manage to suggest
that somehow the limits of what we did as reporters
ought to be defined by what was acceptable to the society in which we were operating, and that we ought to be
very careful about our role. Well, if you begin to play
that game, then you're in serious trouble. I think you define your role as a reporter in terms of what you understand the role of a reporter to be. And if that incurs a
degree of popular wrath, then that's just a consequence
of it.

"But I think that in 1968, we did begin to do what we
should have been doing for years, which is to talk about

what we think the role of the press is. And that's something that we still have barely begun to do. The basic
point that we have never gotten across is that the Presidential campaign is not the property of the two candidates. It ought to belong, in some real sense, to the public. It's the only change every four years when they
ought to be able to get *their* questions answered, and get
the kind of commitments that *they're* interested in from
these candidates.

"The second thing that interests me," Broder went on,
"is the suggestion that you're getting now from some social scientists and psychohistorians that the press ought
to look much more seriously at its role as the chronicler
of critical incidents that shape the personality of these
men who are running for President, instead of just sort
of doing canned feature stories about these guys. But I
don't want to go too far in that, because I'm mortally
afraid of unleasing a bunch of newspapermen who
would fancy themselves as amateur psychiatrists." (Later, in the summer of 1972, the *Post* would assign a reporter named Bill Greider to cover George McGovern,
and he would provide the most sensitive running portrait
of McGovern's personality of any journalist on the
plane.)

Broder was down to the dregs of his Coke.

"The third area in which I think we still do kind of a
poor job is *institutional* reporting," he said. "The story
always tends to be this-guy-versus-that-guy, instead of
the development and change of an institution. That the
story may not be personal combat but the development
and change of an institution is a notion that's very hard
to get into the heads of newspaper people. Because they
want to know 'What's the lead?' But you could look at
the Democratic party, the majority party in the country,
and what has happened to it—and not just Fred-Har-
ris-out, Larry-O'Brien-in, or McGovern-versus-Muskie.
And maybe McGovern wouldn't have surprised us if
we'd done that."

But, Broder said with a sigh, there were not enough resources to handle that kind of story, even on the superfat *Post*—not enough money, manpower, time, or space. He himself had drawn up the blue print for the *Post*'s election coverage, late in the summer of '71, stretching five full-time men from the national staff and a few younger reporters from the state and city staffs so that they would cover all twelve Democratic candidates, plus the two Republican challengers. There was no one to spare for the Democratic party saga.

It was four o'clock. Broder looked again at his watch, announced with finality that he had to get back to work, and led us out of the bar. As we walked the block back to the *Post,* we talked about Martha Mitchell, who had been telephoning reporters to announce that she was a "political prisoner."

Broder shook his head and said something about being disappointed that the papers were running that kind of "shoddy story." I was brought up short. It seemed to me that Martha was getting what she deserved and that the papers were serving their proper function by giving her enough rope. But I had to admire Broder for being so righteous. He had lived in the world's biggest den of thieves for sixteen years, yet he had managed to hang on to an almost Victorian sense of decency. Sometimes when I climbed onto the press bus and saw Broder, I half expected him to be wearing a clerical dog collar. While the other reporters talked tough, he spoke gently. While they hoarded stories, he generously shared the goods. In New Hampshire, he had quietly told Curt Wilkie of the Wilmington *News-Journal:* "You better go out and knock on some doors. It's not there for Muskie." Which, for a journalist, was tantamount to an act of sainthood.

"He's a very conventional journalist," said a colleague, "but by sheer perseverance he really has taken conventional journalism to a new peak; he tells you as much as a well-informed non-genius can tell you. A

Broder column tells you exactly where the political situation is on that given day. It might take a Mailer to tell you what it all *means*, but Broder is almost always on the money about what has happened."

CHAPTER V

More Heavies

THESE FOUR men also deserve special attention:

Jules Witcover of the Los Angeles *Times*

"Jules is like a leashed tiger," said a reporter one afternoon late in McGovern's campaign. "He's going crazy. He can't get his stuff in the paper." We were standing in the middle of a huge pressroom in the Pittsburgh Hilton, sipping beers. Jules Witcover was over in the corner, talking intensely into a phone. He was a tall but unprepossessing man of forty-five, with a weak chin, blank eyes, and thinning hair. He had the pale, hounded look of a small liquor store owner whose shop has just been held up for the seventh time in a year.

"Chances are," the reporter said, nodding toward Witcover, "chances are, he's having a go-round with some editor out there who's just shit-canned one of his articles."

Witcover wasn't doing his best work in 1972. The reason was that the Los Angeles *Times* was cramping his style. All his friends knew it. It seemed to be the story of Jules' life; he had always been better than the paper he worked for.

Witcover was a very straight, conventional journalist, but throughout the year he had tried to inject some analysis into his stories, to interpret the campaign for his readers. Some of his analysis stories got into print. Others were killed by the editors. And sometimes a story would get set in type and then just sit there for one or two weeks. "Well," said a friend of Witcover's, "it's human nature that if you've got one story in type that hasn't appeared yet, you're not going to bust your ass on another. And that happened a lot." On still other occasions, Witcover had the edge on a story, had it a little earlier than everyone else; he would phone the story in, and it would mysteriously turn up in the paper one or two days late, after everyone else had already printed it.

All of this was more or less standard operating procedure for the majority of American newspapers, but it was slow torture to Witcover. He was a gifted, ambitious, hard-working journalist, and he took enormous pride in his work. He had worked like a dog to become a national political reporter. He had gone through almost twenty years of writing for obscure papers, taking long-term assignments he didn't like, and turning out magazine pieces on the side to get recognition. For many years, the Washington press establishment had tended to slight Witcover, because he came from a lower-middle-class background and said "duh" instead of "the." Now he was among the most respected reporters in town.

Having served such a long indentureship, Witcover was deadly serious about his craft. He had given a great deal of thought to his own role as a political journalist, and he was extraordinarily sensitive to the role that the whole press corps played, to its problems and failings.

At the same time, Witcover was definitely one of the

gang. On every press bus, there was always an inner circle of veterans, and whenever Witcover was aboard he was part of the circle. He gossiped in the nether reaches of the bus, drank late, and generally participated in the rituals of the bus. He was a compulsive, driven worker; besides his newspaper and magazine work, he wrote books. When he was going full throttle, he worked early in the mornings, over weekends and during vacations. Like all compulsives, he sometimes let himself go with a spectacular release of energy, such as the night in a St. Louis restaurant when he and Walter Mears stood up on the banquette shouting: "Escargots! We must have escargots!" When the order finally arrived, Mears was in a phone booth filing a story. Witcover threw one of the snails at him, landing it squarely in his ear.

But Witcover sometimes stepped back and examined the press with the fascination of an anthropologist who has just discovered a pristine tribe. Like the songs. The reporters enjoyed writing satirical songs about the candidates. Late at night in some hotel bar, or shivering in the cold, waiting for the candidate to come out of some closed meeting, Witcover and his friends would write these awful lyrics to popular tunes. The lyrics did not read well in print, but Witcover liked to put them in his books—as if they were artifacts, clues to what the press was really thinking. "It's a funny thing," he said one day during the California primary, "I was remarking to some of my colleages just the other day that we privately had Muskie's weaknesses pretty well identified back in January, but we didn't write them hard enough. We kind of gave him the benefit of the doubt. But we wrote songs—satires, parodies—just for our own amusement, and most of the ingredients of those songs were the difficulties that Muskie was having about his temper and his inability to make decisions quickly."

Witcover was not a professional press critic, an A. J. Liebling, he was simply an "activist" reporter. He showed concern for the press's problems in many ways. It was Witcover who had helped Jack Germond to found Political Writers for a Democratic Society. In 1970, he and another reporter had put together the "Washington Hotel Meeting," which was the press's first and last organized attempt to deal with the insularity of the White House. He was the only political reporter in town who contributed regularly to the *Columbia Journalism Review*—a rather conservative publication, but nevertheless the country's major organ of serious press criticism. In his three books (on Robert Kennedy, Richard Nixon, and Spiro Agnew)* he discussed at length the ways in which the press had affected the careers of the three politicians. In his book on Nixon, Witcover blasted reporters, including himself, for not having written more about Nixon's use of media and his relentless evasion of hard questions from the press during the 1968 campaign.

Even in some of his articles for the Los Angeles *Times,* Witcover broke the old convention that the press was not supposed to be seen or heard in campaign coverage. He treated the press as an active force in the campaign, and was quick to sound the alarm when George McGovern tried briefly to shut out reporters. The piece, headlined "McGovern's Campaign Tactics Resemble Nixon's in 1968," ran in early September. It read in part:

On landing in Portland, as local newsmen attempted to question McGovern about reports of disorganization in his campaign, Press Secretary Richard Dougherty broke in and ended the questions.

He led McGovern back to the steps of the plane where the candidate waited for the cameras and then read his prepared statement on the Olympics tragedy. When McGovern finished, Dougherty interposed: "No questions, no questions please" and McGovern was hustled off. A motorcade then went straight to a senior citizens' center in suburban Gresham. En route, reporters in the press bus were given

* *Eighty-five days, The Resurrection of Richard Nixon,* and *White Knight,* respectively.

strict instructions by a local McGovern aide to go directly into the center's cafeteria, where most of the elderly were waiting, and to "stand in one place" against the walls.

He informed the reporters that the average age of the residents was 74 and thus there was "the possibility of a heart attack" if the newsmen created too much stir.

In these first days, McGovern granted some interviews, but only to local radio and TV reporters, with a few representatives of the travelling press permitted to sit in and act as pool reporters for the rest. In this first week's schedule, through next Saturday, there is no provision for any press conference.

All this is reminiscent of the 1968 Nixon campaign, in which nearly all public events were geared for television, where the writing press was given extremely limited access to the candidate. . . .

In this shakedown swing, McGovern is being watched by his travelling observers of the press as much to examine his tactics and style as to record and assess his words. If a pattern of isolation and insulation is established at the outset, it doubtless will create still another public relations problem for the underdog candidate at a time when he can ill-afford any new ones.

Some of the other reporters on the plane felt that this piece was unfair to McGovern. After all, McGovern had led an incredibly open campaign all year long, and Nixon hadn't even begun to campaign yet. They thought Witcover had overreacted to McGovern's few days of inaccessibility. But the article served its purpose. It made the McGovern people very upset, and a few days later, McGovern once again became available for questions.

WITCOVER WAS RESERVED with people he did not know well, and he did not talk easily about himself, at least not to me. Then one night in October, he loosened up. After a long day on the road, almost half of the McGovern press corps had adjourned to a new restaurant called Jimmy's in New York. Witcover and I were sitting on tall stools at the circular bar. Shirley MacLaine was sitting there too. Not one to let an opportunity for propagandizing slip by, she kept saying things like, "Jules, I *know* you just want to smash Nixon and have George win," to which Witcover would gently demur.

A white-haired New York Republican party boss was buying drinks for everyone. "Mr. So-and-so will be hurt if you don't have another," the bartender kept saying every time he refilled our glasses. After a while Witcover began to tell me the story of his life. The verb that he used most often was "scramble."

His father had owned a gas station in Union City. Witcover scrambled to make it out of Union City, via the Navy, Columbia College (on the GI Bill), and Columbia Journalism School (supporting himself with odd jobs). He wanted to be a sportswriter, and he became one on the Providence *Journal*. But his main ambition was to work for a big paper in New York City. The nearest he could get to New York was the Newark *Star Ledger,* a member of the Newhouse chain. Seeing after a year that he wasn't going to make it across the river to the city, he took up an offer to work in the Newhouse Washington Bureau. He spent his career at Newhouse struggling to get national political assignments and trying to get a job on a major newspaper. It took him seventeen years.

While he worked a lot of beats he didn't like—such as writing about the New York delegation in Congress for a couple of Newhouse papers in Syracuse, or covering the Pentagon—he kept scrambling for political assignments. In the summer of 1966, he hustled himself an assignment to travel with Nixon. It proved to be Witcover's big break. One afternoon in Roanoke, Nixon gave him a long interview, which he turned into a piece for the *Saturday Evening Post*. It was the first article to treat Nixon as a serious contender for the 1968 Republican nomination, and it later made Witcover look very good.

After 1966 he began writing daily political pieces for Newhouse. He also wrote more magazine articles, to gain visibility, and he finished his first book, a finely detailed account of Robert Kennedy's 1968 campaign. The book made his reputation. A year later, the Los Angeles *Times* hired him as an assistant news editor. The paper had no national political correspondent. Within a year, he talked the bureau chief into creating the position for him. Witcover was delighted; he finally had the job he wanted on a major paper.

The Los Angeles *Times* was supposed to be among the best papers in America. It was often ranked third, after *The New York Times* and the Washington *Post*. It paid excellent salaries. But it was also a greedy paper which devoted far more space to advertising than to news. As a result the Los Angeles *Times* was rich; in 1972 it made about 42 million dollars after taxes. But the reporters and editors and bureau chiefs had to fight to get their stories into the tiny news-hole.

Witcover arrived while a complicated internal political battle was going on at the paper. One faction wanted to use the limited news space for more local coverage, and wanted the newspaper to be run tightly by the Los Angeles office. This faction was led by Frank Haven, the managing editor.

The other faction wanted the paper to emphasize national news and wanted less interference by the Los Angeles office. This faction included David Kraslow, the Washington Bureau chief, who had hired Witcover.

Haven's faction slowly won out. Haven was a Pasadena WASP, very West Coast, who knew little about national politics. Haven kept asking the Washington Bureau for frivolous stories, or demanding major articles to be written in impossibly short amounts of time, or killing Washington articles to make room for Los Angeles news. Kraslow constantly fought these unrealistic moves. In April 1972, Kraslow was replaced by a Haven protégé, a bland company man named John Lawrence, who had no experience covering politics or government.

It was a staggering blow to the people in the Washington Bureau. They feared that Haven, with his narrow, conservative Southern California mentality, would continue to push serious political news out of the paper. According to his friends, Witcover was deeply shaken by the Kraslow firing, but not so shaken that he seriously considered leaving the paper. That decision was brought on by other indignities.

Several weeks after the Kraslow incident, Witcover arrived in California to cover the primary and was shocked to learn that he had been locked out. He was abruptly informed that two political reporters from the metropolitan staff—Richard Bergholz and Carl Greenberg—would cover the candidates. Haven wanted it this way. So Witcover knocked around for two weeks, chasing after a couple of secondary stories and writing two long analysis pieces that never got into the paper. The rest of the press corps were amazed at the stupidity of the Los Angeles *Times*. It was true that such jurisdictional disputes between metro and national staffs were common, even on *The New York Times;* these disputes were not unlike the feuding between state troopers and the FBI over a big case. But this was something special. For once, the whole press corps was camped out in California and had almost no choice but to read the Los Angeles *Times* (which was nearly impossible to find back in Washington). But, instead of exploiting this great opportunity to show off its star national political man, the *Times* gagged Witcover and gave the job to two reporters whom the press corps considered competent but hardly extraordinary. The whole fiasco made the paper look idiotic and drove Witcover further up the wall.

Witcover became increasingly frustrated as the campaign went on. The paper seemed less and less willing to make space for national news. But what pained Witcover the most was that the paper refused to allow him to analyze and interpret the news. He couldn't understand this. It wasn't as if he were some kind of wild-eyed advocacy journalist. In fact, he deplored the rise of advocacy journalism. He thought that too many of the young journalists who worked for the underground press were undisciplined, lazy, and irresponsible; they went into a story with a fixed point of view which prevented them from digging and looking at all the facts: why find out anything that would contradict their prejudgment of the story? Witcover felt very strongly that the establishment papers had to combat this trend, and that the only way to compete with advocacy journalism was to provide interesting, compelling, responsible analysis based on a thorough review of the facts. If the establishment papers went back to the cut-and-dried formula stories of the forties, Witcover thought, they would bore everybody to death.

So Witcover kept writing meticulously fair analysis stories, and the *Times* kept balking. The biggest showdown came at the end of September over a story on Nixon's non-campaign. As the weeks went by and Nixon kept refusing to face the public, Witcover knew that he would have to write a story about it, pointing out the injustice of a one-candidate campaign. After all, he had slapped McGovern for trying to avoid newsmen. But he kept putting the article off, waiting for a news "hook" that would allow him to write that story in a way that wouldn't offend the *Times*. Finally, at the end of September, McGovern solved the problem for him. Addressing a conference of UPI editors, McGovern accused the press of failing to meet its responsibilities by not forcing Nixon to answer questions on the issues and by not pointing out that Nixon was refusing to face reporters, while he, McGovern, was running an open campaign. It was up to the press, said McGovern, to restore some balance to the campaign.

So Witcover began his story by quoting McGovern's accusations. While McGovern's argument was self-serving, wrote Witcover, it did point up a serious problem: how could the press provide balanced coverage when only one candidate was campaigning? Of course, Witcover went on, the President did have some legitimate reasons for not campaigning—for instance, the risk of assassination, the fact that Congress was still in session.

But then Witcover pointed out the dangers of a lopsided campaign. The public needed a chance to see both candidates questioned on the issues. When only one man campaigned, the whole system was undermined.

Finally, Witcover concluded that although the President might have real reasons for not going out on the stump, he could still hold a press conference in the safety of the White House and answer political questions, something the President had refused to do at the few news conferences he had held earlier in the year.

Witcover, who was by now paranoid about the *Times'* attitude toward analysis stories, showed the Nixon story to several of his friends on the bus and asked them if he was going "too far." All of them found the story very mild. Walter Mears said that with a few minor changes in form, he could have put the story on the AP wire with no difficulty. Bill Greider of the Washington *Post* could not imagine why Witcover was so worried.

The editors in Los Angeles killed the story. They told Witcover that it didn't "come off" and that it was an "opinion" story. Witcover couldn't believe it. He felt that the story was a classic example of the difference between analysis and opinion. He had marshaled all the facts, and drawn his conclusion solely from them. But the editors couldn't see it. Witcover, who was covering McGovern in New York, had long arguments with them over Long Distance. The solution was simple, they told him. All he had to do was get other people to make the same points and draw the same conclusions and then write the article *in their words*. Yes, said Witcover, but that was *reporting,* not *analysis*. It wouldn't have the same impact as an analysis article. The editors asked him again to do it over. He refused. Didn't they see? The piece might be no good in two or three days. The piece was important *now*.

The very next day, Nixon held a press conference at which he answered political questions. One of the main reasons for Nixon's decision to hold a press conference was an analysis piece by David Broder—similar to Witcover's but much tougher—which had appeared four days before. Witcover was now even more miserable, because he knew that both he and the *Times* would have looked very good if his piece had run on the eve of the press conference.

After the fight over the Nixon story, Witcover knew that he would have to leave the Los Angeles *Times*. "I can't stand this much longer," he told his friends. "I'm going crazy." During the Republican Convention, Witcover had been approached with a job offer from the Washington *Post*. He told them that he felt he had a commitment to stay at the *Times* through the end of the campaign; he had helped to plan the campaign coverage, after all, and there were still a few stories he hoped to do. But when the *Post* made him an offer shortly after the election, he accepted.

On January 1, 1973, he joined the *Post*'s national staff. His friends knew exactly why he had made the move. "There wasn't a rat's ass of difference in the money," one of them said, "but the *Post* is a reporters' paper. They give you freedom there, they give you leeway, and Jules would have been a fool not to move."

But the editors of the Los Angeles *Times* never quite understood why they had lost Jules Witcover.

Rowland Evans and Robert Novak, of the Publishers Hall Syndicate and the Chicago Sun-Times

From their office a block from the White House, Rowland Evans, Jr., and Robert D. Novak wrote what was probably the best-read column in America—five times a week it ran in nearly three hundred newspapers here and abroad. Unlike most columnists, they didn't write "think pieces." They wrote "dope pieces," inside information on domestic politics and foreign affairs. Of course, it was close to impossible to dig up sufficient inside dope to make five significant pieces a week. So they were part-time hoke artists. They would take a small incident (which they and they alone had discovered by prodigious digging) and they would blow it up into a campaign crisis. Or they would inflate a small remark into a trend. They claimed to be straight reporters with no ax to grind. Which was ridiculous. Their columns were consistently distorted by their conservative bias.

Evans and Novak made an odd couple. "Rowley" Evans was the gregarious, flesh-pressing member of the team—a smooth, well-connected aristocrat from Philadelphia's Main Line who still talked with a slight case of prep school drawl. A Yale classmate of Mayor John Lindsay's, he was small and lean and still looked like an Ivy Leaguer in his crisp, pin-striped shirts and conservative suits. "For the last fifteen years, Rowley has looked forty-two and just blond enough," said a veteran Washington reporter. "And he's still a Dewey Republican."

He fought with the Marines in World War II, started in journalism as a fifteen-dollar-a-week copy boy on the Philadelphia *Bulletin,* and got to know the Washington scene by covering labor and the Senate for the AP. In 1956, he moved to the *Herald-Tribune*'s Washington Bureau. His career took off four years later when Jack Kennedy became President. Evans, Charles Bartlett, and a few other preppy reporters were old buddies of Kennedy's, neighbors of his in Georgetown when he was in the Senate, and suddenly they were in the center of things. Their people were running the government. They knew everyone at the White House on a first-name basis. Suddenly Charlie Bartlett of the Chattanooga *Times* had a syndicated column, and Jock Whitney, the *Tribune*'s publisher, was offering Evans a column too. Evans realized that he couldn't handle a five-day-a-week column by himself, so he invited Novak to be his partner.

Novak had come up via the AP route, working in Nebraska and Indiana before moving to Washington. As a young reporter at *The Wall Street Journal*'s Washington Bureau, he had quickly earned a reputation for being one of the great political reporters. The two began their column in May 1963. "We had never been social or personal friends," said Novak, "but Evans respected me as a reporter."

The general consensus of the press corps was that Evans was the lightweight of the team. Reporters saw him as the one who kept up the Georgetown contacts and peddled the column to newspaper publishers around the country: He was not exactly stupid, but, well, he was just not that sharp. Which was probably unfair to Evans. It was just that Novak was so highly regarded. Novak might have been a little short on warmth and general humanity, but he was considered a great notebook and shoe-leather journalist, an incredibly hard-working man, almost a machine, who always seemed to know which lobbyist was with which Senator in which hotel room. During his days on *The Wall Street Journal,* he had become almost a legend, and his knowledge of politics was still widely respected.

I saw Novak for the first time on the night of the second California debate. The debate was taking place live on NBC's *Meet the Press,* and Novak was one of the four reporters who had been chosen to fire questions at Humphrey and McGovern. About a hundred reporters had gathered on the cavernous, klieg-lit sound stage in NBC's Burbank studio to witness the event, and they were making a party of it—waving, backslapping, telling stories, laughing. But Novak was standing off by himself. He was short and squat, with swarthy skin, dark grey hair, a slightly rumpled suit, and an apparently permanent scowl. He kept his hands in his pockets and looked at the floor. Some of the other reporters pointed him out and whispered about him almost as if he were a cop come to shush up a good party.

"Novak looks evil," said a gentle, middle-aged *Times*-man. "He can't help it, poor fellow."

"Do you think Novak's going to land his ABM on

McGovern in the first round, or wait?" one wire-service man asked another.

"There's a real tight coil of bitterness in the guy," said a magazine writer. "So much of what he writes and talks about in private tends to reinforce one impression: he's against anything good-looking, anything fashionable, anything slick—and liberalism is fashionable in the circles he travels in. I think that's why he's down on it."

The debate got under way and Novak hit both Humphrey and McGovern with tough questions. As soon as the program ended, I found him and asked for an interview. *Rolling Stone,* I explained, was doing an article on the campaign press.

"No," Novak frowned. "Your readers have never heard of me."

"Well, that's just the point," I said. "We want to inform our readers."

"No," he said, already walking away. *"Rolling Stone* —that's another world."

Another world indeed. Novak had come back from serving in Korea and gone to the University of Illinois in Urbana on the GI Bill, and he considered a college education to be a sacred privilege. He could never accept the idea of students challenging a college administration. He could not stand student revolutionaries or even student activists. In one of their early columns, he and Evans had gone after the Student Nonviolent Coordinating Committee, the radical civil rights group. "SNCC will never be the same after our columns," Novak had proudly told a friend. So he certainly had no love for a magazine devoted to the counter culture.

Later in the year, at the Democratic Convention, Abbie Hoffman and Jerry Rubin, both of them stoned, walked up to Novak and threw their arms around him while a photographer friend of theirs took pictures.

"Leave me alone," Novak barked. "Get away from me!"

Rubin planted a kiss on Novak's cheek. "Unless you pose with us," said Rubin, "we'll endorse *your* candidate. We'll endorse Richard Nixon!" Novak's opinion of the counter culture sank to a new low.

In the early years, however, the column had not been altogether conservative. What had made it such a sensational success was its tantalizing unpredictability. It would contain inside stuff on everybody, no matter who was helped or hurt. Novak prided himself on being a maverick, a loner. He had, for instance, been a great friend of Lyndon Johnson's. One night, several years before Johnson became President, Novak had taken Johnson home after a party. Johnson was blind drunk, and as Novak steered him up to the door, Johnson drawled, "Bob, you know the trouble with you? I like *you* but you don't like *me*." Novak did like Johnson, but in later years he went out of his way to be tough on him. He knew that he was losing Johnson as a friend, that Johnson was beginning to say things like "I never have to be told when Bob Novak's around, I can *smell* him." But he didn't let up. He was very hard on Johnson and very fair. Eventually he and Evans wrote *Lyndon B. Johnson: The Exercise of Power,* probably the best book in print on the subject.

But Novak's insistence on being apart from the crowd, said a friend, also drove him steadily to the right. During the Kennedy and Johnson years, it became smart and fashionable in Washington to be liberal. Attention was focused on the young. And the press community, especially, became actively interested in liberal causes. So Novak, the maverick, deliberately went off in the other direction. The leftist surges of 1968, and especially the campus movements, made him more and more reactionary. In his coverage of the battle for the Democratic nomination, he championed the old-guard party regulars, the more conservative the better. In breathless accounts of closed meetings and campaign infighting, he and Evans repeatedly depicted Muskie as a man in danger of being seduced by foolish liberal advisers. They applauded in November 1971, when "tough-minded" George Mitchell gained full political control of the

Muskie campaign. "What makes this so important," they wrote, "is that Mitchell, unlike other key Muskie advisers, regards the Senator as a centrist who must also reach out to the right."

They were convinced that Muskie would win. Much more than Johnny Apple's news accounts, their columns sensationalized and popularized the notion of the Muskie Bandwagon. They continually relied on old party regulars for their information, and this information repeatedly proved to be wrong. Here are some excerpts from their columns and their biweekly newsletter:

Jan. 19, 1972—[The nomination of Muskie] . . . is just about locked up, we believe . . . incidently, if Muskie loses to Wallace in Florida and Tennessee, those primaries, not Muskie, will lose credibility.

Feb. 16, 1972—Muskie: Despite trouble . . . we still feel he is the odds-on choice for the Democratic presidential nomination . . . the brilliant Muskie campaign strategy of lining up politicians' endorsements has so pre-empted the field that it is still hard to see how he could lose many of them.

Feb. 28, 1972—At best, McGovern cannot hope for more than 25 percent [in New Hampshire], a poor showing in a drab field.

[McGovern got 37 percent of the vote in New Hampshire.]

March 15, 1972—The Florida primary election was a staggering political event. The biggest winner was President Richard M. Nixon . . . the biggest loser was Sen. Edmund S. Muskie, followed closely by the entire liberal wing of the Democratic party . . . Sen. George McGovern's boomlet after New Hampshire is nearly extinguished.

March 29, 1972—Sen. Hubert H. Humphrey is the clear favorite to win next Tuesday's Wisconsin primary, with a close race shaping up for second place between Sen. Edmund Muskie and George McGovern . . . after all the post-Florida scare talk of Wallace coming into the convention with a huge block of delegates, we are having trouble finding very many delegates outside of the South.

[Five days later, McGovern won in Wisconsin, with Wallace second, Humphrey third and Muskie a poor fourth.]

April 5, 1972—Although Sen. George McGovern scored a stunning victory last night in the Wisconsin primary, the real winners are Sens. Hubert H. Humphrey and Edward M. Kennedy . . . Reluctantly Democratic politicians are coming to the realization that Alabama Gov. George Wallace is no longer a merely regionally popular figure, mouthing merely regional issues . . . but like George McGovern, he cannot be nominated in Miami.

And so on. Their reliance on conservative sources among the party regulars and on their own prejudices queered their predictions again and again. Yet they continued to hand out subtle kudos to the conservative advisers in the Humphrey and Muskie camps and demerits to the liberal advisers; the conservatives got complimentary adjectives like "splendid" and "tough-minded"; while the liberals were branded with pejorative modifiers.

They saved most of their venom for George McGovern, however. They called McGovern "the doyen of the Democratic Party's left fringe." They consistently played down his victories and scoffed at his candidacy. They delighted in quoting any party regular who portrayed McGovern as a hopelessly irresponsible radical. After McGovern's Wisconsin victory, for instance, they wrote him off again and quoted a "powerful lieutenant" of Mayor Daley's Chicago machine: "This McGovern's going to have all those woolly heads around him. He might as well forget about the support of our kind of people."

In July a divinity student named Peter McGrath wrote an article entitled "Why McGovern Can't Win: Because Evans and Novak Won't Let Him" for the *Chicago Journalism Review*. McGrath cited Evans' and Novak's record of downgrading, ridiculing and attacking McGovern and concluded that the two columnists did not "trust people who think that politics has a moral component." But he didn't mention the lowest blow of all, the Evans/Novak column that doomed McGovern in Omaha.

The column, which appeared on April 27, about two weeks before the Nebraska primary, was called "Behind Humphrey's Surge." Evans and Novak argued that Humphrey's stock was soaring because "regular Democratic politicians" were desperate to stop McGovern and agreed that only Humphrey could do it. "They fear McGovern as the Democratic party's Barry Goldwater," the column said.

"The reason is given by one liberal senator, whose voting record differs little from McGovern's," they went on. "He feels McGovern's surging popularity depends on public ignorance of his acknowledged public positions. 'The people don't know McGovern is for amnesty, abortion, and legalization of pot,' he told us. 'Once middle America—Catholic middle America in particular—finds this out, he's dead.' "

Now, this was simply wrong. These were not McGovern's "acknowledged public positions." Evans and Novak must have known, if they read the newspapers, that although McGovern favored the granting of amnesty, he was against the legalization of marijuana and his stand on abortion was that it was not a question for the federal government to decide. Whoever the liberal Senator was, he had "long ago endorsed Muskie" and conceded that he would probably "end up backing Humphrey."

In Ohio, Henry Jackson had thrown these hysteria issues at McGovern, and in Nebraska Humphrey began to use them, too. So the Evans/Novak column was a godsend for Humphrey. It was reprinted as part of an advertisement in a popular local Catholic weekly called *The True Voice,* reportedly at the expense of a Humphrey supporter. Omaha is a Catholic city and a lot of people there read *The True Voice.* The ad helped to kill McGovern in Omaha, and the only thing that saved the election for him was the vote of the farmers in outlying counties.

The McGovern people, naturally, weren't happy about the column. "It was a cheap shot," Dick Dougherty, a high-level staffer, said later. "Well, those guys have to write five columns every week, so I guess sometimes they sort of soup things up to get a good story." In Omaha, Dougherty's language had been stronger.

All through the primary campaigns, Evans and Novak kept insisting that blue-collar workers voted for McGovern in the primaries because of "faulty perceptions," because they did not know that he was "radical" on issues like pot, abortion, and amnesty. Once they found out that he was a "radical," said Evans and Novak, the blue-collar workers would repudiate him. McGovern's disastrous defeat in November appeared to prove them right, but most evidence showed that the blue-collar people did not reject McGovern because they thought he was a "radical"; they voted against him because he looked like a chronic bumbler, which is quite another thing. Even if Evans and Novak were correct in claiming that the blue-collar workers had voted for McGovern in primaries because of "faulty perceptions," they never examined the crucial question: assuming that the blue-collar people did not know that McGovern was a "radical," what *did* they think he was?

All the same, Evans and Novak were experienced political observers. Early in the year, they caught some of the serious flaws in McGovern's candidacy—his faulty economic proposals, for instance, and his lack of rapport with the Democratic regulars. But instead of really examining these flaws, they used them vindictively, to prove that McGovern could not win the nomination.

In spite of their steady assault on McGovern, they kept insisting that they were straight reporters and had no conservative bias.

I made several appointments to see Rowland Evans at the Democratic Convention, but had to cancel all of them. Finally, it was arranged that I would phone him at

7:45 in the morning in his suite in the Eden Roc Hotel. "Jesus!" said the sleepy voice. "I'm completely fucked! I have to do two columns and a newsletter today." The interview was short and none too snappy. I wanted to get his reaction to the *Chicago Journalism Review* article.

"I haven't seen it," he said, "but I absolutely disagree with any charge of bias in anything we've written about McGovern. I mean, I've been flabbergasted about the McGovern operation. I thought it was a joke. But we weren't out to get him."

Then what were they doing? Weren't they conservatives?

"*Time* once called us 'zealots of the Center,' " he said. "I don't think that's a bad description. No, I don't think we're conservative. I just think politics moved to the left in the last five years, since Vietnam began to warm up, and we stayed in the center."

The next time I saw Robert Novak was also at the Democratic Convention. He was coming through the front door of the Fontainebleau Hotel to collect his rented car on the huge portecochere outside. "No. 5!" yelled the car jockey. Novak was wearing wrinkled checkered pants, scuffed black buckle shoes and a seersucker jacket that was buttoned too tight over his pygmy belly. As he waited, he acknowledged hellos from passers-by. "Hi, Governor," he said, nodding at an obscure Southern pol.

I went up and asked for an interview and this time he agreed to talk to me if I would drive with him to the Carillon, Humphrey's headquarters. We slid into his green compact Olds and started inching up Collins Avenue, with the air conditioning going full blast. I asked him what he had thought of the *Chicago Journalism Review* piece.

"Well," he said, "I thought obviously it was hostile. But take away the rhetoric and there was a kernel of truth. As he said, I *do* feel that the function of a political party is to win elections. If it can't, it has ceased to serve its function. The Democratic party is in danger of becoming defunct in 1972. I feel most comfortable when there is very little difference between the parties. I don't think the system works very well when there is a great difference, as in 1964. There were a lot of inaccuracies in that Chicago article. He claimed we said McGovern was an ideologue. We never said that. We said he was influenced by ideologues and in some instances bound by them.

"The article did make one point I will fully agree with: Just because we've criticized McGovern doesn't mean we're conservative. Eight years ago, no one would have called us conservative. The *National Review* denounced us because we were critical of Goldwater. I don't think we've changed.

"I mean, Evans had a warm personal relationship with McGovern," he said, rubbing his lips nervously. "They used to have breakfast in the Kennedy years. But Presidential campaigning is a hard game, and all personal friendships go out the window. I was quite close to Barry Goldwater, but he hasn't spoken to me since '64. Lyndon Johnson gave the reception for my wedding in 1962 and then our relationship completely deteriorated during his Presidency."

Novak didn't look at me as he talked, but he spoke fast and volunteered at lot of points. He and Evans had written a lot of critical articles about Nixon, he said, without getting the "cry baby" reaction they had gotten from many McGovern supporters. "Oh, I don't mean McGovern, or Mankiewicz or Hart, I mean the rank and file. They became so accustomed to the uncritical press they received during the first part of the campaign that they were astounded by any criticism.

"I don't want to call McGovern an extremist, but I think some of his positions are radical positions. He denies that, because in American politics, radical is a bad thing to be. Now, the country may be moving in the direction McGovern says it is, but I don't think so. I base that on what we feel the country is about, and we do a lot of traveling and interviewing of rank-and-file voters. We use Oliver Quayle staffers and questionnaires, and either Evans or I go along on every canvassing trip. I actually ring doorbells and fill out the forms myself. We try and do fairly high saturation in what are called barometer precincts—this year I've been in Jacksonville, Milwaukee, Chicago, Queens, L.A., Pittsburgh, Philadelphia, and Detroit. And we found data to indicate that there have been a lot of misperceptions of McGovern's proposals by rank-and-file voters. This country is unhappy, McGovern is right about that, but the country is much more conservative than he is."

We had broken through the worst of the traffic on Collins Avenue, and were coming up fast on the Carillon, so I asked Novak about his fabled sources.

Novak wouldn't name any of his sources and didn't seem to want to talk about them. "Evans and I are switch-hitters," he said. "We write different columns and have different news sources. I use about fifty to a hundred sources regularly, I suppose. I don't really know how many. God bless 'em, though."

Beside Novak, on the front seat, there lay a manila folder, filled with Xeroxes of his columns. On top of that was a small yellow sheet, with his day's schedule typed on it. It said: "3:30, Pierre Salinger, Doral Hotel." No matter what Evans wrote about McGovern, the fact still remained that McGovern needed them more than they needed him. So Salinger was very much at home to Novak, and, the next night, Frank Mankiewicz smiled and smiled and was only too glad to show Evans around the McGovern command trailer.

Later, during the fall campaign, things would change. In September, Novak showed up to follow the campaign for a couple days, and Mankiewicz insisted on banishing him from the Senator's plane, on which all the reporters from the big papers rode, and putting him on the Zoo Plane, with the foreign reporters and TV technicians. Novak did not take this well. At the first stop, he went up to Mankiewicz and protested vociferously. Mankiewicz was implacable. It was the Zoo Plane or nothing.

"OK," said Novak, in his one endearing comment of the campaign, "No more Mr. Nice Guy."

Haynes Johnson of the Washington *Post*

In 1972, Haynes Johnson seemed to be a man whose time had come, for the genre of which he had long been the acknowledged master—the "mood-of-the-country" piece—had suddenly come into vogue. This sudden increase in articles which analyzed the disposition of the American voter actually sprang from events which had taken place four years before, and its origin had much to do with the turbulent state of American journalism in the late sixties.

The whole press corps had been jolted by the New Politics in 1968. The McCarthy surge in New Hampshire took them by surprise, and then the madness for Bobby Kennedy. Then they had received another jolt from the opposite direction—for the event that shook them up the most in 1968, that left the final, bitter taste in their mouths, was the Chicago Democratic Convention. The single most influential piece of journalism that year, among the press corps at any rate, was the column written by Joe Kraft a week after Chicago.

Kraft, a former speech-writer for John Kennedy, was a legendarily aggressive social climber, a member of the set of Georgetown journalists who did much of their legwork on tennis courts and at supper parties. His ambition, combined with a good analytical mind, had won him that most prestigious of showcases, a regular column in the Washington *Post;* his opinions carried weight in the Capital.

On September 3, 1968, Joe Kraft wrote a column in which he asked, rhetorically and repentantly, whether the press did not suffer from certain prejudices.

"The answer, I think, is that Mayor Daley and his

supporters have a point. Most of us in what is called the communications field are not rooted in the great mass of ordinary Americans—in Middle America. And the result shows up not merely in occasional episodes such as the Chicago violence but more importantly in the systematic bias toward young people, minority groups, and the kind of presidential candidates who appeal to them."

Kraft went on to argue that Presidential candidates like McCarthy, Kennedy and even Nelson Rockefeller, who campaigned among college kids and blacks, got all the coverage, while Richard Nixon, who made his pitch to ordinary Americans, "was almost entirely out of the news in the weeks before he walked off with the Republican nomination." Kraft thought that this was because the press was dominated by an "upper-class outlook" which could afford to be indulgent to rebellious Negroes and kids. The press was out of touch with the public.

"In these circumstances," Kraft concluded, "it seems to me that those of us in the media need to make a special effort to understand Middle America."

Joe Kraft had put his prestige behind a fear that many journalists felt but had not wanted to express. Right away, a number of press people joined in the *mea culpa*. Walter Cronkite helped set the tone by giving Dick Daley a nice, respectful interview.

Within the year, both *Time* and *Newsweek* had done cover stories on Middle America. All of this happened before Spiro Agnew had said a single excoriating word against the press.

The Kraft line of thinking had deep and long-lasting effects on campaign coverage. In early 1968, the press had been flying high—reporting the sensational, irresistible story of McCarthy's overnight rise; thrilling to Kennedy's charisma; helping to topple an incumbent President. The press felt its oats when Johnson fell. The bulk of reporters felt that they were powerful as never before, in tune with the country, expressing the feelings of a huge constituency that hated the war. Then, suddenly, Chicago blew up in their faces. Beaten by cops and jeered by delegates, reporters found themselves openly detested as a biased, leftist elite. The violence in Chicago radicalized a few journalists; in Tom Wicker, for instance, it precipitated what can only be described as an identity crisis, and he increasingly became the champion of the young and oppressed. But most of the newsmen were simply shocked and hurt to find out that a majority of Americans thought that the press sucked. They brooded over the wound for three years, along with the editors and network executives. And when they sat down in 1971, around tables in board rooms and city rooms all over New York and Washington, to plan the election coverage, they decided to make "a special effort to understand Middle America."

That was the great leap forward in 1972. Almost every sizeable news organization in America made an attempt, however sketchy or erratic, to canvass precincts, interview families, check out local issues, and find out what the voters were thinking. Everyone talked about getting away from the old system of covering elections by sending out a man to ride around isolated on a bus and report that candidate's speeches. Of course, some reporters had been canvassing for years, but it had not been the official, universal policy of the nation's press.

Now *The New York Times* set up a "grid system," with men in every primary state to explore local political factors and describe the effect that the candidates were having on the electorate; later the paper commissioned a fifty-state survey of voter preferences, which was written up by Johnny Apple. Most large newspapers and chains sent their national political reporters to canvass a few key precincts for a week at the opening of the fall campaign and a week toward the end; usually the purpose of the canvassing was to answer one or two crucial questions, such as whether traditional blue-collar Democrats were going to abandon the party in November. *Newsweek* announced a mood-of-the-country series, but soon lost interest and let it peter out; *Time*'s attempt was likewise half-hearted. CBS and NBC made occasional forays into key precincts. ABC confined its efforts to Columbus, Ohio, which it called the "ABC City"; a special correspondent periodically invaded the privacy of a dozen families there to inquire how they felt about the candidates and the issues.

Of all the news organizations, only the Washington *Post* had a grand design. It consisted mainly of a series of articles based on interviews with 443 registered voters in fifty precincts (chose by precinct-expert Richard Scammon) in the ten largest states. The *Post* could have serialized a good portion of *War and Peace* in the space it devoted to this series. Indeed, the series had the Tolstoyan aim of giving a complete picture of the mood of an entire society. The main architect of this project was Haynes Johnson.

Haynes Johnson was not yet forty, but he was already an institution. In the business, a certain kind of feature that attempted to sum up the national attitude toward specific issues or trends by using interviews with "typical" voters from certain blocs was known as a "Haynes Johnson piece." Haynes Johnson had written his first Haynes Johnson piece in 1960. Having gone to the University of Missouri School of Journalism and received a master's degree in American History from the University of Wisconsin, he became a night city editor for the Washington *Evening Star* at the age of twenty-five, and later a copy editor. But he wanted to write, so he went to the *Star*'s editor and sold him on the idea of a series about Black America.

Johnson spent six months doing door-to-door interviews with blacks all over the country, and he turned out an authoritative series which pleased the editor. So Johnson began to do "Mood of America" pieces for the *Star,* wandering around the country on his own, refining his technique, finding typical labor districts, typical Jewish neighborhoods, typical conservative small towns, and interviewing people in their homes. It wasn't a totally new kind of piece. Ernie Pyle had done much the same thing for Scripps-Howard before World War II, except that Pyle had driven around the country in a battered Ford coupe and approached the whole thing much less scientifically.

During the sixties, Johnson wrote a best seller on the Bay of Pigs invasion and a biography of William Fulbright. He helped cover the '60, '64, and '68 elections, but he did not consider himself a political reporter. He wanted to keep developing his specialty, so in 1969 he moved to the Washington *Post,* where Ben Bradlee let him fly around the country writing more mood-of-the-country pieces. But more important, he and David Broder began to lay out plans for covering the 1972 campaign. The idea was that the campaign coverage of the future would not center on traveling with the candidates, but on gauging the attitudes of the public. So they set up an elaborate system, with questionnaires, computers, key precincts, and a flying squad of reporters. There would be three surveys—one in 1970, one in 1971 and one in 1972 just before the election.

"We wanted to chart the mood of the country over a period of *years,*" said Johnson, "so that when we got into the campaign we would really have something to base conclusions on. We would really have a sense of the major issues and what was moving people." He was sitting in the *Post* cubicle at the Republican Convention, a large, athletically built man with a square jaw and black-framed glasses. "Obviously," he went on, "a problem with the press corps is that there is too much of a tendency to stay in the group, to talk of official sources, to rely on the past, and not to recognize that there are changes that aren't measured in the polls, that aren't measured by getting endorsements. We have the most mature, sophisticated electorate in our history, and it's going to be even more so. And if you don't understand how people's attitudes are changing, how complex they are, it seems to me you miss the whole potential in the country. And that's what the press missed."

The most interesting Johnson/Broder series was the second one, a huge eight-part spread which appeared in

December 1971. It examined public attitudes toward the two-party system, and the professionals' feeling about their own parties. It showed that the parties were breaking into fragments, that bosses no longer controlled votes, that patronage was no longer effective, that few people felt party loyalty, that the public felt a deep distrust of politicians and no affection for any of the Democratic contenders, that powerful grass-roots organizations had grown up around issues like ecology and the war, and that the political situation was volatile and the way was open to new leaders. In other words, Johnson and Broder described the situations that would make it possible for McGovern to win the nomination.

The two reporters used their usual system. They began together, interviewing voters and party pros on tape and filling out questionnaires together. Then they split up for several weeks and worked separately, interviewing from morning until late at night seven nights a week; at the end they finished up together, and then collated the materials back in Washington. The tape recorder was an important tool, because Johnson insisted on reproducing large chunks of transcript in "boxes" alongside the body of the text. "The suspicion of the printed word today is so immense," said Johnson. "If you do a lengthy series on some controversial topic, you find an enormous outpouring from people who don't agree with what you're saying and therefore simply don't believe that you've been there. So we use these transcripts to give the reader a sense of 'By God, whether or not I like it, *that's* what the man said.'" So they had a ward heeler from New Hampshire tell in his own words why nobody came to the party's bean dinner any more. And there was a photograph of the ward heeler drinking coffee in a diner, just to nail down the credibility. There was, over the course of eight days, an impressive array of witnesses—reformers, consultants, bosses, local chairmen, all describing the shaky status of the two-party system.

After finishing the two-party system survey with Broder, Johnson worked with a *Post* reporter named

Nick Kotz on another long series about the American
Labor Movement. He did not catch up with the primaries until late in the spring, and when he did, the pre-
vailing mood he found was one of total apathy. "Despite
all this collective political sound and fury, or perhaps
because of it, this campaign is characterized by public
indifference," he wrote during the California primary.
"You cannot travel across California today without
being struck by the lack of emotion being generated by
the politicians."

On the few occasions when he appeared on the press
bus, Johnson was not exactly everybody's favorite reporter. No doubt this was partly because he gave the lie
to the fuss that the rest of the press was making over the
primaries; he was telling them that the public didn't
care. But many reporters who had known Johnson for
years quite sincerely regarded him as a pompous, con-
ceited stuffed shirt. Resentment of Johnson reached a
peak on the night of George McGovern's nomination,
when Johnson somehow became the only daily reporter
allowed to stay in McGovern's suite throughout the evening. There was some bitter talk of Johnson's being an
"ass-kisser."

While most reporters were impressed with the series
Johnson had written with Broder in December 1971,
they did not think so highly of the series that came out
in October 1972.

Broder helped to research the October series, but it
was written almost entirely by Johnson, and most of the
men in the press corps found it interminable and dull.
There were long articles on the Labor Vote, the Catholic Vote, the Old Vote, the Youth Vote, and on and on.
Many reporters felt that the series simply belabored the
obvious—Nixon was not beloved but held a command-
ing lead nevertheless; America's young people were not
going to vote as a radical monolith; the nation was unhappy and distrustful of politicians. "He tells me what's
happening, but he can't explain it," said one national
political reporter of the Johnson series. "I don't know

whether the whole series is worth it. It's a tremendous commitment of money, it's very expensive to do. It took most of the important guys on their national staff a couple of weeks to do the interviews, and what did they get out of it? A series of blockbusters that nobody's reading. I can't get through it. My friends can't get through it. We all care about that stuff, but I don't know anybody on the bus who's reading it all the way through. So if the press isn't reading it, who the hell *is* reading it? When that first survey came out in 1970, I thought it was just pseudo-sociology. Then I thought that the survey in 1971 made a real contribution. Now I've begun to wonder again."

Many reporters felt that Johnson had begun to parody himself and that his pieces were becoming fatuous. On the night George McGovern lost the election, a bunch of half-drunk campaign reporters at the Sioux Falls Holiday Inn ripped Haynes Johnson's election night wrap-up off the wire machine. One of them read it out loud while the others laughed. It seemed to crown the dismal inevitability of the whole thing. "Once every four years," the piece went, "the American past and present come together. Last night, as always on these occasions, the voters gave their quick, clear and overwhelming verdict on the direction of the American future. It is to be, after all, four more years."

"Jesus," said one of the reporters. "The same Haynes Johnson piece I've been reading for three years. I could have written it myself, word for word."

There was some jealousy in this, but also some truth. Much of Johnson's writing in the fall had been long and dull. But it was also true that the country, in the fall of 1972, was in a dull, passive, contrary and confused mood, and to turn such a mood into interesting reading was close to impossible. Had the election been a cliffhanger, Johnson's pieces might well have been fascinating. At any rate, it was his speciality and he was not about to give it up. It was more expensive and less fun than following a candidate around with the rest of the pack, but it was the only way to draw any useful conclusions from the chaos of an election year. No doubt the *Post* would remain in the vanguard of "Mood of America" coverage until an exciting election came along to make the technique look appealing. Then the rest of the press would follow.

CHAPTER VI

The Newsweeklies

In 1972, *Time* magazine had 4,250,000 paying readers. *Newsweek* had 2,625,091.

Time and *Newsweek* might have looked alike, read alike, and had the same people on the cover week after week. But there was one crucial difference: 1,624,909 readers. Given that monstrous gap to close, *Newsweek* ran a relatively lean, we-try-harder, underdog operation. And *Time,* home free in the circulation race, fairly reeked of extravagance.

Item: *Time* threw big parties at both Conventions, with sumptuous buffets and special perks for VIP's and advertisers. On the first night of the Democratic Convention, *Time* collected the floor passes from all its correspondents and gave them to big advertisers so that the advertisers could walk around the Convention floor and gawk for a couple of hours.

Item: *Time* hired a fleet of fifteen Cadillac limousines that stood ready to whisk *Time* correspondents and messengers to any point in Miami, including Flamingo Park.

("The Zippies all wanted a ride," said a correspondent)

Item: *Time* ran its Convention operations out of a sultan's tent in the Fontainebleau's Exhibition Hall that made every other newsprint operation look like a hovel. On three sides, the *Time* office was fenced in by blue muslin curtains, with a grey-uniformed security guard at the entrance flap. (No other publication had thought of that touch, the security guard.) The fourth side of the office was the back wall of the Exhibition Hall, a riot of red whorehouse flock, adorned with an orchestra of plaster cherubs.

At any given moment, a dozen correspondents sat in a row, staring right into blue curtains and banging out reams of copy, while a crew of shirt-sleeved editors huddled around a complex of steel desks, making tactical decisions. The lines to the Front (at the Convention Hall) were kept open by a telephone operator in a flowered dress who ran a full-sized switchboard and set off beepers in the pockets of stray editors and correspondents; and by a dozen couriers who sat on a row of chairs behind the switchboard—half of them *Time* editors' sons who had reportedly been flown in at company expense. (*The New York Times,* which ran many more words about the Convention than *Time,* managed to get along with no switchboard and no couriers.)

All in all, *Time* brought 130 people to the Democratic Convention, including nine photographers who exposed 400 rolls of film in the first three days. Several senior editors were there, but were not often seen outside of the tennis courts and parties. The senior editors wore hotel haircuts, pin-striped suits and horn-rimmed glasses. "You could switch the senior editors with the Board of Directors of the Chase Manhattan Bank," said a *Time* staffer, "and nothing would change at either the magazine or the bank."

All of the bureau chiefs came to Miami for the week, except for the chief of the Houston Bureau. There just wasn't enough room for him, so as a consolation prize he was flown to Hyannis to babysit with Ted Kennedy. There was room, however, for most of the twenty-three members of the Washington Bureau, which, as *Time*'s largest outpost, filled eighty percent of the "Nation" section every week.

Many of *Time*'s best correspondents worked in the Washington Bureau, reporters like Champ Clark, Hays Gorey, Simmons Fentress, and Dean Fischer, all of whom, it was said, could probably have held down front-line positions on *The New York Times*. Some of them were legends within the *Time* organization, but to the public at large they were about as well known as engineers at Cape Kennedy. Everybody in the *Time* office, for instance, knew that Champ Clark was writing an epic length narrative of the Convention and that every line was uproariously funny. But Clark never saw his narrative, much less his by-line, in print.

Most correspondents had to live with this frustrating condition, which was sweetened by the fact that they made around $30,000 a year. The correspondents filed about 750,000 words every week, and then the editors took over. The editors worked in the New York office, and their job was to throw away about 700,000 of those words. Then they rewrote about 85 percent of the remaining copy.

The Washington Bureau put out a little sheet of its own, called "Washington Memo," which contained some of the gossip and rumors that the correspondents thought unfit to go in the magazine. "Washington Memo" was sent to *Time*'s New York office and most of the bureaus, but each copy was numbered and copies were not allowed out of the office. The "Washington Memo" was supposed to keep *Time* editors abreast of backroom happenings in the Capital, but most correspondents refused to give their best stories to the "Memo." "Some editor will just phone you and try to get you to do a story about some rumor that you put in," said one correspondent, "and you know it's true, but you feel bad because you know you can't ask your source to back you up on it."

There were other gripes that the Washington correspondents sometimes voiced, very privately, about the editors of the Nation section.

"This whole bit about the Eastern Press Establishment has some basis in fact," said one correspondent. "These six or seven guys who determine the final editorial content of the Nation section all sit around New York most of the time. Occasionally, they try to shake them out of their ivory tower. They bring 'em out. They brought the Nation section, lock, stock and barrel—the editors and the researchers—down to Washington last year.

"Now they bring 'em down to Miami, the whole crew, and they assign each one of them to a correspondent, kind of like on the buddy system. The correspondents had a conference the other morning before the Nation section got here and one correspondent said, 'The question I want to ask is about what I would have to call the Helplessness Factor. Are we responsible for picking these people up, taking them around and taking them to the bathroom?'

"A lot of correspondents just sort of ignored their Nation person, and a lot of the Nation people went off and played tennis. A few of the Nation people did make an honest effort to tag along, find out what was going on, and meet the people they were writing about. But for the most part, it was a kingsize waste of money."

The Nation people, in fact, didn't have much contact with politicians and they didn't seem to have heard of the first rule of Old-Fashioned Menckenesque Political Journalism—that all political types ought to be regarded as guilty until proven innocent.

The Nation section's two-week junket to Washington was a case in point. Each morning, the whole section met to be addressed over breakfast by some Washington notable. On the first morning, said a correspondent who was there, the notable was Chief Justice Warren Burger.

When Burger was done with his spiel, the whole table, except for the correspondent, gave Burger a standing ovation. Thinking about it later, the correspondent felt that maybe they had applauded out of respect for the office of Chief Justice. The next morning, however, Ron Ziegler, the former Disneyland ad executive who became Nixon's press secretary, spoke to the *Time* editors. They gave Ziegler a standing ovation too.

It was not just the Nation editors from New York who seemed so completely wedded to the establishment. It was also some of the men who had been in the Washington Bureau for a long time, like the bureau chief, Hugh Sidey. Sidey was known around the bureau as Hugh Sidestep. Sidey was famous for the weekly pieces he wrote about the Presidency for *Life*. The pieces were loaded with "mood" and "color," but they did not have a great deal to say about what was really happening inside the Administration. Some of the reporters in the bureau felt that while Sidey might have had a flair for the *form* of politics, he never bothered really to study the *substance*—the content of bills, economic programs, or major statements on issues. One morning in the late spring, for instance, Sidey had come into the bureau upset and grumbling about McGovern's "confiscatory tax program." Several correspondents had to explain to him what McGovern's tax program really was and assure him that the Senator did not intend to confiscate wealth.

"The meetings they have in the Washington Bureau sound like cabinet meetings," said a correspondent who had recently departed *Time*. "The older men are the cabinet members and Sidey is like the President. They sit around and refer to the Administration as 'we.' Like once I was in a meeting—it was around the time of the May Day demonstrations—and Sidey asked me, 'Do you think we can handle them? Do you think we can keep them from disrupting things?'

"I said, 'No, I think they'll succeed.' And Sidey looked at me as if I were from the Vietcong."

Newsweek's TEMPORARY BUREAU IN MIAMI was just a few feet up the hall from *Time's*. Enclosed on all four sides with blue muslin, it was smaller, humbler and quieter than *Time's* office. No guard and no switchboard. Just a couple of reporters chatting around the coffee urn, a secretary on the phone, and three or four other reporters pecking at typewriters. Most of the editors were back in New York. But if there was less boondoggling around *Newsweek,* and less conspicuous waste, its bureaucracy was still very much like *Time's*. The correspondents whipped out tons of copy, and the New York editors dumped, trimmed, or rewrote almost all of it.

"My copy usually ends up looking like a goddam chicken that's been hit by a fucking truck,"* said John J. Lindsay, a *Newsweek* Washington correspondent, who was known by his friends as "Real John" to distinguish him from the mayor of New York.

"You've got to be happy if they get your facts right," said Lindsay. "Since January I don't think I've recognized a damn thing I've filed. I just pour everything out of the goddam boot. Otherwise, you get a phone call at three in the morning asking you why you left out that the candidate had his teeth drilled that morning."

John Lindsay was a fixture of political journalism, a sensitive and observant man who was deeply dissatisfied with the world and had cultivated a cynical manner to deal with all the hypocrisy that he saw. He was in his late forties, with a thin face and sharp features, and he spoke with the accents of an old Boston ward heeler, for he was one-half Massachusetts Irish. He grew up in a small Massachusetts town and entered politics for a few weeks in his youth, managing a losing campaign for a man who wanted to be state representative from Milford, Mass. "I had a job digging graves at the time, but I didn't have the presence of mind to vote anybody from

* Lindsay later told me that these words referred to his own imperfections as a journalist and were not intended to refer to *Newsweek.*

the cemetery," he said. "It was a clear indication that I wasn't cut out for politics." So he confined himself to writing about politics. He had been on various papers and he worked for ten years on the Washington *Post,* but daily journalism frustrated him because he rarely had time to "take that last step and lock in a story." For this reason, he moved to *Newsweek.*

It was the morning after the last night of the Convention. We were in the Fontaine Room of the Fontaine-bleau Hotel, a blue ballroom decorated with painted statues of busty Marie Antoinette shepherdesses in low-cut bodices. In front of us, the three hundred-odd members of the Democratic National Committee were sitting in gold chairs, waiting for George McGovern, the newly nominated candidate, to come and address them from the stage. Some network crews were hanging around the stage. A couple of dozen newspaper reporters were standing around the back of the room, looking worn out. They had stayed up all through the night, either drinking or writing. Lindsay had filed copy all night but, being an ex-alcoholic, he did not drink. He and I were leaning against a disused bar at the back of the room, hoping McGovern would show up soon. Despite his lack of sleep, Lindsay looked quite sporting in his blue blazer and beige espadrilles, with his horn-rims and greying hair.

"I can't write worth anything," he said with a sad smile, "but I'm a good reporter, I can cut through the bullshit. And there's a lot of bullshit in this business. You'd almost have to get in on a phone line, or something like that, to get the real story—'cause what goes on up there on the platform isn't really what's happening."

Without the aid of any phone taps, Lindsay had a pretty good idea of what was happening, and in the next few minutes I got a sample of some of the political perceptions that are presumably cut from his copy. I have never seen anything like them in *Newsweek.*

Just then, Lindsay was sighted by one of the ubiquitous political fixers who were plying their trade in Miami.

"Hi," said Lindsay. "Who you working for now?"

"Matty Troy."

"Oh, Matty Troy, the liberal Gauleiter," said Lindsay. A perfect description! Matty Troy was a crazy egomaniac who supported McGovern, drank with Jimmy Breslin, and ran the Democratic Party of Queens with an iron fist—a liberal version of one of the Nazi "Gauleiters" who ran German districts in the thirties.

Lindsay and the Troy aide began to discuss the McGovern forces, whom they mistrusted. "Give me an old pol like 'Onions' Burke,"* said Lindsay. "If he was gonna double-cross you, he would wink while he was shaking your hand. But these guys don't even give you a tipoff."

McGovern suddenly appeared at the entrance of the ballroom, surrounded by aides. As TV cameramen crowded him, he edged his way to the gold-curtained stage, where Lawrence O'Brien, the Democratic Party Chairman, was sitting. O'Brien was being kicked out of his job to make way for Jean Westwood, McGovern's choice. McGovern reached the podium and acknowledged the applause of the Democratic National Committee. Then he began to sing O'Brien's praises, saying what a great chairman O'Brien had been.

"Keep looking for the cloud," said Lindsay. "They're gonna take McGovern up on a cloud."

"I would like to thank Mr. O'Brien for his wonderful service to the party," McGovern intoned.

"Not to mention for saving the nomination for me last week," Lindsay said out of the corner of his mouth.

McGovern finally got around to nominating Jean Westwood as the new party chairman. The committee dutifully elected her and she accepted.

Then McGovern nominated Pierre Salinger, his choice for vice chairman of the party. Salinger was

* William "Onions" Burke was once a power in the Massachusetts Democratic Party.

standing underneath one of the sexy shepherdesses. The TV crews trained their lights on him and the cameras whirred. He was obviously thinking over his acceptance speech one last time; everyone expected the committee to vote him in without a peep of protest.

But suddenly Charles Evers, the black Committeeman from Mississippi, was on his feet nominating another candidate, Basil Patterson, a black from New York.

"Black power strikes again," was Lindsay's comment.

McGovern looked agitated. He couldn't oppose a black without looking bad. He leaned toward the microphone and said, "I would like to make a suggestion."

"Take a dive, Pierre, take a dive!" said Lindsay, reading McGovern's mind.

"I think that either Pierre Salinger or Basil Patterson would be perfectly acceptable to this committee," said McGovern.

"I think Pierre just got the signal from George to jump out the window," said Lindsay.

Salinger put up his hand and announced that he wanted to address the committee. He walked quickly to the stage and stood beside McGovern at the podium. Looking deflated, he said brusquely that he sensed it was the will of the committee that Basil Patterson be the next vice chairman.

"He not only sensed it," piped Lindsay. "He saw how many weren't standing up!"

Then McGovern took the microphone to praise Salinger for withdrawing. "I would like to thank Pierre . . ." McGovern began.

"For taking that beautiful parachute dive!" Lindsay said, trying not to laugh out loud. He peered over at the side of the ballroom, trying to catch a glimpse of Frank Mankiewicz and Gary Hart.

"Boy, did the McGovern boys ever bail out on that one," he said. "But tomorrow we'll find out it was a beautiful scheme that Mankiewicz had in his pocket the whole time."

McGovern was still droning on, and Lindsay was get-

ting restless. "I've had enough of this shit," he said finally, and went off to file a story on the meeting.

I looked very carefully in the next week's *Newsweek*,
but I couldn't find a word about the Democratic National Committee proceedings.

CHAPTER VII

Television

THE YEARS since 1968 had been rough ones for TV newsmen. Spiro Agnew had been making it hot for them, ranting about how the networks slanted the news and hinting darkly about what the FCC might do to incorrigible news-twisters. The phrase "media event" had entered the language, and become a dirty phrase. At some time or other in 1972, nearly everybody—right-wing editorialists, left academics, Nixon aides, McGovern staffers, and newspaper reporters—accused the networks of distorting reality. Many newspapermen complained that they would soon be relegated to the role of drama critics; they would merely write reviews of the spectacles staged for the benefit of TV crews.

The TV people were extremely sensitive to all of this hostility, and even they were growing slightly resentful of media events. So in 1972, whenever the setup was too blatantly artificial—like Major John Lindsay milking a cow in Wisconsin or putting on a wet-suit to probe the muck of Biscayne Bay for ecological disasters—the networks often shied away or tried to be the first to brand it a "media event." In California, when McGovern's people began handing out free video tapes of McGovern's speeches to any station that would take them, NBC devoted three and a half conspicuous minutes to a report on McGovern's use of the media. The NBC people even spent a day filming themselves filming McGovern.

During one brief period, in the early fall, when McGovern began staging media events, Cassie Mackin, the NBC correspondent, felt downright insulted. McGovern would spend a whole morning hauling the press corps to some farm in the Midwest just so that he could appear against a background of grain silos when he made a statement about the wheat scandal. "This is a Presidential campaign and we don't need pretty pictures to get on the air," said Mackin. "Why can't they just run their campaign and let us take the responsibility of finding something interesting to say about it? It would be fine with me if they did nothing for the media."

At the same time, TV people were increasingly prone to admit the limitations of their medium. While NBC still had the gall to take newspaper ads claiming that its news program provided "All You Need to Know," many TV journalists were more humble. "I don't think people ought to believe only one news medium," Walter Cronkite told an interviewer during the Republican Convention. "They ought to read and they ought to go to opinion journals and all the rest of it. I think it's terribly important that this be taught in the public schools, because otherwise, we're gonna get to a situation because of economic pressures and other things where television's all you've got left. And that would be *disastrous*. We can't cover the news in a half-hour event evening. That's ridiculous."

Others went even further. "A lot of TV reporters are not really reporters at all," said a CBS correspondent who wished to remain anonymous. "They've come up from local radio and TV stations, and they really don't know much about politics. But all they have to do is run around and dredge up a minute and a half of thought. It makes no difference if they're ignoramuses because there's no space on the program anyway."

A lot of newspapermen would say amen to that. In the early sixties, when the TV people began appearing in large numbers on the press bus, the older newspapermen had regarded them with outright loathing—they were dilettantes, glamor boys, know-nothings. Over the years, the newspapermen had come to treat the TV people with more respect but they were still not prepared to accept them as big leaguers. In August 1972, Lewis W. Wolfson, an Associate Professor of Communications at American University, polled fifty-seven major political journalists, asking them: "Which political correspondents (in print or TV) do you respect the most?" Of the fourteen journalists mentioned most often in the results, not one was a TV journalist.

The print men on the bus did admire a few TV reporters, mostly correspondents who covered Washington full-time such as Doug Kiker (who was a refugee, after all, from the old *Herald Tribune*), Dan Rather, Cassie Mackin, Roger Mudd, and Dan Schorr. These people were good, they dug for news; but still, how could you take seriously a person whose daily output lasted two minutes on the air? In newspaper terms, the TV news amounted to putting out a paper that contained only ten stories every day, with only four paragraphs to each story. In fact, if you put a whole transcript of a network news show into newspaper type, it covered only a third of the front page of *The New York Times*.

The galling thing was not just that these TV people, many of them, bordered on being show-biz celebrities, or that they were pulling down big salaries, or that women threw themselves at some of the TV men (who had been in the living room so often that they seemed like second husbands). The worst of it was that the networks were booming while the newspapers kept dying off.

Yet the newspapermen got along well enough with the TV reporters. They ate and drank together without any conspicuous apartheid. Except, perhaps, for David Schoumacher.

Schoumacher was a tough, somber, extremely aggressive reporter who had a reputation for approaching political campaigns more as an infiltrator than a reporter. He invited staffers out to lunch, took secretaries horseback riding, cultivated anyone who might possibly give him a story. Which sometimes led to accusations that Schoumacher was going too far. Covering Eugene McCarthy in 1968, for instance, Schoumacher had become so obviously immersed in the campaign that supporters of Robert Kennedy complained bitterly that Schoumacher was serving as a shill for McCarthy. Four years later, Schoumacher ran into a different kind of accusation—that of poaching on a fellow reporter's turf.

In January 1972, Schoumacher went out on a Muskie sortie with Jack Germond and a few other reporters. On the plane one morning, Germond overheard one Muskie staffer telling another that Senator Adlai Stevenson III of Illinois was going to endorse Muskie. It was not a great story, Germond thought, but the Gannett papers in Illinois would be delighted to break it. Around noon, Germond's deadline, the campaign party finally arrived at a motel in Tallassee. Germond rushed to the press room and phoned in his exclusive story. The only other man in the press room was David Schoumacher. As Germond was dictating the story, it occurred to him that he should have gone outside and used a phone booth, but he didn't think much about it.

At the next stop in Tallahassee, Germond heard that CBS radio had broken the Stevenson story. They had got it on the air before his papers had even hit the stands. Germond was pretty sore, but his friend Witcover was furious. When they got back on the press bus, Witcover asked Schoumacher where he had got the story. Schoumacher said he had not heard it from anyone in the entourage.

"Well, I couldn't prove he got the story off me," Germond said later. "But, come on, I don't believe in the fucking Easter Bunny."

After the Florida incident, some of the newspapermen regarded Schoumacher with suspicion. They wanted to discipline him somehow, but couldn't think of a way. "What do you do?" said one reporter. "Pull out his plugs?"

The rest of the TV reporters were fairly well liked. It was just that they were . . . different. They were always flying off to the nearest town with a big TV studio in order to edit their film; they missed a lot of dinners and poker games that way. They had to go everywhere chained to a human ball and chain, which consisted of a cameraman, a sound man, a lighting man and sometimes a producer as well. It wasn't really the TV reporters that got in the way, but those cameramen and sound and light people who looked like garage mechanics and dressed in plastic ski parkas and Hush Puppies were always grunting and shoving and stepping all over everyone to get to the front of the crowd. And in the final analysis, the TV reporters were wedded to their cameramen, to pictures.

The TV reporters were the direct descendants of Nathaniel Currier and James Ives, the pioneers of American pictorial journalism. In 1860, Currier and Ives mass-produced cheap, accurate prints (sold at corner newsstands) of Lincoln, Douglas, and Breckinridge. For the first time, the public knew exactly what the candidates looked like. The Currier and Ives operation was a wild success, and it was based on the principle that would become the cardinal rule of TV news: "Don't just tell a story, show it."

Above all else, TV reporters were trained to search for a good picture. Every night, there was a glut of stories pouring into the newsroom, and the surest way to get on the air was to find interesting visuals. If a TV reporter failed to get good footage of the speech, or could not make his sources talk on camera, his piece would probably be killed. Chancellor, or Cronkite, or Smith would take the essential facts of the story and condense them into a twenty-second spiel that would have practically no impact. For years, the networks had slighted stories that were hard to illustrate, such as economic stories. They were just beginning to give such stories the attention they deserved.

A TV story with good visuals could sometimes run a print story into the ground, not to mention a rival TV story with not-so-good visuals. But what a chore it was to get the pictures! "You've got all that claptrap equipment," said Roger Mudd of CBS, "so you can't move as fast as the newspapermen. You're always worrying about this shot or that shot and you can't quite concentrate on what the candidate is saying because you're worrying about the mechanics, and you're thinking *Oh, Christ, we ran out of film!*"

So the test of a good TV correspondent was not primarily whether he was a great political observer. It was whether he could deal with all of the technical problems, guide his cameraman toward the right shots, and put the film together to form a coherent story. When a producer wanted to compliment a gifted TV correspondent, he said, "So-and-so writes well to film." Which meant that the correspondent had a gift for weaving the copy and the film into one neat, indivisible strand of meaning; each picture illustrated a point that the voice was making. The making of a television campaign report was a specialized process that was three parts television technique and one part political journalism.

Take, for example, the California primary. None of the newspapers were printing much about McGovern's welfare plan or his defense budget, so there was no pressure on the networks to get involved in these complicated, nonvisual stories. In California, the basic story was that McGovern had an incredible organization whose tentacles seemed to reach everywhere, and Humphrey had no organization at all; he was a "one-man band." So the networks did takeouts (feature stories) on the Black Vote, the Brown Vote, and the Blue-Collar Vote, which reflected the fact that McGovern's organization was making heavy inroads. "We haven't been doing so much event coverage," said Bob Eaton, a West Coast producer for NBC. "Instead we're doing trends in the campaign, big movements, stories about the state."

Pretty soon the story became not that McGovern was going to win, but how much he was going to win by. Exactly a week before the election, ABC received the results of a poll it had commissioned. The poll said that McGovern had a twenty-two-point lead over Humphrey. The ABC people got cold feet. They decided to wait two days for a "second wave" of polling they had ordered. There were rumors that Humphrey's people were putting enormous pressure on ABC executives, telling them that they would look like idiots when the Field Poll came out at the end of the week. The Field Poll, they claimed, would show McGovern only six points ahead. But an ABC vice president denied that Humphrey staffers talked ABC out of running the first results. "It pays to be cautious," he said. "You don't fool around if you want to keep your reputation intact."

Meanwhile, an ABC employee carelessly let the results slip to McGovern's people, and the McGovern people, being nothing if not shrewd, immediately told CBS. The next night CBS scooped ABC on its own poll: McGovern out front by twenty-two points. ABC was furious, and the night after that, they revealed that McGovern was really only seventeen points ahead (according to their second set of figures). The same day, the Field Poll came out: McGovern out front by twenty points. Four days later, McGovern won the election by only six points. Mervin Field, the director of the Field Poll, said he thought that the poll might have "interfered with the electoral process," presumably by making the McGovern people complacent in the last week and by frightening the Humphrey people into making a desperate last-ditch effort. "In all my twenty-seven years of polling," said Field, "I have never seen the likes of the publicity that one got. The publication itself became a campaign event."*

The day after the Field Poll broke was a Friday, and I spent most of it watching Jack Perkins and John Dancy, the NBC correspondents, filing their reports. Both Perkins and Dancy had been newscasters in Cleveland, Ohio, and worked at NBC as all-purpose, general assignment reporters, not as political reporters. But on Friday, June 2, at least, the situation demanded more video know-how than political wizardry. Perkins and Dancy had ninety seconds each. The hot story was obviously the reactions-to-the-poll story. It was entirely predictable, but still hot. McGovern (covered by Perkins) would be delighted with the poll, but warn against overconfidence. Humphrey (covered by Dancy) would dwell on the fallibility of polls and insist that the election wasn't over yet. So Perkins and Dancy had the job of confirming what everybody knew the candidate would say. The assignment was inevitable, the time limit was set, and the idiosyncrasies of film and TV equipment (and the candidates' schedules) virtually dictated the content of the stories.

Jack Perkins was a tall, big-jawed man who wore goggle glasses and was just as easygoing and bemused as he appeared on TV. When NBC sent him to Los Angeles several years ago, he went native; today he was wear-

---

* The enormous publicity given to the polls may indeed have skewed the results of the California primary election. But it is also possible that the polls were wrong, that McGovern never really had such a huge lead. Almost every publication and network in America chose to accept the polls as gospel and to report McGovern's eventual six-point victory as a "set back." One of the few publications to challenge the accuracy of the polls was *The New Yorker*, which wrote in June 1972: ". . . McGovern's victory by six percent was called a 'set back' for him by most of the press; just as Muskie's victory in New Hampshire was called a 'set back' for him because he hadn't won by the margin that the press had decided he should win by. In both cases, failures on the part of observers were made to seem failures on the part of candidates." At any rate, the press's theory that McGovern had suffered a reversal gave Humphrey and Muskie the courage to continue fighting him after California; their persistence caused a deep rift within the Democratic party.

ing a white necktie, a blue rancher's shirt, tan Levi slacks, a handwoven string belt and Hush Puppies. He was with Bob Eaton, his producer, a short, round-faced man also in his thirties and also dressed West Coast informal—he wore cowboy boots. On Friday morning they were both hovering at the rear of a McGovern press conference in the San Francisco Hilton, where Meade Esposito, the Democratic Boss of Brooklyn, was love-feasting with the Senator. As the conference broke up, I asked if I could follow them on their rounds. Sure, they said, friendly as missionaries. We set off from the Hilton and walked a few blocks to KRON, the local NBC affiliate. At KRON, we walked up a long fluorescent-lit hall to one of the cutting rooms where the processed film was waiting for them.

The cutting room, which was the size of a kitchenette, contained a Bell and Howell projector, a small screen on the far wall, a large boxlike speaker beneath the screen, a counter to one side with a Moviescope film-splicing machine on it, and a middle-aged film editor named Marie. Perkins and Eaton took off their jackets and watched as Marie ran several short reels of film on the projector—footage of McGovern visiting a hospital for senior citizens early that morning, of Perkins doing a "standup" introduction at the hospital, and of a McGovern rally at San Jose the night before. Both men began to splice the film inside their heads.

"I was thinking," said Eaton, "forty-six seconds of your opening and the hospital, twenty of the rally, and that leaves room for something at the end."

"Sounds good," said Perkins.

Marie put the first couple of reels on parallel tracks of the Moviescope. When she moved one of the reels by hand, George McGovern's voice came out of the speaker like a chipmunk's.

"Make him say, 'You've seen the polls,' " Perkins said. Marie wound the reel until McGovern said the words in a little helium voice. (In cutting rooms, politicians are treated like puppets. Later that afternoon,

Marie looked into the Moviescope screen and ordered, "Put your tongue in your mouth, Humphrey!" and then rolled the film until he did.)

Perkins and Marie pored over the hospital footage, looking at the part where McGovern advised his troops against complacency. "Schoumacher got the quote," Perkins said disgustedly. "He wanted to get a nice close-up, so he didn't wait for the news conference, he had to get it right there at the hospital. There's good stuff on McGovern here, but Jesus, we also get these nice close shots of Schoumacher. I'd use the quote from the San Jose rally, but McGovern's shtick there never ends and it gets no response. So we're stuck with Schoumacher."

(Schoumacher would doubtless have smiled his annual smile if he could have heard. The day before, I had overheard him instructing his cameraman to "lean hard on Houston," who was Perkins' cameraman.)

Eaton, who had gone out to call the executive producer in New York, came back and said, "We're fine for a minute and a half. We're go." With that, Perkins and Eaton went to the neighborhood Zims for lunch. Even there, they were not free of the producer in New York. In the middle of a hamburger, Perkins was paged by the bartender—New York had some small question to ask him.

Arriving back at the cutting room, the two men kept on doing sums in their heads, trying to make the film clips add up to 90 seconds. Marie kept offering film clips as if they were hats to try on, and the men kept making technical decisions.

"Do you want Jack here?" she asked, showing the end of Perkins' introductory speech on the Moviescope screen.

"No," said Eaton. "Give me Jack's voice from the A roll, but give me a picture of McGovern on the B roll, with just a little background noise." Marie slipped the A roll film out of the Moviescope and fitted in the B roll. Then she pulled the B roll through the Moviescope while she pulled the A roll over a sound head, so that

Perkins talked while McGovern pressed the withered flesh of an old man.

"That's good," said Eaton.

"OK, just tell me where you want to go out," said Marie, as she continued to pull the film.

"There!" said Eaton. Marie snipped the film with a small scissors and Scotch-taped the loop to the counter.

"Now we cut to the old woman," said Eaton. Marie found the right segment in the B roll.

"Cut it right there, after she says, 'Nice to see you,' " said Eaton. "Then Jack comes in again."

Perkins left the cutting room and went to the newsroom to write his script on one of the giant-type typewriters. He wrote about three pages in type that was slightly larger than the letters in a Dick and Jane book. Meanwhile, in the cutting room, eight or nine loops of film were now hanging from the counter like smoked eels. Marie looked at them doubtfully. "You have me completely confused as to how you're putting this together," she said to Eaton. It was two o'clock—five o'clock in New York. John Chancellor would go on the air in an hour and a half. Eaton began to draw up an outline for Marie.

Perkins suddenly opened the door, flooding the darkened cutting room with light from the hall. New York wanted two thirty-second clips of Humphrey's and McGovern's reactions to Nixon's Moscow trip. The reactions were incredibly boring and Perkins had tried to talk the New York producer out of the project, but to no avail. "They're doing a roundup," he shrugged. The cutting room was getting tense.

Several minutes later, John Dancy, a short, compact man dressed in a light suit, arrived in the cutting room to help prepare the Humphrey footage. Dancy had to do a matching piece about Humphrey. The networks always liked to cover candidates as symmetrically as possible so that no one could accuse them of violating the fairness doctrine.

Perkins had said that the polls showed McGovern

leading with every bloc except senior citizens. Dancy had to say that Humphrey was way behind even with his traditional black and labor supporters, and that he didn't have the kind of money he needed to catch up.

Marie ran the Humphrey footage on the Bell and Howell. There was some wonderful footage of Humphrey raving at a press conference. "I'm not dropping out, I'm about to take off," he piped. He babbled on about Victory in Miami. "Nixon thinks Hubert Humphrey is the strongest threat," said Humphrey. Smoke was coming out of his ears. It was terrific stuff. Better than anything else I had seen, it caught the frazzled desperation that was Humphrey's trademark in the last week of the California campaign. But all this footage landed, literally, on the cutting room floor. It was too long (about three minutes) and too blatantly damning. It wasn't a good match for the light and varied tone of Perkins' piece.

Instead, Eaton and Dancy decided to use three other segments: Humphrey on an early morning talk show (to show that he had to scrounge for free TV time); Dancy interviewing Humphrey in the street about the poll; and Dancy at a Humphrey Labor Rally, telling the camera that "lukewarm labor support has denied Humphrey both money and campaign workers he might ordinarily have expected." Dancy left some final instructions with Marie and went off to write his script. Marie put the segments of film on reels in the right order and sent them to another room where the final splices would be made.

Eaton wandered up the hall to the newsroom and sat on the edge of a steel desk among the wire machines and clattering typewriters. Perkins and Dancy were still working on their scripts. It was getting late, but Eaton couldn't do anything until the control room was ready to "feed" the stories to New York. I asked him whether New York had assigned the stories.

"No," said Eaton, with his customary smile, "this is very much what Jack and I feel is the story. Even more than with newspapers, TV reporting is an individual thing. Just because of the mechanics. They get our story maybe a half-hour before air time; there's no time to change it. They have to rely on the whole thing being produced in the field."

I asked about the thrown-away Humphrey footage. "Surveys have shown that TV news is the dominant factor in deciding undecided voters," said Eaton, who was beginning to glance nervously at the clock. "So I would feel hesitant about doing anything that would influence the outcome. I mean, over the last week we *have* shown that McGovern is ahead, but I spent the fall of '68 with the Humphrey campaign, and I'd be reluctant at this point to write his political obituary."

TV journalists weren't quite the easy riders that Eaton made them out to be. In the world of straight, "objective" journalism, the more freedom you gave a reporter, the more he censored himself. "Freedom" scared a reporter out of his mind, because it wasn't really freedom at all. "Freedom" simply meant that nobody had clearly marked all the pitfalls and booby traps, so the reporter became cautious as a blind man on a battlefield. A network correspondent worried about the FCC breathing down his neck, he prayed that he wouldn't cross some little quirk of the network-news president, and he thought of all the money he was pissing away— about $5,000 for a two-hundred-word story. (The next day, to cover McGovern's whistle-stop train, NBC would use two camera crews and a Lear jet—at a cost of about $10,000, or $5,000 per minute of air time.) To say that TV reporting was an "individual thing" was to say that if a reporter fumbled a story, the shit-hammer came down squarely on his head. There were no middlemen to blame.

Finally, at 3:12 P.M. (eighteen minutes to air time), the director called Eaton, Perkins, and Dancy into the control room. The director, a glowering man with earphones attached to his head, sat behind a huge console in the control room, flanked by four assistants in sport shirts. They were all facing four large TV monitors mounted in the far wall. Perkins and Dancy stepped into a tiny soundproofed booth on the left side of the control room, and sat down in front of a huge, old-fashioned radio microphone. They looked like Bob and Ray.

Down the hall, in the projection room, a couple of engineers had just finished putting the various reels of film on four different projectors. The A roll, the film of Perkins talking at the hospital, was on Projector One. When the director wanted the A roll, he would shout, "P One!" and one of his assistants would hit a button on the console to start Projector One. The Perkins film would show up on a large monitor in the center of the wall, and at the same time it would be fed onto a master tape at the NBC studio in Burbank. Then, at the right second, the director would hit the button to bring in the film of McGovern shaking hands at the hospital, which was on Projector Two, and would point to Perkins, who would read the commentary from his script: ". . . things seem to be going so well that the candidate has taken to warning his followers of overconfidence."

The director had to conduct a crazy little electronic orchestra—cueing Perkins and Dancy in the sound booth, bringing in each new segment of film, bringing up the background sounds of the film segments under the voices of Perkins and Dancy. It would all make one coherent story on the master tape at Burbank, and Burbank would then transmit the whole thing to New York. The director gave all the orders in code, and it sounded like an Apollo launching.

Fifteen minutes before air time. "Stand by," the director said in the tensely quiet control room. "Ready to come up. P One film. Roll 'em."

Perkins appeared on the monitor in rich compatible color, smiling and announcing: "McGovern led in every category but senior citizens—and, as it happened, that is where McGovern began campaigning today."

"P Two background sound," said the director. No background sound came up.

"What happened?" snapped the director. "Where's the sound?"

A voice from the Projection Room came over a loud-speaker: "We'll have to do it again obviously."

Eleven minutes to air time. Perkins was as unruffled as if he were making a telephone call. "We may have to feed live," he explained, "while Chancellor is on the air. Feeding alive is like swinging across a ravine on a rotten rope. We're feeding to Burbank, and they're taping it and feeding it to New York, so there are a lot of switchboards where people can screw up."

The voice on the loudspeaker announced that the projection room was ready. Eight minutes to air time. Everything went smoothly until a "bloom" showed up on the monitor—a flash of light caused by a sudden transition from a dark to a light piece of film. The machine which was supposed to adjust brightness had overcompensated.

Another wait. Five minutes to air time. The director started to call the plays again. Perkins and Dancy read their scripts with perfect smoothness. An assistant director whispered into his headphone telling New York where to put the mats, the cards which said "Jack Perkins, NBC News." They finished, and the director picked up a phone.

"Did they buy it?" Perkins asked.

The director listened to the voice at the other end. "They bought it," he said finally.

Perkins and Dancy got up and sauntered down the hall to the newsroom, where they sat down and watched the news with some KRON people. Chancellor had just introduced the first piece, Irving R. Levine talking about the economy. As the program unrolled, the people in the room dissected it like a journalism school class.

"Three minutes of voice on economic junk, no visuals, and into an ad. And they expect us to beat CBS!" a KRON man bitched.

The roundup of reactions to Nixon's trip came on.

"Mike Mansfield quoting Richard Nixon," grumbled Perkins. "Scintillating television."

Then, at seventeen minutes into the half hour, Chancellor began doing a neat little intro into the California story. The screen showed 46 points, in yellow, for McGovern, and 26 points, in blue, for Humphrey "And here are reports from John Dancy and Jack Perkins," said Chancellor.

"How about Jack Perkins and John Dancy?" said Perkins.

They watched in relative silence.

"Jack got a B minus for starting with a shot of himself talking," a KRON kibitzer said when it was over. "John's visual was much more interesting."

THERE WAS ONLY ONE NOTICEABLE "MEDIA EVENT" in the California primary—McGovern's "Victory Special" whistle-stop trip down the San Joaquin Valley, which the McGovern people scheduled as a stalling measure to preserve what they thought was a twenty-point lead. CBS declined to cover the trip ("We've done train rides to death," Schoumacher told someone); NBC and ABC gave it short shrift.

The Conventions, however, were the greatest media events on earth. The Convention Hall was the world's biggest TV studio, lit for TV with rows and rows of hard white spotlights, wired for TV with 150 miles of electric cable, and with almost every public event staged expressly for TV. The networks dominated the Conventions by sheer numbers. CBS had a staff of 500; NBC and ABC had 450 each. The most popular cliché in Miami was that the Conventions were really conventions of media people; that the reporters were the stars, not the politicians; that the reporters spent a great deal of time interviewing each other about the coverage of the Convention. At the very center of all this attention were the TV people, the biggest stars of all, the most familiar faces in the land. Eric Sevareid, when curiosity prompted him to inspect the Zippie encampment at Flamingo Park, felt it necessary to disguise himself with a false mustache, sunglasses, a Harry Truman/conventioneer shirt, and a cane.

The main attraction of the Conventions was that they brought a mind-boggling collection of rich and powerful people into one small place. So anyone in America with a commodity to sell showed up at the Conventions to try to get a piece of the power and the money. Hookers peddled ass, Mr. Peanut peddled goobers, pushers peddled dope, managers peddled dark horses, and the networks peddled themselves. Since 1952, the networks had used the Conventions as all-purpose promotion gimmicks. As Richard Reeves wrote in *New York,* "The young industry used the conventions to grandly introduce its innovations—coast-to-coast network broadcasting in 1952, Huntley-Brinkley in 1956, the creepie-peepie camera in 1960, then color." The Conventions gave each network a chance to grab a bigger piece of the news audiences away from the other two networks. And the head of each network-news division broke his back for great ratings so that he could prove to his boss that the news division ought to get a bigger chunk of the network budget.

Of course, the network newsmen pointed out the great opportunity the Conventions provided—a chance to study a cross section of the nation, to examine the party system, to present a full spectrum of views, to render, in short, a great public service. That too, that too. But the networks came to Miami because it was good business. In July, the networks did a more expensive job of peddling than anyone else in town—including the Democrats. According to Richard Reeves, the networks spent about eight million dollars on the Convention, while the Democratic candidates and Party spent less than three million.

No small amount of this vast expenditure was earmarked for the press departments of the three networks. Each network had a Winnebago trailer in back of the

Hall, and each Winnebago was filled with about a dozen gnomes whose job it was to sit over typewriters all day and turn out tons of hype to send to hard-up TV editors at newspapers all over America. Any editor with a six-inch hole to plug on his TV page could throw in a handy handout from CBS entitled "The Shimmering Maze Behind the Convention Hall," describing the makeshift CBS Convention offices. Or he could use a release that started: "Mrs. George McGovern gave her first reactions to the California credentials vote in her husband's favor to CBS Correspondent Mike Wallace." The CBS press department hoped that people who read about Mike Wallace's coup would switch to CBS and that CBS's ratings would go up.

These press department trailers were very depressing places. The flacks themselves were wretched, pale, middle-aged men who had the burnt-out look of alcoholics and who invariably wore ascots or loud ties, which only accentuated the blankness of their faces. They would congratulate each other with a false bonhomie whenever a press release showed up on the front page of a newspaper, which sometimes happened. A lot of them were failed reporters, and now they were reduced to touting successful reporters. Yet they were very important. They helped to pump up the ratings. And that was why the networks were in Miami.

The press departments were also supposed to hand out passes to journalists who wanted to observe the network control rooms and to interview the anchor men. But at the Democratic Convention, the press departments were wary of visiting journalists, mainly because of an article that Richard Reeves had written in *New York* just before the Convention started. Reeves had described the frantic preparations that each of the networks was making to capture the best Convention ratings. He had also tossed in some colorful touches, such as the fact that many CBS correspondents considered Walter Cronkite an "air hog."

Many network executives were furious over the article. When I asked a lady producer from CBS to get me a plastic pass I needed to get into the CBS compound, she politely replied, "I won't even ask them, because first of all they'd say no and second of all I'd get my head chopped off—they're still all steamed up and paranoid about the Reeves article." The best I could get out of CBS was a cursory tour of the compound from a lady press officer who kept me on a short leash and jerked me around with a brusque "I'm sorry!" whenever I tried to stray in search of a friendly face who might let me into the control booth.

The CBS tour was awkward, but nowhere near so unpleasant as my dealings with NBC. NBC gave me the bum's rush. My relationship with NBC's press department had been strange and shaky from the outset. Back in April, Cassie Mackin, an NBC correspondent, had arranged for me to get a couple of NBC passes for election night in Wisconsin; all I had to do was find a press officer named Joe Derby who would give them to me. Late one night I finally located Derby, who was drinking in the Ole! Room of the Pfister Hotel with Ham Davis of the Providence *Journal*. Derby was a burly Irishman with grey, curly hair and a Father Christmas face. I introduced myself and Derby peered at my press tag.

"Rolling Stone," he said, looking at me hard. "You underground guys—you're always knocking the establishment. Well, what's wrong with the establishment? I'm gonna get that paper of yours and read what you say, and it better be good." I couldn't tell whether Derby was doing a weird Gaelic put-on or threatening my life, but I laughed and said I would watch what I wrote.

Derby took a new tack. "You guys from the newspapers, you're always putting down the networks, and then you come around asking for help because the networks have all the best resources and you need them." It was true that NBC had a giant computer in Cherry Hill, New Jersey, all primed and ready to spew out precinct analyses, and that every reporter in Milwaukee showed up at NBC on election night to get the teletyped printouts and use the typewriters and phones that NBC had laid out. "But then you turn around and knock the networks," Derby complained.

"Don't worry, I like John Chancellor," I said.

"Listen," Derby said, "you never worked one-tenth as hard as John Chancellor has worked and you'll be lucky to get a fraction as far as he's gotten! You say anything about John CHancellor and he'll put you in the hospital! And if he won't, I will—you wiseass!"

Ham Davis looked alarmed at the heavy turn the conversation had taken. "He's a good guy," he said, pointing to me.

"Naw, he's a wiseass," Derby growled, and then he suddenly surprised me by flashing an angelic smile and putting a big arm around my shoulders. "I'm only kiddin'," he said. "I can see you got a nice face. I just wish you weren't a wiseass, that's all."

In the morning, I ran into Joe Derby again. He was quiet, sweet, helpful, and only too glad to give me two plastic NBC passes. That was the last I saw of him until the eve of the Democratic Convention in Miami, when he offered to get me into the NBC control booth. "I don't have any booth passes right now," he said, "but come back and see me tomorrow." I went to the NBC press trailer for three days in a row, but never found Derby. As I stood around the trailer on the third night, I started looking at the bulletin board for lack of anything else to do. The board was hung with trophies—clippings about NBC Convention coverage from *The New York Times,* the Washington *Post,* and the Miami *News.* I took out my notebook and started jotting down the dates and page numbers of the articles. Suddenly, a tall man with a lantern jaw and sinister tinted glasses came at me like a police dog. "I thought I made it clear the other night that NBC has no interest in cooperating with *Rolling Stone,*" he said very firmly.

"What!" I said, my jaw dropping. The man had never talked to me before except to tell me, on one of my

previous visits to the trailer, that Joe Derby was nowhere to be found.

"I thought I made it clear that NBC has no interest in
cooperating with *Rolling Stone*," the man said.

"So why's that?" I said. "This is news to me."

"I thought I made it clear etc.," said the man.

"Well, so what did I do to offend NBC?" I asked.

"I think you'd better leave," he said threateningly.

I left. A few minutes later I was strolling outside the
press trailer with Dick Reeves and we came across the
man and Joe Derby. We had the same dialogue again,
only more heatedly. Reeves copied it down in his notebook and later wrote it up in *New York*. It turned out
that the man was Bud Rukeyser, NBC's vice president
of corporate information. Reeves got Rukeyser's quote a
little twisted and had him saying: "I thought I made it
clear NBC has no interest in helping publications like
yours." Reeves interpreted the contretemps to mean that
NBC was so out of touch that it couldn't tell *Rolling
Stone* reporters from Zippies.

Rukeyser, who liked to think of himself as a friend of
the Underground Press, was very upset by the article.
He sent a letter to *New York,* saying that the real reason
he threw me out was that I had been "rummaging
through papers" in the press trailer, not because I was
from *Rolling Stone*. So I called up Rukeyser to straight-
en things out. "You know I wasn't rummaging through
any papers," I said.

"Well, I saw you taking notes about the things on the
bulletin board, and I considered that by itself enough to
throw you out," he said. "But as long as we're being so
frank, what about the beer?"

"The beer?" I asked. He'd surprised me again.

"Well, I heard that someone from *Rolling Stone* had
thrown a glass of beer at someone in the Railroad
Lounge, and so when I saw you taking notes from the
bulletin board I frankly figured I had had enough and I
threw you out."

I later asked Hunter Thompson if he had thrown beer at anybody in the Railroad Lounge, which was a private press bar in the Convention Hall. He looked puzzled, and then the memory dawned on him. "Oh, yeah," he said. "They wouldn't let me take my beer out of the lounge so I hurled it into this huge oil drum they had at the door and it made a huge BOOM that you could hear for miles."

Rukeyser couldn't seem to make up his mind as to why he had given me the heave-ho. He told his superiors at NBC that I had been "going through drawers," told *New York* that I was "rummaging through papers," and told me about the beer. But as I walked away from the press trailer that night, slightly shaken, it occurred to me that the networks regarded themselves as omnipotent and sacred institutions, roughly like the Presidency.

Maybe the correspondents didn't, but the corporate heavies did. Later in the year, I would come across the same mammoth PR operation, the same desire to classify the most trivial and worthless information, the same arrogance, and the same mindless lickspittle respect for any higher executive—at the White House, of course. Ronald Ziegler and Bud Rukeyser could have traded places with no trouble. Like a White House press secretary, Rukeyser collected a fat salary for keeping the press from revealing that his employers had a human and fallible side.

As I headed toward the Press Gate of the Convention Hall to begin the tedious business of scrounging for a floor pass, I spotted a friend of mine, a professional political fixer whom I will call Paddy O'Hustle. Paddy had come to the Convention to troubleshoot for three separate clients: John Tunney, Gov. John Gilligan of Ohio, and George McGovern.

"Hey, Paddy," I said. "Can you get a floor pass?"

"Maybe I can," he said solemnly. "Do you know anyone at NBC?"

"Yeah," I said. "I know Cassie Mackin."

"Well," he said, "I'll give you a delegate's pass if you can do me a favor."

"Sure," I said, desperate for a pass.

"You go out there and tell her that Ted Kennedy's supposed to make a statement at eleven, but she can find out about Kennedy sooner if she talks to John Tunney. 'Cause Tunney's Ted's best friend, see, and he knows exactly what Ted's gonna say. And this way, I get Tunney some air time. But for chrissake, don't tell her that."

"OK," I said, grabbing the pass.

"You think she'll do it?" he shouted after me.

"Yeah," I shouted over my shoulder. "I think so."

I had no idea whether Cassie would do it. She was a smart, pretty, thirtyish ex-Hearst reporter who, having been at NBC for only a year and a half, had landed a job that many male correspondents had coveted for fifteen years. She was a "floor person" at the Convention, an assignment that can put rockets on a career. She had developed an iron self-confidence and a touchy professional pride; she bridled at any suggestion that NBC had made her a floor correspondent as a sop to Women's Lib. "Five years ago, they'd have said I was sleeping with the right people," she would snap.

I had seen her the night before, crisscrossing the floor in search of interviewees, and later she had stood alone at the foot of the rostrum, sagging with exhaustion. "I'm so sick of it at this point," she said. "There's no one out there left to talk to." She had developed a waitresslike memory which juggled profiles like orders. She knew the names and salient features of about three hundred county chairmen, delegates, and campaign staffers, and she knew the first questions to ask each of them if an interview should materialize. That night, she had interviewed Kenneth Gibson, the black mayor of Newark; Ted Van Dyk, the McGovern staffer; Joe Duffey, the would-be-Senator from Connecticut; and Dick Gregory, the war protestor, among dozens of others. in most cases, she herself decided whom to buttonhole and what to ask.

Sometimes a voice from the control booth would come through her grey plastic headset to instruct her to ask a certain question. "Reuven Frank, the president of NBC News, came on the headset while I was talking to a kid from Virginia," she said. "He said, 'It's the Harris Proposal he's talking about,' so I asked the kid about that. In fairness to me, that's the only time it happened."

But I couldn't sight Cassie tonight. Armed with my delegate's pass, I elbowed my way through the noisy, hypertense crush of delegates. The only way to make speedy progress through the mob was to yell "Hot coffee!" but so many people were used to the trick that it no longer worked. Celebrities were standing in little pools of charisma. I shoved through delegates who were fighting to snap pictures of Art Buchwald and John Lindsay smoking fat cigars, of Warren Beatty, Germaine Greer . . .

Over by the Texas delegation, Garrick Utley stood out like the Eiffel Tower. His face was lifted toward the rafters, as if in prayer, and his lips were moving. "Jesus," I thought. "The pressure really gets to some of these guys." Then I realized that Utley was talking to one of the NBC telephoto cameras that was perched in the gridwork. One of the reasons that every smalltown mayor, fashion model, Jaycee and publicity hound in America will *kill* to get onto the floor is that, once you have arrived, there is no way to avoid getting on TV. The eyes of the networks are constantly scanning the floor, like the cameras that scrutinize shoplifters at Macy's. If you stand around for a few minutes you will inevitably become part of the background for an interview, or part of an interview.

Finally, I caught a glimpse of Cassie's blond head and pushed my way to the back of the floor where she was standing with her "floor manager" getting ready to question some delegate. A floor manager is a portable bouncer; when the interviews starts, his job is to put out his arms like a tightrope walker and keep passers-by from blocking the camera's view.

"Listen, Cassie," I said, jingling the thirty pieces of silver in my pocket. "I got a hot tip. Ted's supposed to go on at eleven, but John Tunney can tell you what he's gonna say. You could probably get a scoop."

"Oh, that sounds good," she said enthusiastically. "I have to do this thing, and then I'll look for him."

"Great," I said. "He's right over there in the California delegation. He's tall, you can't miss him."

"Thanks a lot for telling me," said Cassie.

"Glad to help," I said.

About an hour later, Paddy O'Hustle came barreling toward me, grinning wildly.

"Did Cassie ever get to Tunney?" I asked.

"No," he said, "but don't worry. I went up to Doug Kiker [also of NBC] and I said, 'Doug, was it you or Cassie Mackin that was interested in seeing Senator Tunney about Kennedy's decision?' Kiker said, 'It was me!' and ran off to find Tunney. Then I went up to Roger Mudd [of CBS] and I said, 'Roger, was it you or John Hart that was asking to see Tunney . . .' and Roger said, 'Must have been me!' Roger got Tunney, too. So in the last hour, I've had Tunney on all three networks and I've got him in *The New York Times,* the Washington *Post* and the Boston *Globe* for tomorrow. I'd call that a good night's work."

Ted Kennedy never had any intention of appearing on television that night, since he had nothing to tell the press. According to [*More*] magazine, a group of bored reporters had asked Dick Drayne, Kennedy's press secretary, if he would join them at a Hyannisport "fish house" at 11 P.M. "When he accepted," [*More*] reported, "an overzealous UPI reporter bashed out a bulletin saying Drayne had called a press conference."

The floor reporters were fueled by a mixture of adrenalin and dogged competitiveness. They had to get to the big stories before the other networks did. One had to compete with the other floor people from one's own network for the jangled attention of the executive producer in the control booth. Yet the floor people stayed remarkably cool and civilized. There was nothing to match the scene in 1964 when Frank Reynolds of ABC had tried to grab Bull Connor away from a CBS producer who was setting up an interview. The CBS producer had punched out Reynolds.

There were a few problems at CBS. One CBS correspondent complained that they had "Walter to Walter coverage." The difficulty, said the correspondent, was that nobody dared tell Walter to shut up. It wasn't really Cronkite's fault. In the midst of the turmoil of the 1968 Convention, some CBS executive had sent Cronkite a note advising him that he was using the word "erosion" too much. Cronkite sent back a note which read, "I QUIT." Now everybody was afraid of offending him.

"When Walter keeps talking and you can't get your story on the air, it's terrible," said the correspondent. "It's not like on a newspaper. If you're a newspaper reporter and some editor kills your story, you get pissed off, sure. But if you're a TV reporter, it's different. Your face is attached to the story. They're not just rejecting some disembodied piece of copy, they're rejecting *you*. So you get horribly angry. Roger Mudd sounded like he was going to quit a couple of times. At the Republican Convention, Mike Wallace quit because they didn't put him on the air when he had cornered Maurice Stans. But that was nothing new. He had quit three times the day before and three times just that afternoon. We all quit all the time."

And in spite of the enormous staffs and elaborate preparations—or perhaps because of them—things still went wrong at the networks. On the first night of the Democratic Convention, CBS fell on its face by announcing that McGovern had suffered a defeat on the South Carolina challenge—which was, of course, a major tactical victory for the McGovern forces. CBS later undertook an investigation to find out the reasons for the failure. The results of the investigation remained top secret, but the main reason was simply that CBS had had a bad night.

Roger Mudd, a knowledgeable political reporter by any standards, was in the South Carolina section but did not know what was happening. Later, he ruefully admitted that he simply had not done his homework. Mike Wallace, who kept asking the wrong questions of Frank Mankiewicz and Gary Hart, did not know either. Neither did Cronkite. All of the floor reporters were supposed to have been briefed by Marty Plissner, CBS's full-time political editor. But Plissner had been too busy preparing delegate counts. David Schoumacher, who was covering McGovern Headquarters at the Doral Hotel, walked into the pressroom there and saw a bunch of newspaper reporters laughing at Cronkite. He managed to get on the air and say that the McGovern people seemed happy with the way the vote had gone. Hearing Schoumacher's report in his earphone, Roger Mudd finally caught on. Off camera, he got Gov. Pat Lucey, a McGovern man, to confirm his suspicion that the McGovern people had thrown the South Carolina vote on purpose. He called this information into the CBS control booth, but it got lost in the gigantic, electronic maw, and Cronkite did not straighten out the story for another couple of hours.

"The thing with television," Roger Mudd said later, "is that everybody's a high-priced communicator and nobody can really communicate. You know, it's a hung-up, inarticulate bunch of people. Even when we put things in memos we can't seem to get through to each other."

As much as any Convention in the electronic age, the 1972 Democratic Convention went its own way, in defiance of the dictates of television. The McGovern people's South Carolina victory depended on a lack of coverage rather than on any manipulation of the medium. And the McGovern people allowed the long, inane Vice Presidential nominations to push McGovern's acceptance speech out of the prime-time hours. The Democrats had a real, spontaneous Convention, with real rifts, boredom, chaos, and chicanery. The network reporters had to struggle to keep up with the happenings. They missed a lot, but they gave a fairly accurate picture of the drama and tedium of the Convention.

At least, the Democrats gave them a show. The Republicans gave them a perfectly scripted TV Convention, and it was as dull as a three-day-long treasurer's report.

"You were lucky to get on the air twice a night," Roger Mudd summed it up, "and even then you felt ashamed to go on with such junk. You know, everybody has their vanity, and you want to get on the air, and you want to show people that you're still working. I was not proud of my work at the Republican Convention, but I've told myself that there really wasn't that much for a reporter to do down there if he was a television man and trapped on the floor. It was *arranged* so there wasn't much to do. You were a prisoner on that floor and every time you got going on something they'd kill the house lights and roll the film so you couldn't broadcast anyhow."

The most interesting story of the Republican Convention took place well off camera. On the second afternoon, a messenger from the Republican National Committee's press office dropped off a sheaf of press releases in the "in" box of the BBC. The BBC was working out of a tiny pasteboard cubicle which was crammed with tables and equipment and was decorated with several gas masks hung on the wall in anticipation of Zippie demonstrations.

The office was being run by the BBC's chief U.S. correspondent, a wiry, forty-nine-year-old jockey-sized man named Charles Wheeler. When Wheeler looked through the papers in the box that afternoon, he came across one unbelievable treasure, a minute-by-minute script of the Convention. The script simply confirmed what everybody already knew, that the Convention was a totally stage-managed coronation of Richard Nixon. But it confirmed it with incredibly damning detail.

The script instructed the speakers when to pause,

nod, and accept "spontaneous" cheers. It stipulated that at a certain point, a demonstration would interrupt the convention secretary in midsentence. And at 10:33, according to the script, the President would be nominated and there would be a "ten-minute spontaneous demonstration with balloons."

Wheeler was still examining this document when three new messengers showed up to demand that he give it back. Wheeler told them that he could hardly consider doing such a thing. The messengers stalked off to fetch the sergeant-at-arms, but they came back instead with a lady from the Republican National Committee press center named Kit Wisdom. She was thin as a blade, had a very sharp nose and spiky dyed hair. She did not argue for long with Wheeler. She simply grabbed the script. Wheeler grabbed it back. Kit Wisdom pulled it out of his hand. Wheeler pried it away from her and pitched it across a couple of tables to a young radio correspondent named Christopher Drake, who might have played the Albert Finney part in an English movie. Kit Wisdom ran around the tables and reached for the script, but Drake poled her off with a straight right arm. "Naughty, naughty, naughty," he said. Finally, she walked away, close to tears.

Wheeler went on the air and told the British people about the script and the scuffle. He was the first reporter to discover the script and the only one to have to fight for it. The Republicans later realized that other copies had been sent out by mistake but despaired of trying to hunt them down. Copies soon fell into the hands of network correspondents, and all of the networks reported on it. ABC gave it good play on its evening news. CBS and NBC did very brief reports on it from the floor of the Convention Hall. None of the networks bothered to mention that the Republicans had tried frantically to retrieve the first missing copy, nor did they mention Charles Wheeler's valiant defense.

That night, I went to the NBC central control booth to watch the NBC executives directing the coverage of the nomination of Richard Nixon. Since the Democratic Convention, phone calls had been made, differences had been smoothed over, and Bud Rukeyser was now willing to cooperate with *Rolling Stone,* or at least with me. So I was led into the NBC complex, which consisted of a dozen or so Winnebagos connected by carpeted bridges. In the center of these was the small wood-paneled control room. At the back of the room were two booths with sliding glass panels—one for Julian Goodman, the president of NBC, who had the power to interrupt the proceedings at any moment via a red phone and over-rule a decision; and the other, occupied by several executives from Gulf, which was sponsoring the NBC Convention coverage.

In the middle of the room, Reuven Frank, the president of NBC News, and George Murray, the executive producer, were seated side by side at a long slim desk that was covered with telephones—blue phones to Chacellor and Brinkley, the red phone to Goodman, beige phones to everywhere else. In the greylit darkness, they were peering at a wall that contained fourteen TV screens—screens for ABC, CBS, and PBS; a screen for the pool camera that covered the podium for all the networks; screens that showed what some of the NBC cameras were doing both inside and outside the hall; and in the middle, two big screens, one showing the actual broadcast and the other, marked Preset, showing whoever was on deck.

Reuven Frank, an intense man with prematurely white hair and a scholarly face, was making comments in a low voice. Murray, with a truckdriver's physique and a fringe of black hair around a balding pate, did all the shouting. Murray was barking commands toward a door on his right that led to the trailer containing all the hookups to the cameras inside the Convention Hall. Somewhere in there, a director named Tony was looking at another set of screens and telling all the cameramen in the hall what to do.

It was about eleven o'clock (the Republican script was running late); the roll call was about to end. Gerald Ford was about to announce that Nixon had been nominated. The delegates were about to go wild in a ten-minute spontaneous demonstration and 20,000 red, white, and blue balloons were about to drop from nets in the flies of the Convention Hall.

"Watch the balloons up there," Murray yelled at Tony. The balloons showed up on the Preset screen. The control room was growing tense. From inside the adjacent trailer, Tony could be heard shouting into a microphone, directing his engineers and cameramen. He referred to the cameramen by number.

"Five, hold five! Hold three. Hold four!"

Suddenly the balloon drop commenced.

"Here they come! Here they come!" shouted Murray. His eyes were glued to the main screen, and he was very excited.

"Go! Start the zooms, Tony!" Murray yelled, getting even louder. "In and out, in and out! Yo-yo! Yo-yo!"

Yo-yo was part of the technical jargon. It meant to zoom in and out very fast. Balloons were dancing all over the screen. It looked like New Year's Eve in Valhalla.

"Switch, switch," Murray screamed. "Go, Tony! Now! Four, five, seven, three!"

The screen jumped with sudden cuts from one delegation to another. There was a giddy collage of laughing faces, banners, standards, balloons, more faces, people dancing in the aisle. Tony was cutting so fast from one camera to another that the screen seemed to whirl.

"That's it, Tony!" Murray lashed him on. "Beautiful! Cut like a maniac! Come on! Faster, faster! No more yo-yo, just cut. One, two, one, two—get the beat, Tony! That's it."

The pandemonium went on for several minutes. Finally, it was over and Murray slumped back in his leather swivel chair, exhausted. Congratulations were exchanged. Murray looked happily done-in, like a virtuoso who has just left the stage after playing a tricky concerto.

Over in the CBS newsroom, they were furious. Everyone there was bitching that NBC had been "editorializing" by making the demonstration look more exciting than it actually was. It was a niggling thing to say, but CBS was right. The demonstration had been a stage-managed bore. The whole Convention was a bore. So George Murray had hoked it up. But he didn't look like a man bent on distorting reality. He had obviously played around with the cameras on the balloon extravaganza to have a little fun. And he had had the time of his life. He had got off on all the shouting and the flashing images. He and the other producers out there in the control room were grown men playing with one of the most amusing electric trains ever built.

ACROSS TOWN, comfortably settled in a large white stucco house in a posh section of Miami Beach, was a very different operation called Top Value Television. TVTV, as they liked to be known, was a collective of twenty-eight young cable-TV reporters who had got press passes to the Conventions, and who had rented the house from a French landlady who did not object to their long hair. Using inexpensive videotape equipment, they made an hour-long documentary about each of the Conventions at a total cost of $25,000—or roughly the cost of a couple of minutes air time on one of the networks. The money had come partly from cable TV stations and partly from private philanthropists. The two documentaries were shown on cable stations across the country, getting an excellent review from the television columnist of *The New York Times*. They were extraordinarily intimate portraits of the Convention and, surprisingly, they reflected no particular ideology. The first tape, on the Democratic Convention, showed Willie

Brown, the slick black McGovern staffer from California, telling his delegation how to vote on the South Carolina challenge and explaining the whole strategy; it showed the making of the challenge that unseated Mayor Daley; it had Cassie Mackin talking about the job of being a floor person and declaring ecstatically, "There's nothing to it, there's nothing to this a woman couldn't have done a long time ago." The tape of the Republican Convention included pep talks from Ronald Reagan, an interview with an embarrassed Eddie Cox, scenes with Vietnam vets, with Paul McCloskey, and with the Nixon Youth preparing for one of their "spontaneous" rallies.

At times, the tapes were blurry, jiggly, and patently nonprofessional. But they gave a robust whiff of the Conventions, and had a caught-by-surprise, off-camera feeling that the networks could not and probably would not want to approach. The most striking thing about the tapes was the absence of narration. Except for a few handwritten titles, the pictures and sounds of the Conventions spoke entirely for themselves; watching a narratorless news broadcast was a strangely exhausting and disturbing experience. There was no easy gloss to take the sting out of what was happening on the screen.

The leader of the TVTV collective was a twenty-nine-year-old dropout from *Time* magazine named Michael Shamberg. When I arrived at the stucco house one afternoon during the Republican Convention, Shamberg was reclining on a sofa, while random activity went on around him. Upstairs, people were viewing and editing new tape. A barefoot girl came in and cried that she had inadvertently erased the best part of the Walter Cronkite footage. Outside by the swimming pool, where azaleas bloomed, a young man was filling balloons from a blue tank of laughing gas and passing them around for his friends to inhale. Inside, the living room was cluttered with cameras, Sony Porta-paks, tape, wires, cables, newspapers and large hand-lettered signs and assignment sheets. One of the signs said:

THE BIG STORIES

1. The Underbelly of Broadcast TV
2. The Vietnam vets
3. Those zany Republicans, young and old
4. The White House family/celebrities

Are *you* on a big story? Does your big story *connect* with the others? Is your Little story part of the big picture?

The Management

Dressed in a loose green T-shirt and gold corduroys, Shamberg looked like a model kibbutznik. He was handsome, lithe, had long black hair and spoke in a sleepy surburban drawl. Shamberg had written a book called *Guerrilla TV* and he believed that cable was the wave of the future. The networks, with their economic dependence on mass audiences and mass advertising, would eventually go the way of the mass magazines like *Life,* he thought. And cable TV—local, decentralized, appealing to small audiences and specialized tastes— would gradually take over. This might not happen until Shamberg was as old as Walter Cronkite, but he was in no hurry. He was simply happy that TVTV's first major project was turning out so well. He liked the network people. They had been very open and cooperative with the TVTV people. It was just that Shamberg believed in a different style of television.

"Look at the economy of production in broadcast TV, with that expensive equipment and unions and shit," he said. "They *have* to produce that stuff. But around here, we're talking about little Sonys that cost only 1,400 dollars and tape that costs ten dollars for thirty minutes and that you can reuse.

"The networks have never understood that the expensive equipment they have dictates a style, which is what's pissing people off. They have to force behavior. When they're on live, or even when they're filming, they have to have something happening when the camera's on. Everything they do costs so much that they can't afford to be patient. That's why they have correspondents who are always talking to give you the illusion that something's happening. They can't wait and really pick up on what's happening.

"We never do that. We just like to hang out. It's more of a print notion. Like, when you do a story, you probably don't do formal interviews as much as you hang out. We're trying to do the same thing.

"The network people are essentially giving people a radio with a screen. If you turn the picture off, you don't miss a thing. They never let you hear environmental sounds. They always make people express themselves in a format determined by the announcer. They never say, 'How do you want to explain the problem? Do you want to take me around and show me or what?'

"Another thing is, they shoot film and take it back to the studio and process and edit it, and the subject of the film never gets any say in it. But we can play a tape back for people immediately. If they don't like it, we'll erase it. People rarely ask you to do that. But you can establish a rapport with people that way if you're working in an alien situation.

"That's how we got our stuff on the Nixon Youth. They were very uptight about us shooting, so we let them see themselves and get a feeling for how they came across, and it relaxed them."

The barefoot girl suddenly returned. She was ready to show the marred Cronkite tape. Shamberg and several other TVTV people gathered on a long curved couch in the living room and watched as Cronkite flickered onto the little Sony set. He was in his shirt-sleeves, leaning back and good-naturedly giving his ideas on Convention coverage. The Cronkite segment was one of the last pieces they had shot for their tape of the GOP Convention, and the team that had shot it kept talking about how nice Cronkite had been and how much they liked him.

Shamberg was relaxed and happy. Like everybody

else, he and his friends had seen the Conventions as a chance for national exposure, and the TVTV people had got that. Now they would move on to other subjects, leaving political journalism behind.

But Cronkite and Co. would be at it every night, and they were slowly beginning to accept some of the same technical innovations that the TVTV people were using. The networks were gradually trying to develop less obtrusive equipment so that their news teams would not change the nature of the events they were covering. NBC and CBS were experimenting with small, light-weight eight-millimeter cameras. They were trying out faster film that needed no bright lights. They were exploring the possibilities of portable tape units like the ones that had given the TVTV people such mobility and allowed them to film people so unobtrusively.

There were young producers at the networks who wanted to make innovations. At CBS, for instance, there as a long-haired, piratical-looking, defiantly hip producer named Stanhope Gould, an enormously energetic man in his thirties, who had been given the two most important assignments of the election year, the Wheat Deal story and the Watergate story. Gould deplored the network tendency toward "Top 40" news, and favored longer, more complex stories. He was looking for new ways to "punch through" to people, and he was willing to use graphics, charts, diagrams, actors playing out skits, anything that would work.

Early in September, George McGovern charged that giant grain exporters and speculators with inside information bought up wheat at low prices before news of the magnitude of the Soviet grain sale drove prices up, and that they did so with the silent consent of the Administration. Cronkite immediately smelled another Teapot Dome scandal and decided that CBS should investigate the wheat deal. Gould worked on the story for two weeks. He assembled a staff of six, including an agricultural expert who knew his way around the Department of Agriculture. He sent crews to Kansas and Texas to film interviews with wheat farmers who were angered by the deal. He filmed experts and government officials in Washington and New York. He and his research team discovered new evidence damning Clarence Palmby.*

There was nothing new about this intensive fact-finding. CBS had a superb research department, including an Elections Unit that sent out a weekly newsletter to correspondents, and the network often assembled stories from stringers and correspondents all over the country. What was unusual about the wheat story was the form that it took. It was in two segments, the first one eleven minutes in length, the second one five minutes long. In the first report, on September 27, Cronkite began by announcing the intention of the report—to find out "who benefited from the grain deal"—and then laid out the whole history of the deal, getting up from his desk to go to a blackboard and use stick figures to show which officials had moved from the Department of Agriculture to private companies. It was almost unprecedented for a network news show to devote such a large amount of time to unraveling a complicated story. It was an admission on CBS's part that the old formats had not been getting through to the people, that you could not report a complicated story like the wheat deal in isolated, two-minute fragments and expect viewers to make sense of it. Instead, you had to pull all the facts together in a sort of illustrated lecture.

By the end of the second report, many Americans understood the wheat deal for the first time. There was an immediate response from fellow reporters. *New York Times*men phoned to say that CBS had told the story better than the *Times,* and no form of praise meant more to network people than recognition from the *Times.* Cronkite was elated; he was reliving his youth as

* Palmby was the Assistant Secretary of Agriculture who moved to a job at the Continental Grain Company after having negotiated the wheat deal with the Russians, but before the deal was made public. Continental then proceeded to close the biggest deal of any grain company, 150 million bushels, three days before the government announced that it was possible to sell grain to the Russians.

a crusading reporter. He ordered another "Special Report," this time on the Watergate Case.

Gould got the assignment again, and he went about it in the same way, checking out dozens of sources, filming all over the country, and helping to prepare a script that used diagrams and stick figures to make the situations crystal clear. In the end, Gould relied mainly on Washington *Post* articles for his information, but again the report pulled together all the stray facts and made a coherent story out of them. The first segment of the Special Report ran on October 27. It began:

Cronkite (standing in front of dark screen showing buildings identified with tags as Watergate, offices of CRP Committee for the Re-election of the President—the White House): Watergate has escalated into charges of a high-level campaign of political sabotage and espionage apparently unparalleled in American history . . .

It was a tought report, which included excellent filmed segments from Dan Rather and Daniel Schorr. It ran an astounding fourteen minutes. Cronkite was careful to mention the Administration's denials of all the evidence, but the graphics told a clear story of political sabotage with a line that led straight to the White House. And there was to be a second report, also lasting fourteen minutes.

There were many complimentary phone calls on the first report, but there was at least one very unfavorable call. It came from Charles Colson, special counsel to President Nixon, and it went to Bill Paley, the chairman of CBS. No one was sure what Colson said to Paley, but Colson managed to change Paley's mind about the second segment. A meeting was held on the subject and CBS executives told Gould that the second segment was too long and had to be cut in half. The executives never mentioned the phone call from the White House. They simply said that the piece was too long. Gould argued against the decision but was ordered to cut the piece.

The abbreviated version of the piece contained all the vital information, but it lacked the impact of the first Watergate report. Gould's method was to lay out the facts slowly and carefully so that they made sense. The second Watergate report, which was to have traced the laundering of the money in the secret fund, cried out for this approach. But in shrinking from fifteen to six minutes, the report became a rushed, run-of-the-mill take-out, difficult for the average viewer to follow.

In the wake of the cutting of the Watergate report, many of the younger people at CBS worried that the news department was abandoning its new approach, that the Wheat and Watergate Special Reports had been two aberrations from the norm instead of the beginning of a hopeful trend. Even more, they worried about the increasing power of the White House.

PART TWO

COVERING NIXON'S CAMPAIGN

CHAPTER VIII

Nixon Before
the White House

EVERY PRESIDENT, when he first enters the White House promises an "open Administration." He swears he likes reporters, will cooperate with them, will treat them as first-class citizens. The charade goes on for a few weeks or months, or even a couple of years. All the while, the President is struggling to suppress an overwhelming conviction that the press is trying to undermine his Administration, if not the Republic. He is fighting a maddening urge to control, bully, vilify, prosecute, or litigate against every free-thinking reporter and editor in sight. Then, sooner or later, he blows. Teddy Roosevelt sued newspapers. Franklin Roosevelt expressed his displeasure over a certain article by presenting its author with an Iron Cross. Lyndon Johnson . . . but there is no sense singling out a few. Every President from Washington on came to recognize the press as a natural enemy, and eventually tried to manipulate it and muzzle it.

But no President ever had any prolonged success at muzzling the press, and most of them came ruefully to accept the press's adversary role as healthy and challenging. In mid-Presidency, Harry Truman served notice that he was "saving up four or five good, hard punches on the nose, and when I'm out of this job, I'm going to run around and deliver them personally." But at his last press conference he said, and sincerely: "This kind of news conference where reporters can ask any questions they can dream up—directly of the President of the United States—illustrates how strong and how vital our democracy is."

Richard Nixon, however, was different. Nixon felt a deep, abiding, and vindictive hatred for the press that no President, with the possible exception of Lyndon Johnson, had ever shared. Nixon had always taken *personally* everything that the press wrote about him. The press, he believed, never forgave him for pulling the mask off its darling, Alger Hiss; so the press tortured him, lied about him, hated him. Over the years, Nixon conceived and nursed one of the monumental grudges of the century, a loathing so raw, ugly, and obvious that it only served to make him vulnerable. To borrow a phrase from Iago, Nixon wore his heart on his sleeve for daws to peck at. The daws had a field day. Painfully, Nixon learned his lesson. He learned to control and disguise his hatred, to use it in subtle ways to defeat his enemies in the press. It was precisely for this reason, because Nixon hated for so long and studied his foes so well, that he had become the nemesis of the press. No other President had ever worked so lovingly or painstakingly to emasculate reporters.

IN 1960, EIGHTY PERCENT of the nation's newspapers and all of the mass circulation magazines endorsed Nixon for President. Which was no surprise, because publishers always tell their editors whom to endorse, and the majority of publishers are staunch Republicans. But publishers do not exercise such neat control over their reporters, and Nixon regarded the press that followed him as a malicious band of thugs and Democrats who had sworn to do him in. Accordingly, he decided to cut them dead.

"*Stuff* the bastards," a Nixon aide told Theodore White in June 1960. "They're all against Dick anyway. Make them work—we aren't going to hand out prepared remarks; let them get their pencils out and listen and take notes."* During that year the Nixon people punished the press for their supposed hostility by withholding transcripts of speeches; late in the campaign, the Nixon people finally realized that this was a self-defeating tactic and began providing handouts. They also inaugurated singalongs. Herb Klein, Nixon's short, smiling press officer, passed out sheet music on the press bus and tried to lead a disgusted chorus of reporters in old favorites. Meanwhile, Nixon stayed aloof, holding few press conferences, making no effort to get his ideas across to the reporters. By the time Nixon lost in November, most of the reporters who had been trapped with him were glad to see him go.

Two years later, Nixon stalked to the microphone at the Beverly Hilton and made his never-to-be-sufficiently studied "You won't have Nixon to kick around any more" statement, which appeared to have croaked him for good. But it hadn't, of course. Five days after the statement, ABC ran a documentary called "The Political Obituary of Richard Nixon." The network got about 80,000 letters in response to the show and most of the writers thought that ABC ought to be hanged by its thumbs. The first benefit that Nixon reaped from his Kamikaze statement was the comforting knowledge that there was a constituency out in the heartland that resented the press as much as he did.

There were other benefits as well. Mainly, Nixon found, over the course of the next few years, that he had succeeded in putting the press on the defensive. His ac-

* *The Making of the President 1960* by Theodore White (New York, Signet Books, 1967), p. 377.

cusations of bias contained some truth. In 1960, many reporters had become shills for Kennedy (as they would later become shills for Johnson, in the honeymoon months following Kennedy's assassination and, later still, shills for Robert Kennedy). The reporters on Kennedy's plane referred to the candidate as "Jack," talked constantly about his "style" and "grace," cheered his speeches, and sang anti-Nixon songs with Kennedy staffers around hotel bars. The Kennedy people encouraged this claque atmosphere. They made the reporters feel like part of the staff, like cherished advisers or bosom friends. Kennedy's standard speech contained an anecdote about a certain Colonel Davenport; often, at the fifth or sixth rally of the day, Kennedy would change this to Colonel Bradlee or Colonel Bartlett, thus sending a winking message to his friends in the press.

If there was ever a gung-ho Winner's Bus, it was Kennedy's in 1960. The reporting was fairly straight. Most of the Kennedy reporters believed, as reporters always believe, that they could be friends with the candidate and still write objectively about him. Some of them pulled it off (just as in 1968, several reporters who liked Bobby Kennedy very much, nevertheless tore him apart for resorting to demagoguery in a speech in Indiana). But the Kennedy reporters did not really stop to examine their writing for traces of creeping anti-Nixon bias. On the plane and the bus they flaunted their personal contempt for Nixon. So what if they made it obvious that they adored Jack? He was going to win, and Nixon was not going to matter any more.

Thus, when Nixon crawled out of his manhole and dusted himself off in 1966, there was more than one reporter who felt like a small-time mobster when he hears that the padrone has got out of the pen and is ready to settle a few scores. Nixon, who was blessed with the acute sensitivity of a paranoiac, knew this. By June 1966, when Jules Witcover interviewed him during a speaking tour of the Midwest and South, Nixon was already claiming that his infamous "last press conference" of 1962 had worked out for the best.

"California served a purpose," he said. "The press had a guilt complex about their inaccuracy. Since then, they've been generally accurate, and far more respectful. The press are good guys, but they haven't basically changed. They're oriented against my views. But I like the battle. I like to take them on in a give-and-take. I used to be too serious about it. Now I treat it as a game. I'm probably more relaxed and not so much is riding on it . . . I have a lot of friends in the press. They tell me, 'I like to cover you. You're news.' I do give the correspondents a lot of news. And I like the press guys, because I'm basically like them, because of my own inquisitiveness . . . The press is very helpful with their questions."*

Nixon had roughly the same number of friends in the press as he did in Alger Hiss' immediate family. His basic strategy (which was to keep himself isolated from reporters) and his basic attitude (which was that reporters were scum) hadn't changed. But he had smartened up and learned one crucial lesson—to "give correspondents a lot of news," in the form of handouts and a few discreet one-to-one interviews.

It was a handout that put him back in the headlines in 1966. In November of that year, Bill Safire, one of Nixon's aides, peddled a handout on Vietnam to *The New York Times*. The *Times* played it on the front page, and once again Nixon was back in the news, just in time to take credit for the Republican Congressional landslide. Then Nixon decided to hide out for a year and stop feeding the press handouts. Instead he fed it George Romney. "I want him to get the exposure," Nixon had said in private. "We have to keep him out at the point."

From the time that Romney began his campaign, with

* *The Resurrection of Richard Nixon* by Jules Witcover (New York, Putnam, 1970), pp. 151–152.

an exploratory stumping of the Rocky Mountain states, the reporters who traveled with him pegged him as a lightweight. The private vocabulary of journalists reeks with obscenity, but the dirtiest word it contains is "lightweight." A lightweight, by definition, is a man who cannot assert his authority over the national press, cannot manipulate reporters, cannot finesse questions, prevent leaks, or command a professional public relations operation. The press likes to demonstrate its power by destroying lightweights, and pack journalism is never more doughty and complacent than when the pack has tacitly agreed that a candidate is a joke. As soon as a candidate shows his vulnerability by getting flustered, or by arguing when he shouldn't argue, the pack is delighted to treat him as the class clown.

Such a candidate was George Romney. In February 1967, when Romney began campaigning, it was generally assumed by the national political reporters that the winning candidate would be the one who could come up with a new and independent stand on the war in Vietnam. Unfortunately, Romney didn't know enough about Vietnam to have a stand, so he had to improvise one, which is always a dangerous game. At first, Romney refused to talk about the issue, but the press hounded him with questions, and Romney could not resist answering. His answers were inconsistent and patently ignorant. The reporters grilled him relentlessly at one press conference after another, and the more he said, the more his credibility crumbled.

Then, in August 1967, Romney went on a Detroit talk show and told the host how he had "had the greatest brainwashing that anybody can get when you go over to Vietnam." The remark was forgotten until the talk show host, greedy for publicity, sent the·transcript to *The New York Times*. The *Times* ran the story on page 28, under the headline: ROMNEY ASSERTS HE UNDERWENT "BRAINWASHING" ON VIETNAM TRIP. The networks, always guided by the *Times,* picked it up. The papers in Romney's home state of Michigan, chagrined at having missed such a big local story, compensated by turning it into a monumental issue. The Detroit *News* called on Romney to withdraw from the race. The "brainwashing" remark encapsulated all of Romney's ineptness in one easily remembered word, and it finished off his chances. He kept on campaigning until the end of February 1968, in the same way that a dead man's fingernails keep on growing.

Meanwhile, Richard Nixon had not been obliged to answer any questions about Vietnam, because Romney had been getting all the press's attention. Now, about three weeks before Romney pronounced himself dead, Nixon rolled the stone back from his own tomb and came out. He announced his candidacy before a well-attended press conference at the Holiday Inn in Manchester, New Hampshire. "Gentlemen," he said, "this is *not* my last press conference."

That night, he gave a party for the reporters at a motel in Concord. He drank with them, joked with them, offered big hellos to old acquaintances, offered candid observations, and generally acted like Conrad Hilton at a Hotel inauguration. Then he got up on a small chair and told a lousy joke about the weather, which received (according to one witness) "polite titters and more than one grimace." He announced that there would be statements handed out every day and ran down the details of his press operation. He emphasized that he would be accessible; he would give interviews and briefings and the press would always be kept informed of his whereabouts.

The next morning, the reporters woke up and couldn't find Richard Nixon. Then a Romney staffer tipped them that Nixon had got up early and quietly driven off to the nearby hamlet of Hillsboro to tape a "completely unrehearsed" discussion with a carefully selected contingent of townsfolk and farmers, for use in TV commercials. Some of the reporters protested to

Nixon staffers, who blithely explained that the commercials were being taped secretly so that the press wouldn't inhibit the participants.

The reporters bitched among themselves, and lodged some more protests with the Nixon staff, but they were anxious not to break the tenuous truce with Nixon— Henry Kissinger would as soon rush to insult Le Duc Tho. Conscious that the press had blown its credibility by openly despising Nixon in 1960, they were in no hurry to get into a pissing match with a notorious skunk. So a compromise of sorts was struck. The next day, a Nixon bus took the reporters to the Hillsboro Community Hall and they were allowed to wait outside while Nixon continued to tape his commercials. The door was guarded by a private security force.

The Hillsboro caper set a precedent for the whole campaign: no newsmen at tapings. Which meant that the reporters could not cover the real campaign. Nixon's advisers had the revolutionary notion that they could run their candidate from the safety of a television studio, thereby eliminating the meddlesome press. People would believe the version of Richard Nixon that they saw on TV, rather than the version that the reporters presented, secondhand, in the newspapers. Besides, TV had long since eclipsed the newspapers as a means of reaching the electorate.

Nixon's TV campaign was definitively documented in Joe McGinniss' *The Selling of the President,* a year after the fact. Many reporters resented McGinniss's book when it came out. They thought it made them look like fools. "McGinnis made it look like he discovered the TV thing," said Walter Mears, who had traveled a great deal with Nixon in 1968. "Well, come on, that's ridiculous. We knew what was happening and we all wrote stories about it."

These stories, however, did not have much impact. Perhaps it was because they did not make their point quite as forcefully as McGinnis, who wrote that Richard

Nixon "depended on a television studio the way a polio victim relied on an iron lung."

The main problem was that the press took Nixon's campaign at face value. They did not see it for what it was—a charade designed to divert attention from the real campaign, which consisted of stage-managed question and answer shows on television.

Nixon fed the reporters a phony campaign, and many of the reporters ate it up. Nixon kept showing off a group of "young intellectuals" he had gathered around him, people like Len Garment and Dick Whalen who had no real influence on the campaign. Nixon made a great fuss over his "youth movement" in order to create the impression that he was building up his own New Frontier. More than one reporter was taken in by this ruse and helped to create the myth of the New Nixon, while Nixon's brightest staffers, long since disillusioned, sat back and laughed.

Nixon gave the reporters a lot of news—rallies, a few press conferences, infinite handouts. He also gave them a great running story, the perennial loser winning for once. However, he did not give them a position on Vietnam.

The first question of the whole campaign, asked by a reporter at the first press conference in Manchester, was: "What are you going to put forward to the American people as a policy toward Vietnam?" Like Romney, Nixon had no policy on Vietnam. But he did have a terrific answer, and he had no qualms about repeating it an infinite number of times. The answer was double-talk. It contained no substance. But it sounded good to the housewives and cab drivers who questioned Nixon on the TV panel shows. After all, they were amateurs at the art of cross-examination.

The pros on the press bus at least knew that Nixon wasn't saying anything. But somehow they never ganged up on Nixon the way they had on Romney. In nine months of trying, they failed to make him cough up a stand on Vietnam. Some, like Jules Witcover, tried very hard.

At a press conference one day in late February, for instance, Witcover thought that Nixon had left himself open on some point in one of his answers about the war. When the conference had ended and Nixon was about to get into his car, Witcover ran up to him in the snow and began to ask a follow-up question. A look of alarm spread over the face of the aide who was standing next to Nixon, and before Witcover could finish, the aide had shoved Nixon into the car. Witcover got the front seat on the bus, and sat watching the back of Nixon's head during the ride to the next stop. When they arrived, Witcover jumped out of the bus and tried to talk to Nixon again.

"No soap," Witcover said later. "Couldn't get to him. They hustled him off. Just the idea of your going up there and confronting the candidate—the guys around him were startled, they couldn't believe their eyes that you were doing this. And they learned very, very quickly, and it didn't happen much after that. They just didn't let you do it."

Witcover was one of the few reporters who felt any urgency about pinning Nixon down on Vietnam during the spring. Most of his colleagues were far more worried about *who was going to win* the nomination—would Rockefeller take Nixon? The Vietnam issue could wait. But then Nixon had the nomination, and he became even more inaccessible than in the primaries. All of a sudden, the men who had seemed so powerful with George Romney felt very impotent. Excuses were made. If only Humphrey would attack Nixon on the war, said the reporters, then we could use Humphrey's charges to corner Nixon and make him answer. But Humphrey wanted to avoid the Vietnam issue for his own reasons. So the two candidates had a tacit agreement to lay off the war. What could the press do?

It never seemed to occur to the reporters that they

had a duty to stand up and take the place of Nixon's non-existent opponent.

"It's easy to look back now and say, 'Jeez, this was very important and you didn't ask the guy about the war,'" said Witcover. "But he would have press conferences and we'd ask him about the war, and he'd slough it off, you know. And after a while you get tired of asking the same question. That was really what it was more than anything else. We just didn't continue to go at it.

"I remember one guy who did was Ted Knapp. God, right up to the end, every time he got a shot at Nixon, he'd ask him about the war. Got to be a broken record. But most of us, myself included, figured, 'Aw, it's no use, we're gonna get the same runaround.' And you know, maybe we would have continued to get the same runaround, but at least we should have made more of an effort."

Ted Knapp, the man who had the quixotic habit of always questioning Nixon on the war, was the chief national political reporter for the Scripps-Howard chain of newspapers. He was a dapper, fastidious man, with wavy grey hair and a soft, ruminant, cultivated manner of speaking. He never spoke harshly about anyone, including Richard Nixon. Reminiscing in 1972, he was almost fatalistic about 1968. "I feel that the persistence of our questioning him, though unsuccessful, was largely responsible for his shying away from us, and for his having a limited number of news conferences, both in the campaign and during his Presidency," he said. "I remember one press conference in particular, on a Sunday morning in Pittsburgh, after his nomination in 1968. There was repeated questioning on how he intended to end the war and a refusal to accept the pat answer that he had been giving. I'm 90 percent sure that after the news conference there was quite a spell when he was totally unavailable."

Richard Nixon learned a lot about the press from the 1968 campaign, far more than the press learned about him. He learned that the press was still on the defensive because of '60 and '62. He found out how to undermine reporters in subtle ways. He discovered that he could be an effective performer on TV, and that he could use television to get around the press. The main lesson he took from the campaign was that he could isolate himself from the press with no dire consequences to his political well-being; he could refuse to come to terms with the major issue of the day for nine straight months without risking a mutiny from the press.

As President, he lived by this lesson. He held only twenty-eight press conferences in his first four years of office, by far the most abysmal record in modern times. In the campaign year of 1972, he held only seven press conferences, and only two of those dealt with political matters. This should have come as no surprise to the reporters. It was they who had let him know that he could get away with it.*

---

* However, though nobody succeeded in smoking out the incumbent, in 1972 David Broder did nevertheless try to make the Democratic candidates commit themselves to weekly press conferences. "The point at which we have maximum leverage on these guys is the point at which they declare their candidacy for the White House," Broder said later. "At the first conference that the candidate has after announcing, I would like to see the question routinely asked: 'Are you willing to commit yourself *now* to holding weekly press conferences throughout your campaign and during your Presidency if you are elected?' Just get them on record. I've argued this for some time, without any success at all. We did ask that question of Humphrey, Muskie and McGovern when they came to lunch at the Washington *Post* in early 1972 and we got fairly good responses." Broder and Jim Naughton also tried to pin Muskie down to frequent press conferences at a late-night, off-the-record bull session at a motel in Portsmouth, N.H., in February.

CHAPTER IX

The Old
Squeeze Play

OCTOBER 17, 1972. Not a very extraordinary newsday in the annals of the White House press. Having breakfasted at their suburban homes and their houses in town, and then perhaps stopped at the office to scan the *Times* and the *Post,* they began to arrive just after 10:30. From the direction of the National Press Building (only four blocks off), they came strolling up Pennsylvania Avenue in ones and twos, past the Treasury, past the Quakers and crazies, and finally they came to the Northwest Gate, where there stood a white guardhouse. Fishing for billfolds, they pulled out their plastic laminated White House passes—a little color picture of the bearer in the middle of each pass—and waved them at the sergeant on duty.

The sergeant, who was not a bad sort, smiled at the regulars from behind the plate-glass window and pressed the button which springs the catch in the wrought-iron gate and, with a push, they were inside the fortress. From there, they trudged up the driveway toward the west lobby; if they had held a straight course, they would have walked smack into the full-dress Marine who stood at attention on the porch of Henry Kissinger's chandeliered office, but instead they veered to the left, up the path a few yards and through the French doors of the pressroom.

Pressroom? It looked more like an antechamber of a fat Wall Street law firm. Just the kind of venue that made the Nixon staffers feel at home, even if it was not quite what the press was used to. Before the Nixon regime, the reporters had camped out in the West Lobby, piling their coats, hats and cameras on a huge circular Philippine mahogany table, fighting for lounging privileges on the one beat-up sofa, and wandering in and out of the press secretary's office. The reporters also had a small pressroom just off the lobby, which was crammed with desks and contained forty telephones. For purposes of identification, each of the phones rang on a different note. Often, all of the phones rang at once, producing a jangled symphony that the old hands grew to like.

The White House reporters found the lobby very cozy, but in 1970, Ronald Ziegler announced that he was going to move the press to "more comfortable quarters" in the Executive Office Building, across the street from the White House. A number of reporters complained loudly, accusing Ziegler of trying to banish the press and cut off their access to White House staffers. Ziegler indignantly denied this, but he did come up with another plan—fill in the West Wing's swimming pool and turn it into a press room. Lyndon Johnson had liked to strip down and plunge in with publishers and network executives, but skinny dipping was not Richard Nixon's style and he did not object to giving up the pool.

Even then, some of the reporters worried that the new setup would deny them access to Ziegler's office. "You will always have access to my office," Ziegler solemnly promised them. Somehow the promise got lost in the move. Ziegler's office was now well off the main pressroom, and the reporters had to run a gauntlet of remorselessly efficient secretaries to get to Ziegler.

The White House decorators boarded up the old pool and redid the place in various businesslike shades of brown: beige walls, beige drapes, beige sofas along the walls, big chestnut-colored chairs, tan carpet. The ashtrays were cleverly disguised as Roman urns, the table lamps were made out of China vases, and the walls were hung with Currier and Ives snowscapes. At the front end of this long rectangular room was a darkwood lectern, with a light blue curtain on the wall in back of it. An elegant waiting room, in short, steeped in just that flavorless, impersonal gloom that one associates with all rooms where people are made to cool their heels.

ON THIS TUESDAY MORNING, there were already a dozen reporters here, talking about nothing, or reading the *Times,* or simply looking bored. At the rear of the main room, a short corridor led to another room. On the right wall of this corridor, there were coathooks and a row of glass "bins" that contain the day's handouts—a radio statement by the President, a fact sheet on a bill that he had signed, the schedules for Edward Finch Cox, Tricia Nixon Cox, Julie Nixon Eisenhower, and Mrs. Richard Nixon.

The next room contained rows of padded cubicles, each equipped with a typewriter and two phones for all of the major newspaper and news-chain correspondents. At the rear, there were three larger booths, one for each of the networks. The left wall was lined with phones for foreign correspondents, most of whom did not rate cubicles; these were direct lines to the Washington Bureaus of British newspapers, European newspapers, and Iron Curtain news agencies. On the left of the room, another corridor led to a smaller, dark green room which contained candy and soft-drink machines, a coffee maker, three wire tickers, and a round table where the TV tech-

nicians had already begun the daily game of gin rum-
my. There was a story that Eddie Folliard, having
emerged from retirement to be given a tour of the plush
new premises, shook his head in disbelief and said, "I'll
have a drink, but I won't go upstairs."

Back by the handout bins, a flight of stairs led down
to another collection of booths and cubicles—booths for
each of the radio correspondents and cubicles for the
lesser papers. Also, another row of wall phones—the
Avenue of the Rising Sun, it was called, because the
phones belonged to the Japanese correspondents. Three
or four Japanese showed up for every briefing, took co-
pious notes, and then mysteriously drifted away; nobody
knew what they thought or what they wrote, largely because nobody within memory had bothered to inquire.
The Avenue of the Rising Sun was a quiet place, except
when a major textile agreement was announced. On
those occasions, the Japanese stampeded for the phones
and screamed the details across bad connections to their
home offices. Fay Wells, the dowdy correspondent for
the Storer Broadcasting Company, once produced a legendary thirty second spot by saying, "This is how Japan
got the message when the White House lifted the United
States trade ban with the People's Republic of China,"
and then opening the door to hold out the microphone
and record twenty seconds of shrill, hysterical Japanese.

It was an odd congregation, the White House press
—a strange mixture of professional witnesses, decree-
promulgators, cheerleaders, hard-diggers, goldbricks,
and gadflies. There were shadowy figures like Trudy, a
small birdlike woman who worked for a Jewish newspaper in St. Louis and who seemed to do nothing but receive dozens of mysterious phone calls on a downstairs
pay phone; or Alan Lidow, the correspondent for Gene
Autry's Golden West Broadcasting Company, who had
never been known to ask a question at a briefing, and
who seemed to be present mainly so that the FCC would
not forget the existence of Golden West.

Roughly 1,500 reporters paid dues to the White

House Correspondents Association, an organization whose sole function was to sponsor an annual dinner held in the banquet room of one of the large Washington hotels. But only sixty or seventy of these reporters regularly attended the daily White House briefings.

The regular White House correspondents could be divided into two basic types. There were the old-timers, who had come into the job as a sinecure, a reward for long years of faithful service; to them, the pressroom was one more quiet men's club. And there were the young, ambitious types, the future Tom Wickers and Max Frankels, who saw the job as a showcase for their talents. If they did well, they would move up to become bureau chiefs and editors. No ambitious young man wanted to stay in the White House forever, because the job was a slow death.

"It is a strange, airless kind of work," said Russell Baker, who had covered the White House in the fifties and early sixties. The White House was like a Stuart court, Baker thought, and all the correspondents lingered like courtiers in the antechambers. The President's aides were like sycophants who protected the monarch, fed the courtiers information that would make the Great Man look good, and nursed the ego of "this monstrosity, this Queen Bee" who was at the center of court life. Whenever he left the White House to cover a story on the Hill, Baker felt as if he were climbing out of a closed sewer and going up onto a mountain, into the fresh air. "There were 435 people up there on the Hill," said Baker, "and they *all loved to talk.*"

Nevertheless, some reporters thrived in this suffocating palace atmosphere. They began to think of themselves as part of the White House, and they proudly identified themselves as being "from the White House press" instead of mentioning the paper they worked for. They forgot that they were handout artists and convinced themselves that they were somehow associates of a man who was shaping epochal events. The walls of the White House press complex were covered with memen-

tos of the past, framed and yellowing photographs: a
line of somber men in straw boaters and high collars
with Woodrow Wilson in the center, like a Sixth Form
and its Master; a larger and merrier group with Franklin
Roosevelt; a loose circle of men in Hawaiian shirts and
Bermudas, laughing with Harry Truman in Key West;
several rows of men in flannel suits posing formally with
Ike on the White House lawn.

The faces of these men were infused with a funny expression, a pathetic aura of pride, a sense that they were
taking part in the colossal moments of history. Now
most of these moments were forgotten, and no one remembered a word that any of these men had written.
The strikingly said thing about all these pictures was the
anonymity. Except for the Presidents, not a single face
was familiar. They were journalistic Prufrocks and they
measured out their lives in handouts. Deferential, glad
to be of use, they enjoyed some prestige in their day, but
none of them had passed into legend as a great reporter
—with the exception of Merriman Smith.

MERRIMAN SMITH came to the White House in 1941, a
young United Press reporter of twenty-seven with slick
black hair, a pockmarked face, and a moustache he had
grown to make himself look older. He remained on the
beat until his death in 1970. A straight, old-fashioned
reporter who thought that his job gave him "a front seat
at the making of history," he reported what the President said, whom he saw, and where he went. No interpretation or analysis. But he stood out from the pack
because he had the aggressiveness, resourcefulness, and
sometimes the ruthlessness of a great police reporter. He
was prolific: he once filed 30,000 words of copy in a
twelve-hour period on a Presidential train trip. He was
fast: he could write a story in his head in the thirty seconds it took him to run from the Oval Office up to the
UP's phone booth in the pressroom. His sprints to the
phone booth were legendary. He trampled anything or

anyone in his way; he once slipped and dislocated a shoulder on the way to the phone but dictated for an hour before passing out from the pain.

He went to incredible lengths to score small scoops. It was rumored, for instance, that he always was the first reporter to know that Nixon was going to go to the Western White House, because he had cultivated a clerk at a San Clemente motel who called him whenever the whores came up from Vegas in anticipation of the arrival of the Secret Service.

For years, he doggedly hung on to his seniority privilege of sitting in the middle of the front seat of the pool car on Presidential trips. He was in this cherished spot on November 22, 1963, in the Dallas motorcade. When he heard the sound of gunfire, he grabbed the radiophone (which was on the transmission hump, directly in front of him) and started to dictate. Jack Bell, Smith's rival from the AP, was in the back seat. After Smith had dictated four pages of copy, Bell demanded the phone. Smith stalled, saying that he wanted the Dallas operator to read back the copy—the overhead wires might have interfered with transmission. Everyone in the car knew that Smith had a perfect connection— they could hear the operator's voice coming over the phone. Bell started screaming and trying to wrestle with Smith for the receiver. Smith stuck it between his knees and hunched up into a ball, with Bell beating him wildly about the head and shoulders. UPI beat the AP by several crucial minutes on the story, and Smith won a Pulitzer for his coverage of the Kennedy assassination.

In later years, Smith watched with alarm as the White House turned into a massive public relations operation, exercising more and more control over the distribution of the news. But by that time, his personal problems had begun to outweigh his professional ones. "Hell," Lyndon Johnson told Smith in 1966, "I don't have anything like the troubles you have—you lost your boy in Vietnam while you were going through a divorce from your first wife, behind in your taxes, poor-mouthing me on the

Merv Griffin show to make money for big tuition bills —I've got it a lot better than you have."* Smith also had a bad drinking problem which increased as the White House job wore him down physically. In 1970, he learned that he had incurable cancer and shot himself with a pistol.

Unlike most reporters, Smith left behind a legacy of books. In these books, he chronicled an era of White House reporting that now seems heartbreakingly simple and innocent. In the forties, the reporters gathered once a week in the Oval Office to throw questions at the President for as long as they pleased; and the President, only a few feet away on the other side of a huge desk, responded with wit and candor. Presidential advisers still roamed freely and talked to the press. Reporters were still allowed to badger every visitor who left the President's office. The reporters felt a patriotic affection for the President, and did not mind engaging in what Merriman Smith called "a friendly conspiracy" to keep the public from finding out that Roosevelt was confined to a wheelchair.

The pressroom, in those days, was as raunchy and intimate as a police shack, and the reporters knew each other well, drank together in the long afternoons, and played pranks on each other.

NOW, IN 1972, THE WHITE HOUSE PRESS COMPLEX was as flavorless as a large insurance office, so impersonal that the people downstairs scarcely knew the people upstairs. It had lost the sour camaraderie of the police shack—except for an obscure little group of six men who were permanently hunkered down in a corner of the downstairs room. At almost any hour of the working day, you could find them reading the papers and grumbling articulately, slumped in a circular arrangement of armchairs and sofas, with their feet up on the central

* *Merriman Smith's Book of Presidents,* edited by Timothy G. Smith (New York, Norton, 1972), p. 61.

piece of furniture from which they took their name, the Knights of the Green Ottoman. The six Knights were united by a bond of vague discontent—with the White House operation, with their jobs, or simply with themselves.

There was Don Fulsom, the UPI audio man. Fulsom was an open, friendly thirty-four-year-old with a long face who was considered a troublemaker by the White House staff. A question of his attitude. He had been fired from his first radio job, at a station in Buffalo, N.Y., when he began the news on Easter morning by saying: "Today, millions of Christians around the world are celebrating the alleged resurrection of Jesus Christ." In private conversation, he never called Nixon anything but "the Trick."

In the next armchair sat Jim McManus, Westinghouse's correspondent, a neatly dressed man with a lean, almost Jesuitical face and a quiet manner of speaking. He was one of the few men ever to walk out of a White House briefing in protest.

On the sofa was Howard Norton, sixty-one, grey-haired, wearing a white shirt and a White House tie-clasp. In 1947, his investigations of racketeering had won a Pulitzer Prize for the Baltimore *Sun*. Now he filled the minimal needs of *U.S. News*, which, being almost a house organ for the Administration, did not demand much investigative reporting. Norton did not say a great deal, but when he talked he was very frank. "This job," he said, "has ruined more good reporters than any job I know."

Then there were Al Sullivan, a USIA reporter in his thirties who had some surprisingly unofficial-sounding opinions about the White House; Gil Butler, about the same age, the reporter for TV station WTOP, who was chuckling over a volume of Mencken; and finally, Gary Axelson, a plump young man who was sorry that his employers at Metromedia had promoted him from the State Department beat, where he used to be able to dig up good stories. At the White House he found only frustration.

It was quarter after eleven on this Tuesday morning, and the Knights were getting restless. They were making the ritual joke about tranquilizing gas. The gas, they said, came out of the vents above the sofa before every briefing and subdued nettlesome reporters. "Well, I guess they got us just about comatose enough," said Fulsom, squirming in his chair. "They can bring out Ziegler now."

McManus looked at his watch. "Looks like the old squeeze play," he muttered.

"Yeah," said Sullivan, "the old squeezeroo."

"What is the squeeze play?" I asked.

"Well," said McManus, like a teacher going back to a familiar lesson, "the press briefing is scheduled to begin at eleven. You will notice that it is now eleven seventeen. Inexplicably, the briefing starts late more often than not. Now, if anybody is going to get a telephone and make any sense out of the information they have and still get it moving on the wire or over a broadcast facility, the briefing simply cannot be allowed to run beyond fifteen minutes until twelve. At the absolute outside, say ten minutes until twelve. And if it was the Second Coming, you could probably make it two minutes to twelve, but you'd bust into everything, just absolutely break into all the wire circuits. I mean, it would *have* to be the Second Coming.

"Noon is a crucial hour for newspapers across the country. You see, most of the papers that these wire services do business with are one-edition dailies. The services have got to get that copy out to them or it's simply not going to get set in type. And they've also got their eye cocked on their broadcast clients when it comes up to major newscast hours, like noon.

"The point is that if you are a press secretary, you use all these little tricks. You start the briefing late, you compress the time, you increase the anxiety in the room. Then, you throw out something that the wires are going to want to run with, but that not everyone else necessarily wishes to run with, so that the wire reporters are at odds with the other reporters."

It almost boiled down to a formula: the more troublesome the briefing promised to be, the later it started. A week before, on October 10, the Washington *Post* had reported that the Watergate bugging incident was merely one facet of a massive spying and sabotage campaign set up by the Republicans, and the *Post* identified a young lawyer named Donald Segretti as one of the operatives in the campaign. Two days before, the *Post* had charged that Nixon's appointment secretary, Dwight Chapin, was Segretti's contact in the Administration.

Because of these articles, Ziegler had had a great deal of trouble with the press. Smelling blood, the reporters had momentarily come to life, stinging him with question after question about the Watergate, Segretti, and Dwight Chapin. Ziegler had piled up record numbers of "no comments" which the wire services dutifully counted. He was beginning to look ridiculous, like a gangster who takes the Fifth when the DA asks him his address. So the briefings got later and later.

As the delay grew longer, the Knights continued to beef about the White House system. It was all they had talked about the previous week, and it was all they would talk about in weeks to come. They complained about Ziegler's penchant for setting up ground rules— bringing out someone like John Ehrlichman, and then telling the press that they could only question him about one limited subject. "If any governor tried that, he would be laughed out of office," said Al Sullivan, who used to cover the governor of New Jersey. "But a lot of these guys are caught up in respect for the White House, so they respect the stupid ground rules."

McManus, who at one time covered the governor of Indiana, nodded in agreement. "This Watergate thing has been going on for weeks now, and all we get is no comment. And what has happened? Do you see the publishers breaking down the gates of the White House, or the editors jamming the switchboard with protests, or the reporters screaming with rage? Nothing. Nothing at all."

"What can you do about it?" I asked.

"I don't know," said Sullivan, shaking his head. "I don't know."

"We should hold Ziegler there for four or five hours and make him *run* out of the room," said McManus.

At 11:23, a voice came on the PA system. "There will be a briefing in the briefing room," it said. It was a sweet female voice and Don Fulsom knew it well because it belonged to a secretary with whom he once had a run-in. About a year ago, when Ziegler had quietly dropped the regular afternoon briefings, Fulsom was one of the few reporters who bothered to protest. The secretary, who heard him protesting, called him a creep. So Fulsom mentioned in his radio report that a "White House staffer called a reporter a creep." The secretary had refused to talk to him ever since.

By now everyone was rushing into the briefing room, the stenographer was seated and ready to take transcript, the Signal Corpsman was at the sound console, adjusting the controls of the PA system, a deputy press secretary and three female secretaries were standing by in case Ron Ziegler needed any additional information, and Ron Ziegler was standing at the podium, smoking nervously and looking wary.

In fact, with his pudgy, baby face, he looked like nothing so much as a high school teacher who is a little too young to command total respect. He began the briefing, but some of the reporters in the back went on talking, so a certain sternness came into his voice, as if to show them that he didn't care. And like a high school assembly, the briefing started out with a long series of tedious announcements: the President met with labor leaders from twenty-four countries; his remarks would be posted. There was a photo opportunity with the President and the members of the National Advisory Coun-

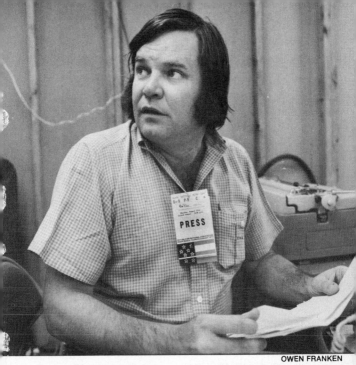

R. W. Apple, Jr., of *The New York Times*

ANNIE LEIBOVITZ/*Rolling Stone*

David Broder of the Washington *Post*

Senator McGovern with Rowland Evans, Jr.

Robert Novak

ANNIE LEIBOVITZ/*Rolling Stone*

Haynes Johnson of the Washington *Post*

STANLEY TRETICK

Front row (from left to right): Jules Witcover of the Los Angeles *Times,* Walter Mears of the AP, Senator McGovern. Back row: James Naughton of *The New York Times* (left), Gordon Weil of McGovern's staff (right).

Ham Davis of the Providence *Journal* (left) and Curtis Wilkie of the Wilmington *News-Journal* (right).

ANNIE LEIBOVITZ/*Rolling Stone*

BOB MCNEELY

Carl Leubsdorf of the AP (center with tape recorder) and
James Doyle of the Washington *Star-News* (right rear).

cil on Drug Abuse Prevention; a press release on the meeting would be handed out later.

The announcements went on for several minutes, with everyone fidgeting and coughing and making few notes. Then Ziegler announced plans for trips to Philadelphia and New York State later in the week, and everyone perked up a little and wrote down the itineraries. From there, Ziegler moved on to announcements about seventy-one bills that Congress had sent the President, and about legislation still pending, like the spending ceiling. "Now the eyes of many people in this country are on the Senate to see if they will meet their portion of the responsibility to keep taxes down and inflation under control by acting affirmatively on the spending ceiling legislation." Blatant propaganda, and everyone was going to sleep, but someone asked Ziegler if his remarks were meant as a form of pressure on the Senate and Ziegler said yes, and handed out some more propaganda. There were some intelligent and well-informed questions about other bills, but Ziegler told the reporters to save their questions until he had finished making his announcements.

Then he dropped the big sop of news he had been saving: "I'd also like to tell you now at this time that the President has asked Dr. Kissinger to go on from Paris to visit Saigon to review with President Thieu the status of the Paris negotiations." The questions began, dozens of little questions of detail—when was Kissinger last in Saigon? who will be going with him? had he wrapped up the Paris talks for good? "See," said McManus, "if there's a danger they'll ask about the Watergate, all he has to do is pitch them something about Kissinger, and the wires can hardly wait to get it on."

For a few minutes, everyone focused on Henry Kissinger's trip. They asked some probing questions and some stupid ones, but the striking thing was the high school atmosphere that pervaded the briefing. It was as if they were all chafing under the teacher's authority, and they wanted to humiliate him without getting caught. So whenever anyone asked a question that carried the slightest hint of naughty disrespect, they all giggled. When Ziegler's microphone suddenly started to vibrate wildly, causing him to back off in alarm, someone shouted "Sabotage!" and there was a great laugh from the whole class.

The microphone, after all, was one of Ziegler's most effective weapons. It made him sound booming and authoritative, and it made the questioners, who spoke in unamplified tones, sound comparatively timid and mousy. I was standing next to the ancient representative of a formerly great Midwestern daily, who arrived every morning befuddled with drink and proceeded to pore over the *Times* sports section during the briefing. As he turned the pages, which he did absent-mindedly, they made a noise like a four-year-old jumping in a pile of leaves. Consequently, the reporters standing around him could not hear many of the questions asked at the front of the room. But they could hear Ziegler's replies coming out of the four hidden speakers in the room.

The questions continued. Someone asked whether Kissinger used an interpreter. "I can't provide you that information, but Dr. Kissinger does not speak North Vietnamese," said Ziegler. A wave of mocking laughter and comment moved back through the room. The question was asked twice more. "Ron, why can't you tell us whether he uses an interpreter?"

"I'm not prepared to discuss the talks in any way whatsoever," Ziegler said curtly.*

* Ziegler made a habit of refusing to answer even the simplest and most innocuous of questions. Most of the White House reporters convinced themselves that Ziegler was merely a "mouthpiece" for the Administration and was not given enough information to answer these questions. My own impression, however, was that he refused to answer these questions out of simple spite. At the briefing for Monday, October 16, for instance, Ziegler repeatedly refused to say whether Donald Segretti had ever been employed by the White House. Then, after several minutes of questions on the subject, he suddenly said: "Donald Segretti has never been employed by the White House." Marty Schram and I later asked him why he had not

After a while, the wire people began to get edgy. Fran Lewine, the No. 2 AP correspondent, tried to end the briefing. "Thank you," she called out in a bored singsong from the back of the room. The rest of the group roared with disapproval. "Wait a moment, wait a moment," they all grumbled. So the briefing moved on to other questions, important questions. Fulsom asked whether the President had found out yet if those were American bombs that had been dropped on the French Consulate in Hanoi. (He had not.) McManus followed up and asked if the President did not have an interest in finding this information out. (He would receive and had received information along this line, but the Defense Department was the place to ask that question.)

Phil Potter of the Baltimore *Sun* asked Ziegler about the President's trip to Atlanta two weeks before. Potter was an unreconstructed hawk of retirement age who frequently got into noisy arguments about the war at the Press Club bar, but he asked good, tough questions. Potter said that during the Atlanta motorcade, he twice saw somebody, "apparently a security agent," grab or tear down a McGovern sign being held by a demonstrator. He wanted to know if that was approved. In his blandest tones, Ziegler answered that "our policy is the total opposite of that kind of activity . . . we are opposed to any violence at all." (Two weeks later, at a rally in California, Curtis Wilkie of the Wilmington *News-Journal* would see Dwight Chapin instruct a pimply faced young Nixon supporter to go and bat down the signs of the McGovern supporters.)

Someone else followed up, saying that the incident had been widely witnessed and asking if Ziegler was sure that it had not been condoned. Ziegler showed his first flash of anger and spoke sternly: "That was a public

saved everyone a lot of time by answering the question immediately. Ziegler responded with some doubletalk about how he had been "making a case, establishing a position, making it clear that I wasn't going to *dignify* the question with a comment." Then he smirked and said: "You can't just have the news funneled to you."

motorcade on a public street and I don't have a comment or any basis on which to judge that situation or comment on it. I've given a response to you in terms of what our policy is on this over and over again. I've stated it and I think it's clear."

It was clear that they wouldn't get anything out of Ziegler on that subject, so they moved on. John Osborne of the *New Republic* asked a question about Clark McGregor. Fulsom came back to the French Consulate question. "Is the President concerned that it's taken so *long* to get a report to him on whether these were American bombs?"

"Uh," said Ziegler, beginning to seethe. "The uh . . . a very complete investigation of that is being conducted."

More intricate questions about Kissinger's travels. And then finally, for the first time in almost twenty-five minutes, someone got around to asking about the scandals.

"Ron, is there anything new on the Dwight Chapin affair?" called out Peter Lisagor of the Chicago *Daily News*.

"Nossir," said Ron tersely.

"Thank you, Ron," shouted a harried wire service man.

The room erupted in protest. Ziegler started to walk away from the lectern. "Wait a minute! Wait a minute! Ron! Ron!"

McManus got the floor. "Ron," he said, "there's a great straining in the back of the room to go tell the world about Henry Kissinger. Now, if we're going to end this briefing, let's have a briefing at three o'clock."

Ziegler was furious. His voice was cold and hoarse. "The normal procedures that we will follow and are going to follow is that the wire services will cut this briefing off," he said, his anger eating away at his grammar. There were shouts for attention.

"There will be a posting at three o'clock," Ron concluded, and began to leave again.

"Now, wait a minute, Ron," shouted Robert Pierpoint of CBS. Pierpoint was probably the hardest and most persistent interrogator of any of the network men. (The briefings drove him crazy, but he blamed "the system," not Ziegler: "It's kind of fruitless to make life difficult for Ziegler. But I do it. The reason I do it is that I want the people who read the briefings, including, hopefully, once in a while the President, to know that I am dissatisfied with the situation.")

"The wire services have no more right than any of the rest of us," Pierpoint said angrily. "You've just given them that right. Now, we have other questions that we would like to ask."

"I did not just give them that right," said Ziegler, and curiously he sounded just like an angry Richard Nixon.

"It has not been a right that they had before," said Pierpoint.

"It has been standard procedure," said Ziegler in cavernous Nixon tones.

"Since you took over, it's been standard procedure," said Pierpoint. "Now, several of us have questions we've never been allowed to ask and we'd like to go into it if you're not going to see us at three o'clock." And before Ziegler could stop him, Pierpoint was sliding into another question about the peace talks.

Ziegler was icy. "Uh, I'm not prepared to, uh, be responsive to that question, Bob," he said.

"Yeah, but . . ." Pierpoint began to ask another question, but Jim Dickenson of the *National Observer* had already begun to talk, asking another question about the Atlanta incident, and Ziegler had recognized him to spite Pierpoint.

"Well, wait a minute," said Pierpoint, in a high plaintive voice. He sounded as if he were about to cry with frustration. "Jim! . . . aw, Christ!"

Dickenson wanted to know whether the White House had tried to determine whether the sign-destroyer in Atlanta was a government security agent.

No, said Ziegler, because the White House had only

been informed of the incident by Phil Potter after it took place. Pierpoint raised his voice again and got in two more questions about the Paris talks. Ziegler answered them curtly.

"Ron, I have a question I've been anxious to get in, and I don't believe it's been asked," said John Osborne.

He spoke in a gentle Southern accent from his seat in the middle of the room, and his voice carried a quiet authority. The others listened carefully, because Osborne had the reputation of a man who knew what he was doing. Born in Corinth, Mississippi, sixty-six years ago, Osborne had grey hair, a prominent nose that gave his face a mole-like appearance, and a shy manner that hid an iron will. Having worked for newspapers in the South and for the AP, he became a National Affairs writer at *Time* in 1938 and quickly rose to become Foreign News editor. He was a controversial figure around the Luce offices, a man of strong and often dogmatic convictions. Militantly pro-Soviet during World War II, he later did a complete about-face and became a terrifyingly hard-line cold warrior. In 1951, he wrote in an editorial: *"Life* sees no choice but to acknowledge the existence of war with Red China and to set about its defeat, in full awareness that this course will probably involve war with the Soviet Union as well."

Over the years, he had mellowed. "He is," said a former *Time* associate, "one of the few men I know who keeps improving with age." In 1961 he left *Time-Life* to free-lance and by 1968, through a process he claims is too complicated to discuss, his views had changed sufficiently to allow him to sign on as one of the two full-time writers on the liberal *New Republic*. Since then, he had devoted all his energies to observing the White House, writing a weekly column called "The Nixon Watch."

Osborne had been the only journalist in America to give a consistent, clear, comprehensible picture of Nixon's machinations, aspirations, successes, and failures. He was a meticulous craftsman, and he pieced this picture together like a restorer filling in the missing portions of a Greek vase. He searched for clues in statements, speeches, or simply in the air around the White House, and every Wednesday morning he sat down to write a 1,000–word column that was witty, discursive, personal, and full of educated conjecture. It was this speculative tone which made "The Nixon Watch" so much more useful than anything that appeared in a newspaper, for conjecture was a necessary tool in cracking the secretiveness of the Nixon Administration. And Osborne was scrupulously fair. His even-handedness, discretion, and unobtrusive manner appealed to many of the Nixon staffers, who were constantly surprised to receive praise from the *New Republic* when praise was due. So they sometimes cooperated with him to the extent of letting him come into their offices and ask a question or two. It was said that Ziegler's boss, Bob Haldeman, actually liked John Osborne. Which might have been the reason why Ziegler treated him with respect.

*　　　*　　　*

ON THIS TUESDAY, Osborne asked the best question of the day. The *Post* that morning had implied that Herbert W. Kalmbach, Nixon's personal lawyer, and a fund collector for the Committee to Re-elect the President, had access to the Watergate "secret fund." Incredibly, no one had mentioned the subject yet.

"Two related questions," said Osborne. "First, this Mr. Kalmbach of Newport Beach. Is it a fact that he is Mr. Nixon's personal attorney? And two, has Mr. Nixon been in touch with him in the last two days?"

Ziegler gave him a detailed and courteous answer, saying that Nixon had not been in touch with Kalmbach in months.

Someone else asked whether the White House had tried to contact Kalmbach to determine whether there was any truth in the *Post* story.

"To my knowledge, there has been no contact with Mr. Kalmbach," snapped Ziegler.

Then Sarah McClendon spoke up. Ziegler saw no need to be courteous with her. Sarah McClendon was a frumpish woman in a purple pants suit and a star-in-circle earrings, with tousled platinum hair, and a sweet, toothy smile. At the outbreak of World War II, she had sold her clothes for twenty-one dollars traveling money, left her hometown of Tyler, Texas, and joined the WACs. Her only pair of shoes had high heels, and she drilled in them for two weeks. She was sent to Washington to work in the WAC PR operation. After the war, she married, was deserted by her husband, and went to work as a legwoman for a Washington correspondent, nine days after having given birth to her daughter. She did not tell the correspondent about the baby for fear of being fired.

After years of struggling, she became a correspondent herself, doing piecemeal work for several radio stations in the South, writing for a handful of Texas newspapers and the North American Newspaper Alliance, and turning out a weekly newsletter. She also became the comic relief at Presidential press conferences. Whenever they were in a tight spot, Kennedy, Johnson, and now Nixon would point to her with an indulgent smile and wait for her to ask some stupid, irrelevant question, which, it was true, she sometimes did. But no matter what she asked, all the male reporters laughed.

Sarah McClendon was vulnerable because she was a woman in a male chauvinist profession and she did not work for a large paper. Lyndon Johnson thought nothing of getting her fired from several of her Texas papers so that she could be replaced by Les Carpenter, a Johnson shill.

In the spring of 1972, she had investigated some questionable government contract dealings by Strom Thurmond and Harry Dent. She wrote up her findings for the NANA syndicate, but when Dent found out about the article he made such loud and horrible threats that NANA not only tried to kill the story in question but stopped running her other articles for the next year and a half. A thousand such bullyings and petty cruelties had not daunted her. She had a revenge of sorts; she was now as tough as any reporter in Washington, and she was not afraid to ask a question for fear of sounding silly. It was no coincidence that some of the toughest pieces on the 1972 Nixon campaign came from Sarah McClendon, Helen Thomas of UPI, Cassie Mackin of NBC, Marilyn Berger of the Washington *Post,* and Mary McGrory. They had always been the outsiders. Having never been allowed to join in the cozy, clubby world of the men, they had developed an uncompromising detachment and a bold independence of thought which often put the men to shame.

But the men still tittered whenever Sarah McClendon asked a question, and Ziegler still treated her as if she were a wino who had wandered in off the street (although he was always very sweet to her *after* the briefing, which only disgusted her more).

"Ron, was Mr. Kalmbach the man who took Mrs. Martha Mitchell to the hospital to have her fingers sewed up after she was pushed against the glass?" asked McClendon.

"I don't know," said Ziegler, as if he were trying to shake off the village idiot.

"You don't know. Could you find out that for me, please?"

"No, I won't."

"Why not?"

"It's not part of the White House information."

McClendon started to argue, but Ron began talking over her as if she didn't exist.

"On this briefing matter," he said, "I'd like to select Pierpoint, Bill Theis [of Hearst], Jack Horner [of the Washington *Star*]—who's the current president of the White House Correspondents Association?"

"Ed Poe."

"Edgar Poe [of the New Orleans *Times-Picayune*],

and Aldo Beckman [of the Chicago *Tribune*] and Jerry Schecter [of *Time*], to, uh . . . ."

"Put a woman on there!" yelled Sarah McClendon.

"Fran Lewine . . . to gather together and make a recommendation to me as to how these briefings will end. The standard procedure we've been following over the last three years is that the senior wire-service reporter has been cutting it off and the press has responded to that. If you want to designate another procedure to do that, that's all right with me, but we're not going to have this type of chaos in future briefings. I gave in to it today because there seemed to be some question of understanding these rules. But I'd like to establish a procedure and if that group will meet and make recommendations for me, we'll follow them."

Various voices began to argue. Ziegler was furious.

"I don't want to discuss it here in a public briefing," said Ziegler, "but those people who are named, please form yourself as a committee as you would and make recommendations to me to how these briefings should be run."

"Well, Ron, who gave you the right to name a committee like that?" asked McManus, prompting some giggles from the crowd.

"Well, uh, the right to put some decorum into these briefings so that this doesn't take place again."

"Will your committee also look into the possibility of returning to the twice-a-day briefing schedule?" asked Fulsom.

"That's a decision that I will make—and *I'm* the committee on that —and will post this afternoon," said Ziegler.

"Well, it seems that that's part of the problem, Ron," someone said. "If we were having a second briefing, this question wouldn't come up."

"As far as this briefing is concerned, and I'm ending it, it's ended!" said Ziegler. He was pale and shaking with anger.

There was silence as Ziegler began to stalk out to his own office. Then somebody very cautiously shouted: "Four more years!" Everyone gave a great laugh of relief.

McManus came up, closing his notebook. "Have you got the picture now?" he asked softly.

Yes. The image was quite clear. The White House Press had all the solidarity, effectiveness, and maturity of the French Chamber of Deputies.

Ziegler had called in the old squeeze play, but he had squeezed a little too hard, and it had blown up in his face. The newspapermen and the TV men had been pushed too far and had openly rebelled against the traditional privilege of the wire services to end the briefing. Ziegler hadn't counted on that, hadn't expected the press to break one of its own time-honored rules. He had lost control of his class—terrible humiliation for any teacher.

But no matter. Nothing was lost save face. Within a few minutes everything had returned to normal. Though the briefing had gone well beyond noon, no one had turned into a pumpkin. Most of the reporters simply walked back to their cubicles and filed something about Henry Kissinger, a quick and easy story. Then they left and had a good lunch. When they returned, about two o'clock, there was, as usual, little to do. John Osborne sat in his captain's chair and took some notes from transcripts of past briefings, which are kept in a looseleaf notebook. Other reporters sat around and read the *Evening Star*. The Knights of the Green Ottoman snoozed like tycoons on an ocean liner.

A little after lunch, the members of Ziegler's committee met in the briefing room and had a cordial discussion. Every so often, you could make out a clear phrase among the low voices: " . . . be firm about it . . . three points . . . Ron shouldn't be the one to say no." Later in the afternoon, the following communiqué was posted.

To All Hands:

A special committee of correspondents has recommended to Press Secretary Ronald L. Ziegler that all new briefings continue to be terminated by the Senior Wire Service Correspondent present.

However, in case of breaking deadline stories, anyone has the right to request that the briefing be postponed while those stories be filed—unless *THE MAJORITY OBJECTS*.

A request also was made to Mr. Ziegler to resume the 2-a-day briefings to provide additional time for correspondents to ask questions.

THE COMMITTEE

Around three o'clock, some of the reporters began looking at a pair of little white plastic stars on the wall. (There was a pair upstairs and a pair downstairs.) The stars were lit with a flickering light. When the light stopped flickering, it meant that there was a "lid" on the day's news—there would be no more briefings, announcements, or press releases. Downstairs, Don Fulsom was reading the paper, but his peripheral vision noticed the flickering cease. "That's the lid!" he said. Within ten minutes, the place was almost empty.

CHAPTER X

Divided They Fall

THAT AFTERNOON, McManus came back early from lunch and went to Ron Ziegler's office. He had a long, calm discussion with Ziegler and urged that the second daily briefing be instituted again. Ziegler listened and, of course, did nothing to revive the afternoon briefings.

When McManus finished treating with Ziegler, he came out and slumped in one of the captain's chairs in the middle of the empty briefing room. He began to talk to me quietly and almost sadly about the White House. "This morning Ziegler said that his interest was in decorum in this room," said McManus. "Well, I don't believe we ought to stand around this room and shout at each other, but the reason the people were shouting in this room today is that they were being denied the right to ask questions. And that's all we really get to do around here. We're sequestered.

"The press secretary has the power to obviate these problems, but instead he plays on what I call our structural incompetency. The weaknesses of our structure are just like a series of levers and any press secretary can manipulate them with ease, if he cares to. I mean, it's as if he's been handed five dogs conditioned by the Pavlovian method and a tinkle bell."

Ziegler had no qualms about playing on the weaknesses of the press. That was, after all, one of the main functions of a flack. And, at thirty-three, Ziegler was the compleat flack. He started as a press agent for the Southern California Central Republican Committee and later, as an executive at J. Walter Thompson in Los Angeles, he touted Disneyland. In 1968, he had watched public relations men win the election for Richard Nixon, and now he saw them beginning to rule the world. His old mentor at J. Walter Thompson, the haughty and automatous Bob Haldeman, was now the second most powerful man in the White House. While many flacks were former journalists who secretly loathed themselves for sinking into the whoredom of press agentry, Ziegler gave every sign of considering public relations a profession superior to journalism; after all, journalists merely wrote what flacks told them. "He was never torn, as some of his colleagues who had been newspapermen often were, between protection of his candidate and the public's right to know," Jules Witcover wrote of Ziegler's performance in the 1968 campaign. "That was journalism school stuff; on the field it was 'us' (the Nixon team) against 'them' (the press)."*

Ziegler was the perfect spokesman for the Nixon Administration. He was totally loyal to his boss and he treated the press with a bland contempt that was quite genuine and unaffected. At the briefing lectern, he was smug, condescending, and relentlessly evasive, often refusing to answer the simplest and most innocuous of questions. He talked in a kind of flackspeak that would have given Orwell nightmares. He sometimes accused reporters of "trying to complexify the situation," and he

_____
* The Resurrection of Richard Nixon by Jules Witcover (New York, Putnam, 1970), p. 376.

reversed White House positions by the simple expedient of announcing that he had "misspoken" himself in the past.

After the briefings, of course, Ziegler came on as a nice guy, a regular fellow who could tease and be teased. And most of the White House correspondents actually fell for Ziegler's act. Like Bob Semple of *The New York Times*. One afternoon, I was sitting next to Semple in the White House press plane, sipping wine and eating grapes, and I asked my standard question, which was: When are you people going to mutiny?

"Well," Semple assured me, "we'll get tee'd off. And it's gonna be over the issue of when can we ask the guy [Nixon] some questions. Ziegler's very, very good at his job. I don't mean very good about giving out information, but he's a marvelous buffer. And actually I kind of like the guy because he has a redeeming sense of humor. Ron is capable of saying, you know; 'Why am I doing this? Here I am on a plane and this is my whole life, and I don't ever see my wife . . . ' So, you know, he's capable of taking on the complaints of the press."

Of course, Ziegler never did anything about any of those complaints. But at least he was sometimes there on the press plane, and the reporters could go up and actually talk to him, provided they weren't on his ever-expanding shitlist. They usually couldn't get in to see anyone else on the White House staff, and Nixon didn't like to give press conferences. So Ziegler was the only President they had, and they tried very hard to like him.

A few people, like McManus and Fulsom, thought that Ziegler was a royal phony and a menace to the press, and they let him know it. And on one long flight in October, Helen Thomas of the UPI put her cards on the table. She was sitting in the cramped rear compartment of the President's plane with four other pool reporters when Ziegler came back to banter and remind everyone what a good guy he was. Helen Thomas started in on the Watergate scandal. "Lies," she said, "we get nothing but lies. And someday those lies are going to catch up with this Administration." Ziegler kept smiling and saying things like "Gee, Helen, I can't agree with you there." Suddenly Helen Thomas gave Ziegler a very hard look and said, "I'll say one thing for you, Ron. You've never lied to us directly. *But I don't know how you stomach your job.*"

But Thomas, McManus, and Fulsom were like the last people to crack in a Prisoner of War compound. Here was this awful little POW camp, with an officious pouter pigeon of a junior officer—the camp commander's favorite—who bullied the prisoners, studied their flaws, rewarded their failures, beat them for their successes, and encouraged them to turn each other in. And yet, under the mind-bending strains of four years' captivity, nearly all the prisoners had convinced themselves that the little bully was really not that bad a guy. They were grateful for the times when he kidded around with them.

In a way, one could not blame Ziegler for openly disdaining the White House press corps. They were such a bunch of patsies. If they bought his act, they would buy anything. Ziegler, and the men from whom Ziegler gladly took orders, consistently harassed reporters in the most petty and most underhanded of ways. And yet, the reporters never cried "foul" and never mutinied. A few cases of harassment, such as the Daniel Schorr affair, received a good deal of publicity.* But smaller examples of harassment happened almost daily at the White House. These dirty tricks can be divided into several categories, including divide-and-rule operations, freeze-outs, sheer balls tactics, and tax scares.

---

* After doing a critical piece on the Administration, CBS's Schorr had been investigated by the FBI on the phony pretext that he was being considered for a "high government post."

DIVIDE-AND-RULE

Divide-and-rule was one of Ziegler's favorite tactics.
One example was the way in which he used the Henry
Kissinger story to set up a fight between the wire-service
reporters and the straight reporters. At other times, Ziegler played on the simple fact that one reporter will always cut another reporter's throat for even the most
trivial scoop. In this way, Ziegler drove Jim Doyle out of
the White House.

In 1969, having served for several years as the Boston *Globe*'s Washington Bureau chief, Doyle moved into
the chair recently vacated by Haynes Johnson at the
Washington *Star;* one of Doyle's assignments was to
cover the White House on Saturdays.

During the rest of the week, the job was done by Gar-
nett "Jack" Horner, who had served on the *Star* since
1937 and had covered the White House since the early
Eisenhower days. Jack Horner was a White House lifer,
the permanent secretary of the White House Correspondents' Association. He was an overweight sexagen-
arian who looked like Charles Laughton, and every
morning he sat in a captain's chair in the middle of the
briefing room, resting his wattles on his chest. Not that
he was a lazy man—he scurried around all day protecting
himself by filing new leads and inserts on every handout that issued forth from the White House propaganda machine; he was an absolutely thorough and "objective" stenographer, recording every official happening,
never tainting his copy with the smallest speck of insight.

He was also a remarkably complaisant man. Once,
when Horner was part of the pool on Air Force One,
Lyndon Johnson invited all the reporters up front to
have a chat. Horner plumped one soft question after another into Johnson's lap. After the conversation, as the
reporters were making their way back to the rear of the
plane, Johnson said in a stage whisper that half the

plane could hear: "Boy, that Jack Horner really is a big ass-kisser, isn't he?"

Horner was always so pleasant and helpful around the White House staff. Whenever Ziegler started stumbling through a particularly tortuous answer, Horner always came to his aid with: "Ron, aren't you merely trying to say . . . ?" He also liked to make life easier for the President, and he once sought out Ziegler before a press conference and asked, "Is there any fertile ground we should plow tonight?"

In contrast to Horner, Doyle was young, restless, liberal, and unhelpful in his questioning.

One Saturday afternoon in the spring of 1970, Doyle was sitting around the White House pressroom when the *Star* called to say that a report had just come over the wire from the Chicago *Tribune* to the effect that Robert Finch was quitting his post as Secretary of Health, Education and Welfare in order to become a White House aide. The *Star* wanted Doyle to get the report confirmed and find out more details. Doyle found Gerald Warren, the deputy press secretary, and started questioning him about Finch's impending move. Warren, an innocuous, spindly, bankerish type, kept protesting that he couldn't say anything about the matter himself and couldn't take the problem to Ziegler. So Doyle decided to let the problem wait until later in the afternoon and went off to cover an Agnew press conference on youth and drug addiction.

When Doyle returned to the pressroom, Jack Horner was sitting in the *Star*'s cubicle. Horner was a man who never missed a chance to come in and work for overtime pay. Without saying anything to Horner, Doyle went to a phone and called the *Star*'s city desk.

"Jack Horner's here," he said.

"Don't worry," said the man on the desk. "We'll tell you why when you get back to the office."

Doyle drove back to the *Star* and asked why.

"Well," said the man on the desk, "Ziegler gave Jack the Finch story, so Jack's going to do it. He gave it to

Jack on the condition that he doesn't let you or anyone else in the pressroom know about it."

Doyle was incredulous. "You mean," he said, "that you're letting a guy set ground rules against another guy on the staff?"

"Well, just this once," said the desk man. "It won't happen again."

"You're damn right it won't," said Doyle. "I'm not going back to the White House. Ever." And he never did go back, although he occasionally covered a Presidential trip.

Meanwhile, Jack Horner continued to accumulate gold stars on his wrinkled forehead. Ziegler fed him one exclusive after another as a means of punishing the *Star's* competitor, the fractious Washington *Post*. Shortly before the 1972 election, Horner's exemplary behavior earned him what he called the biggest beat of his life, an exclusive interview with Richard Nixon. There was only one ground rule—Horner was not allowed to print the questions he asked the President. Which meant that Nixon could virtually ignore Horner's questions and simply spew out his carefully prepared remarks. Horner was being used as a funnel, but he did get his scoop. As he sat there in the Oval Office, feeling the delicious whirr of the little tape recorder that he always carried strapped to his waist like a pacemaker, Jack Horner must have thought to himself: "What a good boy am I."

THE FREEZE-OUT

Stuart Loory was the *Herald Tribune*'s Moscow correspondent for several years in the early sixties. Later, he covered the White House from 1967 until 1971 for the Los Angeles *Times*. He left partly because Ziegler and other White House staffers made things uncomfortable for him whenever he wrote an unflattering or unorthodox article about the Administration. "I found great similarities between covering the White House and the

Kremlin," he said later. "When the Kremlin was unhappy with you, they shut you out. They didn't invite you to press conferences. They didn't let you travel. The White House put the same kind of pressures on you when you wrote something they didn't like. The way Marty Schram was treated, for instance, was a typical Russian tactic."

Marty Schram was the White House correspondent for the Long Island daily, *Newsday*. He was a serious-minded, rabbinical looking young man who wore black-rimmed glasses and a Groucho Marx moustache. In the summer of 1971, Schram helped Newsday's Pulitzer Prize-winning team of investigative reporters to carry out an exhaustive investigation of Richard Nixon's best friend, Bebe Rebozo.

The investigation resulted in a six-part series, carefully documented with maps and charts, which laid out the shady business dealings of Rebozo and his friend Sen. George A. Smathers (D.-Fla.). "The deals made by Bebe Rebozo and the Smathers gang have tarnished the Presidency," *Newsday* declared in an accompanying editorial.

When the series came out in October 1971, Ziegler was asked to comment on it.

"We have absolutely no concern about the integrity of Mr. Rebozo, and I'll have no further comment on those stories," said Ziegler. Then he put the freeze on Schram.

Without ever mentioning the Rebozo series, Ziegler suddenly began to act as if Schram did not exist. He refused to talk to him, except to give curt and rude answers when Schram asked a question at a briefing. If Schram tried to broach a question after a briefing, Ziegler would cut him off with a brusque, "I don't have time now," and walk away. When Schram made an appointment to see Ziegler about the problem, Ziegler kept him waiting for an entire afternoon and then left via a back door.

Ziegler steadfastly refused to admit that this treatment had anything to do with the Rebozo series. In February 1972, reporters who were not on the list to go to China were summoned to Ziegler's office, one by one, to receive the bad news. Schram was among those called. Ziegler made a number of excuses as to why there was no room on the plane for *Newsday*. Schram pointed out that *Newsday* met all the criteria that had been set up, while many of the papers on the list did not. Ziegler made more excuses.

"Come on, Ron," said Schram. "It's the Rebozo series."

Ziegler denied it.

"Well, then, what is it, Ron, what's the reason?" Schram kept asking. Ziegler kept answering that certain, uh, decisions just had to be made.

Even after the China trip, Ziegler continued to exclude Schram from pool assignments. This banishment did not cripple Schram, but it did hurt him because he liked to embellish his features and takeouts with the kind of atmosphere and fine detail that could only be gathered by observing Nixon at close range. He still collected information from several friendly sources he had cultivated on the White House staff, but it pained him whenever he saw the pool trooping into some state dinner, the pool members being mostly "hard news guys who didn't give a shit about the background stuff."

Almost a year after the Rebozo series appeared, Nixon went to campaign in Nassau County, where *Newsday* was delivered to seven out of ten homes. As usual, Schram didn't make the pool. "But what am I supposed to do," he shrugged, "act wounded? They shouldn't choose the pool, anyway. The press should choose it."

SHEER BALLS

Every so often, when bullying and intimidation failed, Ziegler and his superiors would resort to a tactic that can only be described as sheer balls. They would tell a lie so Stalinesque in its grandeur or would make a demand so preposterous that the reporter in question was struck dumb and did not know where to begin his counterattack.

One of the most spectacular examples of White House ballsmanship was the attempt to convert Nicholas von Hoffman at the time of student uprisings over the invasion of Cambodia and the shootings at Kent State. Nick von Hoffman was a prematurely grey-haired forty-two-year-old columnist for the Washington *Post* who voted for Nixon in 1960 and 1968 for reasons which he has never been able to explain satisfactorily. People who discovered von Hoffman's voting record were invariably surprised by it, because von Hoffman had been slamming Nixon all over the *Post*'s "Style" section ever since the inauguration of the column (and of Nixon) in 1969. One of von Hoffman's charms was his maverick inconsistency, but his stands were invariably radical and he himself described the content of his column as "bolshie drivel."

After the invasion of Cambodia, he wrote a column saying that the situation was so appalling that "the Washington monument went limp." So it came as something of a shock to von Hoffman when the Nixon White House attempted the old Lyndon Johnson hustle of soliciting his advice to try to bring him on as a member of the team. Even Johnson, who used to spend whole afternoons cajoling reporters, would never have taken on a hard-core radical like von Hoffman. Von Hoffman wrote an account of the incident for the *New American Review,* and he swears it's all true. (He didn't write it for the *Post* because the *Post* refused to print the exact language he had used.) The article deserves to be quoted at length:

The crew-cut press aide who stands at parade rest while Ziegler does his monologue begins inviting people backstage. I am approached and led into Ziegler's office. Outside the window is Nixon, hands behind his back, talking to Kissinger, strolling on the lawn, maybe still grooving on his crisis euphoria or maybe he's already crashed. The four at

Kent State have already been killed; two more will die at Jackson shortly.

John Erlichmann [sic] comes into the room . . .

"I'm sure John would like to hear your ideas," Ziegler says.

"Suppose you're right about Vietnam," I begin, and they make as if I'm about to give them the unique word, instead of being one among who knows how many reporters they've run through their office. Most of us believe against certain knowledge that if only we could get in there and tell them, they'd listen. So I am in the White House and the President's man has said he wants to hear. You don't have to be a politician to be infatuated with your own possibilities.

"Suppose you're right about Cambodia," I continue, "suppose you're right about the military situation, suppose you're right about everything, don't you see you still can't fight this fucking war?" I fancy that the word hasn't been spoken in the building since Lyndon Johnson. I also imagine that bad language may make them pay attention. "In a democracy, see, fifty-one percent is good enough to build a road or exempt the oil companies from taxation, but not to fight a war. You gotta have ninety percent for that, and you boys didn't pull that in the election. That cocksucker was elected to end the war, not spread it."

Ziegler is a two-expression man, blank and smiling. No frowns, no pensive looks, no screwing up in distaste, it's the blank or the smile. The blank is for when you're speaking; the smile is for when you're finished and he's about to talk. Having a conversation with him is like playing tic-tac-toe with a computer.

"People'll feel differently when it works out. Opinion'll change when it's a success," Ziegler says. An efficient organization silences all opposition by declaring high quarterly dividends.

"Millions of people don't give a shit if it's a success. Christ almighty, they don't even know where Cambodia is much less want to conquer it."

The President has gone from the lawn.

"We know that. We're pulling out. We're withdrawing. Vietnamization is working."

"Oy!"

"As people see that the President's policy is a success, they'll support him."

"If you keep pushing this way, these kids are going to burn down the country. Get off people's necks."

Erlichmann says something to indicate that things are nastier than he'd like to see them. There is more talk about the stock market, the businessmen, the different kind of people who've had it. Erlichmann agrees it is serious, remarking it has probably cost Governor Rhodes of Ohio the primary. I repeat the prediction of bloody trouble. Erlichmann replies, "We're counting on leaders like yourself to keep things calm."

Leaders like who?

We're doomed.

TAX SCARE

In 1969, Jules Witcover wrote a book about Nixon's 1968 Presidential campaign called *The Resurrection of Richard Nixon*. The White House, getting wind of the project, called up all of Witcover's sources and instructed them not to talk to him any more. Fortunately, Witcover had already completed most of his research.

In 1970, when the book came out, Witcover went on *The Dick Cavett Show* to publicize it. Cavett asked him whether the Nixon people had been cooperative, and Witcover recounted how the Nixon people had tried to stop him by cutting off his information. A week later, Witcover's wife received a phone call from an Internal Revenue Service agent who announced that Witcover was going to be audited.

Witcover had to take time off and assemble all his tax materials. An IRS agent looked through every check Witcover had written in the last year, and found nothing amiss. For weeks, Witcover tried to make the IRS tell him why he was being audited, what in specific they were looking for. The IRS never came up with an answer, except to say that they were testing a new system and that his name had been chosen at random. Witcover, however, was convinced that he was the victim of a political audit.

Witcover was not the only journalist to receive a visit from the taxman. At the time of *Newsday*'s Rebozo series, Robert Green, the head of the paper's investigative team, had his tax returns audited by the IRS. So did William Attwood, the publisher of *Newsday,* and David Laventhol, the editor. The IRS also examined the newspaper's financial records.

DAY AFTER DAY, Ziegler and his superiors frustrated and harassed the White House press corps in petty ways. Yet the correspondents refused to stand up and defend each other. No one, for instance, ever lodged a protest in behalf of Marty Schram or investigated the IRS audit of Jules Witcover.

Meanwhile, the White House kept building up a powerful public relations machine whose function was to compete with the press, to go over the heads of the press and straight to the people. The White House sent off tons of mailings to newspapers and individuals. The White House frequently demanded and received free network television time so that the President could present his arguments to the public and even so that the Vice President could attack the press.

The Nixon aides were advertising people, Dan Rather said as he sat around the pressroom one afternoon; they knew ten times as much about the media as the Johnson people had. They had known that if they squawked enough about post-speech analyses by network correspondents, they could make the networks back down. And they knew dozens of little tricks which allowed them to use television to their own advantage, said Rather. For instance, in October 1972, Nixon hardened his stand on amnesty in a speech which he made over the radio. CBS had a clip from an old TV interview in which the President had put forth a much softer position, and Rather would have liked to have shown the two statements side by side to demonstrate that Nixon was toughening up his position for political reasons in an election year. But to do this, Rather needed a *picture* of the second statement. The White House people had realized this, and that was the reason Nixon had made the statement on the radio.

So the voice of the White House grew stronger while the voice of the press became weaker.

One morning in September, as we were flying out to California on the White House press plane, I tried to find out from Peter Lisagor why the press corps was so docile. Lisagor was a fixture of Washington journalism; as the veteran "special" correspondent of the Chicago *Daily News,* he could write more or less what he wanted. While his White House articles usually opened with a "news peg" from the daily briefing, rather than the kind of "trend" lead that John Osborne favored, Lisagor was nevertheless very good at standing back and putting official statements into perspective. When Ziegler announced the end of the draft, for instance, Lisagor carefully pointed out in his lead the political implications of the move—its appeal to young voters. At the same time, Lisagor was a living monument in the Washington press establishment, a former president of the White House Correspondents Association, and a man who did not like to rock the boat too hard.

"Why not a mutiny?" I asked.

Lisagor stopped typing on the lightweight portable he had set up on the tray in front of him.

"Well, you see," he said, in his polite way, "because the White House people managed successfully to put the press in the ambivalent position of being an entity separate from the public interest or the public, the press has not much to stand on."

"When did you first see that tactic used?"

"Well, it was first articulated by the Nixon Administration. The others had accepted the notion that the press was a legitimate vehicle for disseminating information to the public. But the Nixon Administration gave the press an identity of its own, separate from the public interest, and then began to characterize the press either as friendly or hostile or what have you."

As Lisagor continued to talk, it became clear that he felt the Nixon people had maneuvered the press into a kind of Dien Bien Phu, isolated and abandoned without any hope of rescue. If Nixon wanted to make himself inaccessible, there was nothing the press could do. "It can't sue him," said Lisagor. The press had no legal rights, except for the First Amendment, which was a thin reed. It wasn't an institution set up by the Constitution. It could kick and scream, but that didn't produce any results because "the public doesn't give a damn about our problems." The only thing the press could do, Lisagor concluded, was to work more vigorously to ferret out information from the government, "recognizing that no Administration owns the public's business—that it *is* the public's business, and that the public is the proprietor of it."

But not many White House reporters got around to ferreting out information. One problem was that the White House swamped them with press releases. Perhaps a greater problem was the beat system.

The ideal way to find out what was going on inside the White House was to approach it from the outside— drive over to State or HEW, for instance, and look up some Young Turk who had just had a pet program sold out by Haldeman or Ehrlichman in order to placate some right-wing governor; the Young Turk would be angry and would gladly tell the whole story. But usually a White House reporter didn't have time to cultivate sources outside the White House. The White House was his beat and he had to stay there to protect himself in case a story broke, and also to fill in his colleagues on other beats when they needed information from the White House.

Bob Semple, for instance, used up large portions of every working day getting the White House reaction to various developments for fellow *Times*men on the Hill or at the State Department. If he could not get a comment from Ziegler, he would have to sit down and write a summary of past White House statements on a certain bill (if he was helping out the man on the·Hill) or a certain international situation (for the man at State). Which meant that Semple was tied down to his desk at the White House. Although some newspaper editors and bureau chiefs had begun to talk about freeing up their White House men to do more investigative work, this was not being done during the first Nixon Administration.

Since few of the White House correspondents had opportunities to ferret out information, since they *were* largely sequestered from staffers and outside sources, they needed decent briefings and press conferences if they were going to do a creditable job. Above all, they needed a revival of Presidential press conferences. In the days of Franklin Roosevelt, the weekly sessions in the Oval Office were considered indispensable by the White House correspondents. Arthur M. Schlesinger, Jr., wrote in *The Coming of the New Deal*: "By according the press the privilege of regular interrogation, Roosevelt established the Presidential press conference in a quasi-constitutional status as the American equivalent of the parliamentary question period—a status which future Presidents could downgrade to their peril."*

For years, political scientists, political reporters and historians like Schlesinger considered the Presidential press conference an unshakable institution. Nixon changed all that.

"What we assumed, and it seems sort of dumb in retospect," said David Broder, "was that just because the press conference had grown up from Wilson on and seven or eight Presidents had adhered to it, it had somehow become institutionalized. It's not institutionalized at all.

* *The Coming of the New Deal* by Arthur M. Schlesinger, Jr. (New York, Houghton Mifflin, 1959), p. 562.

In fact, you could effectively say that Richard Nixon has abolished the Presidential press conference as an institution. He may grant two or three a year, but when they're that infrequent they don't really mean anything."

There was a school of thought, led by John Osborne, that held that press conferences did no good anyway. Osborn thought that Nixon was "altogether too good for the common good at using press conferences to present himself and his policies in a favorable light." Other reporters echoed him, saying that reporters never were able to follow through on a line of questioning and pin Nixon down, that too much time was wasted on trivial questions. But many of these reporters had forgotten, or had never known, what a real press conference was like.

"You have to go back to the Kennedy period or even the Eisenhower period to see what a Presidential press conference *system* really looks like," said Broder. "The key thing is the frequency. If you have them weekly—as was the custom under Roosevelt, Truman, and Eisenhower—it doesn't make any difference if you blow ten minutes on some trivial thing or if you don't get to follow up on a question, because the President is going to be back there the next week and you'll have another chance. You can look at those old press conferences and get a very acute sense of what was agitating public opinion at the time, of what questions were up for political discussion. Now obviously, if you're down to three or four a year, the press conference doesn't serve that function at all. You just get scatterings of bits of information. But on a weekly basis, it serves an extremely important function. It requires the President to think about what *other* people may have on their minds."

FOR THE CORRESPONDENTS to do a proper job of covering the White House, they needed regular Presidential press conferences and they required briefings from a press secretary who was not in love with the art of obfuscation. The only way to extract these necessities from

the Administration was joint action—a petition or a
boycott, supported by the whole White House press
corps, that would put pressure on the Administration to
change its smug ways.

But whenever I suggested joint action to reporters
around the White House, they looked at me as if I had
suggested cutting off their typing fingers. They invariably launched into speeches about how reporters were
fierce individualists who defied any attempt to regiment
them. Everyone made basically the same speech, but
Dan Rather made one of the best. "You know," he said
when I broached the subject of joint action, "journalists
by their nature are not an organized lot. The average
journalist, including myself, is a whiskey-breathed, nico-
tine-stained, stubble-bearded guy, and journalism is not
a business that attracts very organized people." Rather
was wearing a beautifully tailored blue suit and he gave
off the healthy glow of a man who has just emerged
from a hotel barber shop. I had never seen him smoke
and I doubt whether, on a typical day, his strongest ex-
halation could budge the needle on a Breathalyzer.

But the curious thing about political journalists is that
they often work as a herd when they should act as individuals, and they claim their right to perform as individuals when they should close ranks and act as a group.
The most sheeplike herd in Washington—the Pentagon
press corps—boasted the loudest of its individuality; the
reporters at the Pentagon bragged that they were so independent that they had never formed even a ceremoni-
al organization like the White House Correspondents
Association.

But it was not just the worst reporters who shied
away from joint action. Some of the best and the toughest also had qualms. "We're all reluctant to gang up,"
said Jack Germond. "Ganging up is a bad business. I
mean, there aren't many guys I want to gang up with.
I don't agree with their methods. I have a different
judgment on what I think is news. I have a different
judgment on what I think is a fair way to go at some-

thing. I have a different judgment about my ability to beat them on my own, so why should I join up with them?

"There are occasions when some kind of ganging up is necessary, I suppose," Germond conceded. "And Nixon's campaign in 1968 was probably one of them."

"Let the editors fight those battles," said Jules Witcover. "We're in the trenches every day and we're just trying to get access. It's like professional football. You start going straight in and it doesn't work, so you loop and you stunt and you just see how the game goes. This business of getting together and forming a committee or boycotting or something else—that doesn't deal with the ongoing changes. It's just constant and you've just got to keep making your moves and being aware that they're doing those things, and try to cope with them on your own."

"But Jules," I said, "that doesn't seem to work. The White House keeps getting away with murder."

"There's nothing wrong with looping and stunting if everybody does it, but there are not enough guys who do it," Witcover admitted. "There are not enough guys who see this happening. I think there are still too many guys who just cover a campaign like it's an evolving set of speeches."

Most of the reporters seemed to perceive, however dimly, that they were the people's representatives in the executive mansion and that the President had no right to keep them in the dark and to use the media solely for his own ends. But at that point they balked. They would not admit that this extraordinary situation called for extraordinary action by the press; they refused to consider a strike, a boycott or any kind of dramatic gesture that would point up the gravity of the crisis. "There's just an awareness that this would be a politically unwise thing to do because you'd leave yourself open to attack," said Jules Witcover. Nixon had the reporters so thoroughly on the defensive that they forgot that they, as a body, had considerable power and that they had certain rights.

It was not as if pressure had never succeeded in the past. In 1967, during the Johnson Administration, Ben Bradlee, the executive editor of the Washington *Post,* decided to fight the system of backgrounders.* Bradlee instructed his reporters to "fight like hell" to get everything on the record, and he got *The New York Times* to go along with him. A few days later, when the White House tried to hold a backgrounder on the Common Market, the *Post*'s Carrol Kilpatrick and the *Times'* Max Frankel protested and insisted that they had to know why the briefing was for background only. The briefing was put on the record. Having won a small victory, however, the *Times* and the *Post* did not keep up the fight, and backgrounders continued to flourish.

During Nixon's first term, there was only one group effort to deal with the White House, the "Washington Hotel meeting," and all the reporters involved went out of their way to explain that they weren't trying to gang up on the President. The Washington Hotel meeting took place in December 1971, when Nixon had avoided holding a press conference for nineteen consecutive weeks. When Nixon finally announced that he would hold a press conference on December 10, Jules Witcover and Stuart Loory, who were both then working for the Los Angeles *Times,* decided that it would be a good idea if some White House reporters got together and discussed how to make Presidential press conferences more productive.

Witcover and Loory realized that if they weren't careful, the White House would try to brand the meeting a "press conspiracy," so they did everything they could to make the meeting open and innocent. They got John Osborne, whom the White House regarded as if he had won the Nobel Peace Prize, to chair the meeting. Then they phoned about forty reporters and invited them to

---

* Backgrounders are small press conferences where government officials give out information on the condition that it will not be attributed to any source. Using backgrounders, officials can float trial balloons or simply lie without assuming any responsibility.

come. Some simply refused to consider the invitation, fearing the "conspiracy" charge. Others consulted with their editors and agonized for days over the decision. Bob Semple consented to attend, but only as an observer. Witcover and Loory considered setting up a miniature press section for him—a separate table, with a typewriter and free drinks.

Finally, twenty-eight reporters met one December morning for a coffee-and-cruller session in a room on the mezzanine of the Washington Hotel, a second-class place just up the street from the National Press Building. The meeting was as innocuous as a student council session. The first subject they discussed was whether it was cricket for them to meet. They agreed that it was. Then they talked for over an hour, arriving at a consensus on two points: it would be nice if somebody would ask the President at the upcoming press conference whether he intended to see the press more frequently; it would also be nice if reporters were more diligent in following up each other's questions, so that the President could not slip by with an evasive reply. Some of the reporters had misgivings about asking the President about the press conference situation—the viewing public might be offended to see the press taking up time with an "inside baseball" type of question. But eventually everyone at the meeting agreed that it was a good thing to ask because it was in the public interest to have more press conferences.

It was a very informal meeting, with everyone gulping coffee and smoking. At the end, John Osborne was asked to go over to the White House and tell Ziegler about the subjects that had been discussed and the conclusions that the reporters had reached. When Osborne appeared in Ziegler's office that afternoon, the press secretary smiled and said that he already knew about the meeting. Osborne gave him a short summary of the discussion and Ziegler said "Fine," thanked him, and led him out of the office.

Of course, Osborne's mission did no good. Soon after

the meeting, Herb Klein (the White House director of communications) wrote an article for the Op-Ed page of *The New York Times*, hinting darkly that the reporters had been up to no good: ". . . some of the reporters who were there took pains to say they were not part of a cabal or conspiracy and that in no way did they discuss either the order or the subject matter of the questions that would be asked at the forthcoming conference. Whether or not they did, the timing of the meeting did nothing to enhance press credibility."

Later, Allen Drury, *The New York Times*-reporter-turned-conservative-novelist, painted an even darker picture in *Courage and Hesitation,* his semiofficial book on Nixon: "A group of major correspondents, fantastically, has actually held a secret meeting, their ostensible purpose to arrange the sequence of questions, their real aim to get Dick Nixon."

It was true that the press conference on December 10 was probably the roughest one Nixon ever had to face. "But that meeting didn't make it rough," said John Osborne. What made it rough was the fact that Nixon had piled up a lot of things to answer for, like calling Charles Manson "guilty" before the trial, firing Walter Hickel, and letting unemployment rise. Two or three reporters asked nasty questions, but there were very few follow-up questions, and Nixon dodged the tough ones with his customary skill.

Nixon always had the advantage at these conferences. The reporters were disorganized and many of them suffered from stage fright in front of the live television cameras. Nixon, on the other hand, spent several days preparing himself, polishing answers to possible questions; he even memorized the seating chart so that he knew exactly where to point whenever he felt the need for a soft question from a friendly or notoriously incompetent reporter.

Toward the end of the half-hour press conference on December 10, Herb Kaplow (then of NBC) asked whether the President would hold press conferences more frequently in the future. Kaplow phrased the question very tactfully, and Nixon gave his standard reply, right out of one of the loose-leaf briefing books he'd been studying for three days. Of course, he had an obligation to inform the American people, but there were several ways—press conferences, formal reports to the nation, television chats with one or two correspondents. He thought that the American people had a right to hear his views directly, not just through the press. "And I think any member of the press would agree on that," he said. He would like suggestions on how to keep the nation informed without dominating television too much, as some had charged. Maybe the answer was "more conferences in the office."

"But," said Nixon, "you make the vote."

A few weeks later, Peter Lisagor, acting as head of the White House Correspondents Association, sent a list of suggestions to Nixon via Ziegler. Ziegler announced that the President was "pleased." The list was promptly forgotten. None of the suggestions, including a plea for weekly press conferences, was adopted.

Thus, in the long run, the Washington Hotel meeting was a flop.* It was like a resolution by the General Assembly of the U.N.—there was no clout behind it, so it was ignored. If there was a conspiracy in Washington, it was a White House plot to cripple the press, not a press conspiracy to get the President. The White House conspiracy, if anything, *demanded* a counter-conspiracy from the reporters to regain their rights. But the White House reporters refused to assert themselves, except to

---

* There were also a few smaller, less formal attempts at organized resistance, all of which failed. For instance, on the eve of the China trip, Charles Wheeler of the BBC tried to organize a boycott of a cocktail party the White House was giving for correspondents who weren't going to Peking. "My God," Wheeler said later, "they had made space for parish newsletters with circulations of seven hundred and fifty, but they weren't allowing any foreign correspondents to go. And then they tried to buy us off with a cocktail party. So I phoned around and said I didn't think we ought to go to the party. But several people went anyway, just for fear that they would miss something."

write a few sniping, ineffective articles about the lack of press conferences. Later, during the 1972 campaign, Nixon naturally felt free to seclude himself.

And even the best of the White House correspondents despaired of making the President account for the actions of his Administration. John Osborne, for instance, wrote a column about a press conference which Nixon held on August 29, 1972. A couple of reporters asked Nixon about the Watergate, and Nixon skated around the issue for a while, finally concluding with a statement that "no one in the White House staff, no one in this Administration presently employed, was involved in this very bizarre incident."

Osborne noted that nobody bothered to ask Nixon about John Mitchell, Hugh Sloan and other assistants who were alleged to be involved with the Watergate affair but were no longer "presently employed" at the White House. "He was not asked, either," Osborne went on, "whether with all of these investigations on he now knew who had ordered the bugging and why it was ordered. I stood within 10 feet of him and didn't even try to ask that simple and obvious question." Later in the article, Osborne summed up by saying that the thing he would always remember about "Mr. Nixon's first 'political press conference' of 1972 was his handling of the funds and bugging matter and our failure to handle him as a vulnerable candidate should have been handled. It was a lesson in the mesmerizing power of the presidency."

BUT MESMERIZING POWER had nothing to do with the case of Clark Mollenhoff. Mollenhoff was a fifty-one-year-old bull of a man, with greying closely cropped hair and glasses, who had been drafted by the New York Giants in 1943, but gave up a pro football career to enter journalism. An Iowan who still spoke with a Midwestern nasality, he joined the Des Moines *Register* and gradually earned a reputation as the toughest investigative reporter in Washington.

He prided himself on having "no ideological hangup." He fought injustices in the State Department and the Agriculture Department and in 1953 he began to expose labor rackets and convinced Robert Kennedy to enlist the Senate Government Operations Committee in the battle against labor racketeering. As Jimmy Hoffa was led off to jail in 1967, he spat on Clark Mollenhoff. Nobody could intimidate Mollenhoff, not even Presidents. Eisenhower once told him to sit down at a press conference. He stayed on his feet. In time, he won every prize in the business, from the American Legion's Fourth Estate Award to the Pulitzer.

For all his success, Mollenhoff was unpopular among some of his colleagues. In 1964, when he was heir apparent to the presidency of the National Press Club, a group of members mounted a successful stop-Mollenhoff movement. Many people found Mollenhoff dogmatic and egotistical. Moreover, for an investigative reporter, he had a curious weakness for participating in government. Under Kennedy he served on the U.S. Advisory Commission on Information Policy while still writing about the Administration. While covering the Goldwater campaign in 1964, he wrote a memo bringing one of his pet injustices to the candidate's attention; Goldwater based a speech on the memo. Finally, in 1969, he became an ombudsman for the Nixon Administration, a $33,500-a-year bureaucrat who was supposed to warn the President against corruption within the ranks of the Administration, investigate complaints, and ferret out wrong-doings in past Administrations. Mollenhoff resigned after a year. His detractors said that he was eased out after making a fool of himself by clumsily and stubbornly defending the nomination of Clement Haynsworth to the Supreme Court. *He* claimed to have left because the Nixon staffers engaged in "foot-dragging" over things he "was suggesting for their own good."

Two years after Mollenhoff had quit the White House and returned to his desk in the Motel Modern surroundings of the Des Moines *Register*'s Washington Bureau, the Watergate affair broke. Mollenhoff was appalled at the implications of the break-in and once again started suggesting moves that the White House ought to make for its own good. But this time he was suggesting them in the public prints. In a long series of tough columns, Mollenhoff called on Nixon to set up a bipartisan panel which could investigate the affair and clear the Presidency of all taint of wrongdoing. He also charged that the Justice Department could, if it wanted to, force at least one of the indicted men to tell who had financed the operation—by granting immunity from prosecution.

On October 5, Mollenhoff was typing in his plaque-studded office when the news came over the bureau's wire machine that Nixon was holding an impromptu press conference in the Oval Office. Mollenhoff dashed the four blocks to the White House and arrived while the press conference was still in progress. But he was not allowed to go in. Standing around the empty White House pressroom, Mollenhoff began to smolder. He was convinced that the White House had purposely avoided notifying him for fear that he would badger Nixon with questions about the Watergate.

Later that afternoon, Mollenhoff stormed into Ziegler's office to give the press secretary "a piece of my mind." Mollenhoff accused Ziegler of trying to block the "tough, informed questions" which he had been raising in his column for weeks. Then he began to question Ziegler about the financing of the Watergate burglary. He asked if Ziegler seriously believed that Gordon Liddy and James McCord, two of the arrested men, had used their own money on the project.

"No," said Ziegler.

"Then where did it come from?" asked Mollenhoff.

"Why, I didn't think there was any question but that the money came from the Committee," said Ziegler.

Mollenhoff was startled. He couldn't believe that the White House press secretary would admit that the Watergate break-in had been financed by the Committee to Re-elect the President. So he asked again.

"There is no question but that the money came from the Committee," Ziegler repeated.

The next morning—October 6—Mollenhoff had a story on the front page of the *Register* based on the Ziegler quote. Reporters immediately began to phone Ziegler about the quote, and Ziegler read all callers a prepared statement which said that the quote was a "misinterpretation" of what he had told Mollenhoff.

"I said I have no personal knowledge of any aspect of this matter other than what I have read in the press," Ziegler's statement continued. "Therefore I am not in a position to draw any conclusion or to make any authoritative statements whatsoever, and the reporter for the Des Moines *Register* was so informed."

That evening, Ziegler called Mollenhoff and read him the statement, too.

"Well, are you denying that?" Mollenhoff asked him.

"Well, no," said Ziegler, and repeated that he had not been authorized to say anything, and that he didn't know anything about the Watergate.

"Well, if it stays within that context and it's clear it's not a denial, that's fine," said Mollenhoff.

But many papers treated Ziegler's statement as a denial, which angered Mollenhoff. A week after the story appeared, he went to the morning White House briefing to battle openly with Ziegler and to defend his own reputation as a journalist.

The briefing began with some pleasantries from Ziegler and an announcement that the President would make a radio speech on crime the coming Sunday. There was a long string of questions on the Paris peace talks. Then Mollenhoff, standing at the front of the room about ten feet from the lectern, initiated his exchange with Ziegler.

Mollenhoff: Ron, there has been some dispute about our conversation as of last Thursday, and I wanted to go over that with you here to make sure there is no misunderstanding about what you are denying. You are not denying the quote itself, that there is no question but that the money came from the Committee, is that right?

Ziegler: I have issued a statement on that, Clark. I will stand by it.

Mollenhoff: My story has been questioned on this. That is important to me. It is an important point relative to the Watergate investigations. I want to go over this. I want a confrontation out here where we have witnesses, where the question of accuracy is settled.

Ziegler: I have issued a statement and I stand by it.

Mollenhoff: I don't want you to get away that way. I want to go over the context in which this was said. You said this on defending the Administration on the general thoroughness of the investigation. You said that the question had been answered and that there is no question but that the money came from the Committee. We had just gone over the $1,600 that Liddy had in his possession. We had just gone over the $3,500 that was spent for the electronic devices by McCord in connection with the Watergate bugging.

At that point, you said—I raised the question about the sources of this money, and we had agreed that it was absurd that they would spend their own money for this—and at that point you said, "There is no question but that the money came from the Committee" and there was not any question about what money it was or what committee it was. Do you challenge that?

Ziegler: I have issued a statement and stand by it.

Mollenhoff: That is the kind of crap we have been getting out of this White House all along. You may not know anything about this, but you have been denying implication of the White House and the Committee people on top for the last two months. I was not aware that you were unauthorized to speak on the subject, because certainly the press conferences up to now have indicated that you were.

Ziegler (looking around the room): Any other questions?

Somebody immediately popped up to ask a question on the bombing, leaving Mollenhoff stranded and shaking with anger. Ziegler was pale and his pudgy face was drawn, but the bombing question and some subsequent queries about campaign plans gave him a chance to calm down. Mollenhoff kept raising his trembling hand and coming in with more questions, but Ziegler kept putting him off. Nobody helped him. In the back of the room, a reporter shook his head as Mollenhoff came in for his third attack. "There," said the reporter, "is the male Sarah McClendon." Everyone in the room knew all the details of the Mollenhoff affair, which had been reported in the Washington *Post*. Most of them probably believed that Mollenhoff was in the right.

But Mollenhoff was a comic figure to his colleagues. He had thought that he was too good for journalism, but he had failed as a mandarin in Nixon's White House. He was like a cocky kid who had left his small town for good, proceeded to fail dismally in the Big City, and was now forced to come back to the small town covered in shame but putting up a good front. So no one was anxious to defend him. They watched him for a while as he flailed against Ziegler, and then, instead of demanding that Ziegler answer Mollenhoff's questions, they stepped in with questions of their own. "Ron," someone said, sounding faintly bored, "may I change the subject?" Nobody seemed to care whether Ziegler denied the quote or not. That was Mollenhoff's problem, not theirs.

Mollenhoff was no proponent of joint action. "If they don't have the guts to do it individually," he said later, "there's no point getting together to rig a conspiracy to get them off their asses." But he did expect some help from his fellow newspapermen. He kept looking around in a beseeching way, until someone in the back of the room finally asked Ziegler: "Did Clark Mollenhoff quote you accurately in that story?" Ziegler said he had already given a response on that point. The subject was dropped.

Mollenhoff managed to get off one parting shot.

"The speech Sunday on crime—will that include the Watergate?" he asked Ziegler.

At the end of the briefing, a group of reporters gathered around Mollenhoff to slap him on the back and shake his hand. "That a way, Clark!" they said. "That was certainly some performance! It sure is good to see someone take on Ziegler like that!"

The White House press corps always admired a show of fierce individualism.

CHAPTER XI

Nixon's Campaign

EVERY SO often in the course of the fall campaign, Jules Witcover appeared at a White House briefing in his black, funereal raincoat, looking like a cut-rate version of the bad fairy. He would wait until the questioning started to hum and then, with his eyes all blank and innocent, he would catch Ziegler's attention and ask, "Ron, what did the President do today as a candidate for reelection? Did he do anything?"

Ziegler would bristle and fight the impulse to snap, and then he would give a very composed answer detailing all the Presidential duties that Nixon would discharge that day, and he could completely ignore Witcover's question. Witcover would come back a minute later with something like, "Ron, *as a candidate,* did the President read the *Times'* story on Segretti?" Witcover never could get over the fact that all the White House staffers took offense the moment you said or even implied that Nixon was a candidate for President. Around the White House, it bordered on treason to call Nixon a candidate;

the big plan was to run him as the President and try to bury the fact that he was a politician. Ziegler tore up the English language looking for euphemisms for the word "campaign." Someone would ask him about one of Nixon's upcoming campaign trips and Ziegler would answer, "Yes, on Monday the President will go to New York to, uh, *follow the schedule we've announced.*"

Whenever he could, Witcover liked to remind the White House that Nixon was running for office. Dan Rather, for his part, began signing off his reports with the tag line: "This is Dan Rather with the Nixon campaign at the White House." Some of the better political writers around Washington, like Peter Lisagor and Jack Germond, tried in their articles to point out the political motivation behind each of Nixon's Presidential acts. Nevertheless, it was difficult to keep writing political copy about a stubborn non-candidate, a man who made only eight token campaign outings during the entire fall.

Nixon had already taken a couple of these trips when the White House press office, which had been ignoring my pleas for accreditation, did a sudden, mysterious about-face. On September 26, a stern, no-nonsense White House secretary phoned to say that I had passed the requisite security check and could ride the press plane on the Presidential Trip to New York City, San Francisco, and Los Angeles. The trip had already begun, she said, but I could catch the Presidential party if I got out to Liberty Island in New York Harbor on the double.

I got there just in time to see the press coming into the island in three Chinook helicopters, the kind that were used to carry troops in Vietnam. The choppers circled the island three times so that the cameramen on board could get aerial shots of the Statue; you could feel the blades pounding the air.

Meanwhile, the 36th Army Band played Sousa marches. I was standing in back of the crowd—which consisted almost entirely of plaid-uniformed girls from Catholic schools and little boys in yarmulkes from Hebrew schools, all of whom were broiling and screaming for Cokes in this shadeless park right beneath the Statue's backside—when the White House press corps started charging single file through a hole in a nearby hedge. The wire-service men and the regulars headed straight for a row of phones that had been set up on a table at the rear of the park. They had just found out that Henry Kissinger and Xuan Thuy had decided to extend the peace talks for one more day. Robert Pierpoint's sound man hastily removed the mouthpiece of one of the telephones and wired a tape recorder to the inner workings of the receiver so that Pierpoint could phone the story into CBS radio. Pierpoint shouted into his microphone above the crowd noise, but the sound man kept looking at the dials on the tape recorder gesturing that something was wrong. "Come on, New York, the sound level's too high," the sound man yelled into another phone. "I *told* you the sound level was too high!"

"Christ," Pierpoint said to no one in particular. "When you try to work with these guys, they *do* not understand that we are under tremendous pressure."

Ziegler came bustling through the throng of reporters. "Lisagor!" he shouted. "Lisagor! This *is* the first time the talks have ever been extended. All the others have been one-day sessions. But, just off the record—don't push it too much." Ziegler accompanied this advice with a vague but ominous cranking gesture.

Lisagor, who was chatting with Carroll Kilpatrick, the tall, grey-haired Washington *Post* correspondent, did not seem greatly excited over the information that Ziegler had checked for him. "I don't see many Negroes in the crowd, do you, Carroll?" he said.

"Hey," he continued, "have you heard Claudel's title? He's head of Frogs for Nixon."

Claudel was Henri Claudel, the French Consul General, who had come to present some citation to the American Museum of Immigration, which Nixon was officially opening this afternoon. Nixon was using the occasion to show how much he admired America's Heritage Groups—such as Italians, Ukranians, Poles, and especially Jews. Nearly half an hour after the press arrived, Nixon himself finally appeared to the cheers of the schoolchildren and proceeded to give a speech about how immigrants made America great. The speech contained all the old "melting pot" clichés. Most of the reporters crammed themselves onto a wooden platform in the middle of the park and craned their necks for a look at Nixon.

Suddenly a small group of antiwar veterans, who had apparently crashed the rigid security of this by-invitation-only affair, began to shout "Stop the bombing, stop the war!"*

Nixon stared into the cameras on the wooden platform. "I have a message for the television screens," he said. "Let's show, besides the six over here"—he pointed to the war protesters—"the *thousands* over here." He gestured to all the schoolchildren, who were dutifully screaming "Four More Years!" Then the protesters were dragged away by the police.

Jack Germond was pacing the pavement at the back of the park, studying a tip sheet. "Jesus," he said, "this is the ultimate media event. Nixon at the Statue of Liberty! It's a piece of fiction. I just hope we get into the OTB parlor before five o'clock. I got a good horse in the eighth."

Frank Lynn, *The New York Times'* specialist on New York City politics, was covering the New York leg of Nixon's trip in accordance with the paper's tradition that a reporter from the New York office takes over whenever the President is in the metropolitan area. Bob Semple, the *Times'* White House man, immediately recognized that the day's story was Nixon's blatant grab for the ethnic vote. He tactfully suggested this to Lynn, and he also warned Lynn that the speech which Nixon was sched-

---

* Months later, some of these veterans told *The New York Times* that the New York office of their organization, Vietnam Veterans Against the War, had mysteriously received invitations in the mail a few days prior to the ceremony.

uled to deliver that evening would harp on a hackneyed theme which Nixon had put forth dozens of times in the past—that America must maintain a strong defense. The next morning, Lynn led his story with the sentence: "Calling for the maintenance of a strong defense establishment President Nixon urged Americans last night 'never to send the President of the United States to the conference table with anybody as head of the second strongest nation in the world.' "

(Several weeks later, seeing Lynn at another Nixon function in Westchester, Semple felt a curiosity welling up inside himself. He wanted to know why that lead had ended up on Lynn's story. Semple sensed that he shouldn't question Lynn about the matter, but he could not resist. He had a second or third martini and then went over to Lynn and asked, "Say, Frank, did the desk rewrite that story of yours . . .?" The moment the words were out of Semple's mouth, he saw a look of shame in Lynn's eyes and knew that he shouldn't have asked.)

Later that afternoon, after the speech was over and the President had taken off in his helicopter to go to a meeting with "Jewish leaders," the press was taken back to Manhattan on a Circle Line ferryboat and then bused to the Commodore Hotel. Dan Rather went back to Manhattan on a specially chartered tugboat. For some reason, there was a chimpanzee on the deck of the tug, and he was persuaded to clap his hands at the press assembled on the deck of the ferry. Which called for repartee from the press. "Hey, Dan," they yelled, "is that your producer?"

The monkey provided the best moment of the afternoon. The bus ride through the city was depressingly quiet. There was a pall of defeat and futility over the White House press corps. Inside the White House, their broken, sheeplike behavior seemed somehow natural. But here, in the world outside, it was painful to watch. Three thousand miles away another bunch of reporters were careening about the West Coast with the Mc-

Govern campaign. They were suffering from a blinding fatigue, but at least there were signs of life on the McGovern bus; there was noisy speculation about the prospects of a candidate who made mistakes and acted in unpredictable ways. But here in New York, the White House correspondents knew that nothing unpredictable would happen. The word that appeared most frequently in their pool reports was "uneventful." They were too resigned to the tedium to fight it. During the fall, the only major acts of protest and defiance came from the shock troops—reporters from outside the White House press corps who were only covering Nixon for a little while.

That evening, the buses picked up the reporters at the Commodore Hotel and took them across town to the Americana Hotel, where Nixon was going to address a thousand-dollar-a-plate dinner. At the top of a wide stairway, uniformed guards directed the guests to a huge ballroom on the right and the press to a smaller meeting room on the left. Total Quarantine for the press.

Lyndon Johnson, in the halcyon days when he was still wooing reporters, used to invite three or four of them, and their wives, to almost every state dinner. It gave the reporters a big thrill to see their names on the official invitation list, and on the Washington *Post's* society page the next morning. Johnson knew that this was a simple enough thing to do—letting the press in with the white folks every so often—and it earned him an enormous amount of good will. But Richard Nixon was hardly ever willing to spoil his parties by inviting the press. He didn't mind having four hundred Youths for Nixon crash the party that night. (They kept yelling "Four More Years!" on cue.) But he wanted the press out of sight.

The eighty reporters in the pressroom lined up for paper-dry turkey sandwiches and a shot at four bottles of whiskey (which were cleaned out by the first fifteen men in line). The myth dies hard that the Nixon operation is first-class all the way. But it died for me that night. The food was stale and scarce. Although the President was staying at the Waldorf, the press was billeted for the night in the Commodore, a grimy, seedy railroad hotel whose main distinction lay in having pioneered the technique of piping sexually explicit films into hotel rooms. Some of the men had been to their rooms and caught the porno classic *Vixen,* which the Commodore was featuring that week. *Vixen* was already a topic of conversation.

"Did you see the scene with the trout?"

"Isn't that something?"

"Naw, that's famous. Haven't you ever heard of the trout scene?"

"Four more years in the Commodore, that's what we need!"

THE PRESSROOM was set up like a classroom, with three rows of baize-covered tables facing a podium and three Sony television sets which were set up at the front. Most of the reporters went about setting up their Olivettis on the tables, sipping drinks from a cash bar, and talking shop. One of the local reporters appeared at the well-guarded door with a guest from the dinner across the way—a suburban Marie Antoinette, dressed in a smart neo-Moroccan pant suit. The lady sniffed delicately at the scene, taking in the dozens of slouching, puttering figures. "They don't seem to be doing anything," she said. "Why don't they report something?"

As if to satisfy the lady, the Sony monitors began to buzz and lit up finally with the image of a tuxedoed Robert Dole, the Chairman of the Republican Party. As Dole spoke, a wave of comment gradually rippled through the room. The absurdity of the insult was sinking in. Dole was speaking from a dais not two hundred feet away, just across a marbled hall, yet the press was not allowed to see him live—except for a four-man pool. It was no big deal to see Robert Dole once again in the flesh, or even Nixon, but the restriction was so petty that it began to loom large as a taunt.

"I looked forward to a Convention full of surprises and excitement," Chairman Dole was saying, "and those of you who were there know just how exciting it was. Tonight we are fortunate to have a video tape of the most exciting moments of the Convention, and we are going to show it to you on these big screens." There were different reactions to this statement in the pressroom. There were a few reporters who probably agreed; one or two others may have concluded that Republicans simply had unusual criteria for excitement; but most of the reporters were stunned by the enormity of the lie. The room began to reverberate with jokes about the "exciting moments" being shown on the monitors— Sammy Davis hugging Nixon, Pat taking a bow, Nixon's banal acceptance speech. Ralph Harris of Reuters, a small, rumpled, grey-headed Englishman who had been stationed at the White House for many years, stared at the monitor and shouted: "Throw Nixon out of work!" John Farmer, a political writer for the Philadelphia *Bulletin,* looked at his typewriter and kept repeating, "You can't cover this guy. They won't let you." Peter Lisagor shook his head and walked off to join the other pool reporters in the ballroom. "I've got to smell this crowd," he announced. "I've got a feeling you really got to smell this crowd to know it."

These comments were mostly muted because Ron Ziegler was on the prowl, pacing up and down the aisles between the rows of tables. Not that there was any crack in Ziegler's bland smile to show he was picking up hostile vibes. No, Ziegler was like an expert floorwalker who would spot a shoplifter, walk calmly to the nearest phone, ring Security, and adjust his pocket hanky as the security thugs dragged the shoplifter away.

Ziegler was now hovering around the front of the room, where Jim Doyle was sitting. Doyle had locked horns with Ziegler at a briefing earlier in the evening.

Doyle kept asking whether "the candidate" was going to have a press conference during the trip. Ziegler became furious and finally snapped: "Don't worry, we'll tell you if there's going to be any news conference, Doyle!"

"Hey, Ron!" Doyle now shouted at Ziegler. "Do *you* get to go inside?"

"Yes," said Ziegler, staunchly oblivious to the sarcasm. "I'm going in with the Youth for Nixon. I'm going in right now." And in he went.

Meanwhile, the Exciting Moments movie had ended and the action had shifted to the simultaneous fund-raiser in Chicago, linked by closed circuit, where Anne Armstrong, the Party's Vice Chairman, was introducing Spiro Agnew. "All day long," she said, "I've been trying to think of one word to describe Vice President Agnew."

"I'll bet it's shithead," said Doyle, in a loud voice. "It'll bring down the house."

Anne Armstrong listed a number of virtues she associated with the Vice President. "And he can transmit these qualities to others," she said.

"Like a leper!" said Doyle.

Just then, Gerald Warren, the deputy press secretary, appeared at the door. He was in a floorwalker's suit like Ziegler's.

"What's it like inside, Gerry?" Doyle asked him. "You been inside?"

Warren slumped his shoulders and let his tongue hang out. "Hot!" he said.

"Nice to know there *is* an inside," said Doyle.

At 10:30, Nixon entered. The reporters watched him on TV as he made his progress through the lobby, came up the stairs, stepped onto the dais, acknowledged applause, and started to speak. There was a low steady clatter in the room now. The reporters were intently taking transcript on their portables. All in a day's work. Listen for the lead and file the story. Here and there, people were quietly boiling with indignation—mostly people who were not regulars at the White House. Cassie Mackin sitting in the front row taking notes, looked grim. "Isn't this incredible?" I said to her.

"The Republicans certainly have things organized, don't they?" was all she said.

"Why do they just sit here and take it?" I asked.

"They've been worn down," she said, very low. "We need some new ones."

Nixon was making his standard speech, embellished with little winks, gestures, and turns of phrase ("Now, in very personal terms, may I tell you . . .") that implied that he understood that a very special bond existed between him and the fat-cat audience. Nixon's behavior with these people bordered on crassness and cried out to be described; it was a story in itself. But, as far as I could tell, such a story did not suggest itself to the reporters who watched him, and certainly none ever got into print.

About halfway through his speech, Nixon got to the part where he announced how happy he was that young people could vote. It was significant, Nixon congratulated himself, that "right here in this room, at this great dinner where it costs, I understand, a great deal to sit down and eat, that the young people were able to come in and at least enjoy the speeches."

That was too much for Doyle. The needle in his bullshit detector hit the red zone. He was up on his feet shouting at the tube. "How about the press!" he screamed. "How about the press!"

"You're not young, Jim," somebody said. "You gotta be young to get in." But Doyle went on yelling at the monitor, half joking and half off the handle.

"This is terrible! This is awful shit. I just want to take a look at him! Is he alive? How do I know he's alive?" People stopped typing for a moment, turned around in their chairs to look at Doyle, assured themselves that he wasn't really dangerous, and then went back to their jobs. Doyle sat down and looked around him, half expecting to see everyone else up and raging. All he saw was the White House press corps, hunched over the baize like blackjack addicts, taking down every word Nixon uttered. At the end of the trip, Doyle wrote a piece about the "surrealistic atmosphere" of Nixon's isolation, but the article failed to match the fire of his outburst.

After the dinner ended, Cassie Mackin went out into the hall to do her "standup" in front of the NBC camera crew. She got as far as the second sentence, and then she doubled over in a fit of laughter and had to stop. The guests were being allowed to leave through only one of the doors, but were trying to get out through all of them. The beautifully dressed people still in the ballroom were actually pounding on the doors, and the security guards and police were leaning against these doors from the other side.

"They're banging on the doors to get out!" Cassie kept saying between paroxysms. "I'd love to see them break the doors down!" Then she would compose herself, signal the cameraman, try to do her introduction and collapse in laughter again. It was not healthy to flaunt that kind of an attitude around the Nixon people, and one didn't have to be prescient to predict that within forty-eight hours Cassie would run afoul of the Thought Police.

The next morning, the reporters were bused to La-Guardia. They walked past Nixon's blue and silver plane, which the White House people insisted on calling "The Spirit of '76," and boarded an oversized Eastern 727 which was at once tackier and less comfortable than either of the McGovern press planes. As I came to the top of the ramp, I met Cassie Mackin again. "Welcome to the Spirit of 1984," she said.

There were four or five assistant press secretaries aboard—Tricia Nixon replicas in neat skirts and blouses. They sat in the first-class section with typewriters and a mimeograph machine, and about halfway to Oakland they began passing out the prepared text for the speech that Nixon would make at a thousand-dollar-a-plate lunch in San Francisco. They also handed out the text of the speech the President would give that night in Los Angeles. Since both speeches ran about ten legal-sized pages in length, the White House press people had helpfully prepared a page of salient excerpts from each of the speeches.

I was kneeling on a seat in front of Lisagor and Bob Semple, turned around so that I could talk to them. Semple was typing away on his portable Olympia and sipping wine when the handout arrived; he immediately scanned the excerpt sheets and looked alarmed. He underlined a sentence from the Los Angeles speech that went: "Those who call for a redistribution of income and a confiscation of wealth are not speaking for the interests of people . . ." Nixon was obviously referring to George McGovern, but at no point in either speech did he actually mention McGovern's name.

"There is some pretty sleazy operating going on in this thing," said Semple. "I don't understand it. The guy obviously isn't reading us." He laughed. "I mean, I don't think McGovern is calling for confiscation of wealth, do you?"

Semple began to read the San Francisco text. He underlined a sentence which referred to certain "proposals that would put the United States in the position of having the second strongest" Navy, Air Force and Army in the world. "It would be a move toward war," the speech said. The author of these nefarious "proposals" was not identified.

"All right," said Semple, "let's say we use a lead saying President Nixon declared today that Senator George McGovern's defense policies represented—you know, this is simple, wireservice stuff—*a move toward war*. Now how long do you think it would take for McGovern . . .?" Semple laughed, apparently at the idea of McGovern launching an indignant counterattack. "I mean, that's tough business."

"Well," said Lisagor, "that's how it's gonna be handled."

"It's an interesting question," Semple went on enthusiastically. He had curly brown hair, a long, smooth, boyish face, and blue eyes that widened and lit up whenever he grew excited about something. "I think just to put that in your lead is not necessarily serving Nixon's purpose—not when you're using outrageous statements like that."

"Even outrageous remarks seem to help Nixon this year," I pointed out.

"And to be recorded flatly, it helps him more," said Semple, completely contradicting his first position.

"Yes, but I don't know why that is," I said.

"I can tell you why," said Lisagor. "It's because Nixon is one of the best students of journalistic formats of any politician we've had in a number of years. He understands the one-dimensional format of the wire service, where you can't qualify anything and where you've got to go with a hard punchy lead, and that's what this speech is designed to do."

"Well, I'm trying to work out a way around it," said Semple firmly.

"Share it with me," Lisagor said drily.

"Well," said Semple, looking at the handout again, "I may just say that he came to California and played on very familiar themes in terms that seem to admit to no debate, that show no consideration for the complexity of the issues."

Semple thought that over for a moment and then added, "Yeah, but then the desk will go like this." He made a ripping sound and tore up an imaginary piece of copy.

"Yeah, right," said Lisagor.

"Yeah," said Semple, to me. "But not because the editors are pro-Nixon. It's just the rules—and they're good rules. But I'll tell you about that later." And he went back to his wine and his typewriter, leaving me to talk to Lisagor.

"The rules of objectivity are such," said Lisagor, "that a man can make political capital out of them by being clever in the way he presents a particular issue." Joe McCarthy, said Lisagor, was the prime example of a

man who had taken advantage of the rules. McCarthy
made outrageous accusations, knowing full well that the
wires would print his statements deadpan, with no quali-
fications and no counterstatements from the people he
accused. McCarthy had understood what made a headline, what made a good lead. Nixon knew these things,
too. He knew that the "move toward war" statement
would make a good, crisp lead for the wires.

(Nixon also knew that his attack on McGovern
would get good play, while McGovern's defense, coming
a day or two later, would not have as much impact. Nixon himself stated this law of journalism back in the fifties, when he saw himself as a victim of attacks from the
left. "A charge is usually put on the front page; the defense is buried among the deodorant ads," he said.)

"All politicians make these simplistic charges," said
Lisagor.

"It becomes a problem for the press to put these
charges in proper perspective. But a lot of reporters feel
that they've discharged their obligation if they just report what the man said."

IN THE NEXT THREE DAYS, Bob Semple wrote three stories about the trip—one for the *Times* of September 28,
another on September 29, and a final piece for the Sunday "Week in Review" section on October 1. In his first
piece he wrote:

The President discussed neither his programs nor his
opponent's in detail. Instead, he employed broad strokes to
paint the South Dakotan as a willing captive of the left who
had isolated himself from Mr. Nixon's vision of the American temperament.

But not once did Semple write that Nixon had *wrongly* accused McGovern of wanting to confiscate wealth
and weaken the country militarily. In effect, his stories
said that Nixon had begun to use strong rhetoric and

had thrown some tough accusations at McGovern, but then McGovern was doing the same thing to Nixon. We talked about the stories while he was writing them, and at one point Semple said: "You can say that Nixon's attack on McGovern was couched in severe language and general terms, but you can't then write—'and bore no resemblance to what McGovern has been saying.'"

SEMPLE WAS NOT INTIMIDATED by the White House; it was just that he was a model *Times*man, and therefore painfully conscious of the rules of objective journalism. He came from a large, close-knit, cultured Midwestern family. (His father, who ran the Wyandotte Chemical Company, not only served as president of the Detroit Symphony, but also sat in as second clarinetist several times a season.) Early in his teens, he was sent to Andover, where he ran the school paper. Later, he went to Yale, became chairman of the *Daily News*, and acquired an accent somewhat similar to that of William Buckley, who had held the same position in an earlier era. After graduating he studied history at Berkeley for a year and flirted with the idea of going to law school. But he could not face the prospect of more schooling; he rejected the professions one by one until he finally settled upon journalism *faute de mieux*.

In 1961, he went to work for the fledgling *National Observer;* two years later he wrote to James Reston, asking for a job on the *New York Times*. He was hired and served a two-year apprenticeship as a deskman in the Washington Bureau. By 1965, he was lobbying heavily for a job as reporter, and Tom Wicker, who was then bureau chief, finally made him the No. 2 man at the White House. From then on, he rose quickly, for he wrote gracefully, worked fiendishly hard, and charmed everyone with his open, good-natured manner. In late 1967, Wicker assigned him to cover the long-shot candidacy of Richard Nixon.

Semple would later think that he had been a good

choice for the assignment, for he was able to convince the Nixon people, who hated the *Times,* that he was looking at the candidate with "a fresh eye." In one of his first pieces, Semple wrote that the old, Red-baiting Nixon had vanished. "In his place," wrote Semple, "stands a walking monument to reason, civility, frankness." (Even in June 1973, after the Watergate scandal had broken, Semple claimed that he was not embarrassed by this early assessment. "I guess I'm victimized by the same thing as Scotty Reston," he said. "I'm perfectly prepared to believe in redemption.")

Later, after Nixon had won the nomination and launched his Presidential campaign in earnest, Semple became less enchanted with him, but found it hard to express his doubts within the narrow, hard-news form of reporting preferred by the *Times.* In the fall of 1968, a mildly worded piece he wrote pointing out Nixon's trick of declaring "moratoriums" on issues he did not wish to discuss was greeted with skepticism by the editors; they balked at running it. The *Times* was loathe to break away from the traditional, simplistic forms of election coverage, and Semple had to fight for over a week to make them accept a piece which contained so much analysis. Though he continued to write such pieces over the course of the next four years, he did so with extreme caution, for he shared the *Times'* fear of mixing conjecture with straight news. Although he admitted in 1973 that the press needed some new form of journalism to deal with the obscurantism and dissimulation of the White House, he was always leary of pioneering such forms himself. "I just didn't know how good I was at it," he said.

When Semple followed Nixon into the White House, his belief in redemption continued to spring eternal. Though he realized, and wrote, that Nixon's staff was concerned mainly with re-electing the President, he still searched for higher motivations. In April 1970, for instance, he wrote a magazine piece about John Ehrlichman in which he depicted the Nixon aide as a "compas-

sionate and easy-going" middle American who was seeking to push Nixon away from the right and toward the middle of the road on issues such as welfare and civil rights. Not all of Semple's colleagues agreed with this appraisal.

"Why are you so nice to Ehrlichman?" Marty Nolan asked him. "He's just a sleazy arrogant thug like the rest of them around here."

"I think there's such a thing as being too cynical," Semple replied.

Even in 1973 Semple did not feel compelled to apologize for the gentle treatment he had given Ehrlichman. He had been writing about the "substance of ideas, pieces of legislation" rather than about Ehrlichman's character, he said. He had avoided denigrating Ehrlichman's character in order not to affront Ehrlichman. "I had to keep lines open to Ehrlichman to find out what the hell Nixon was doing."

Semple prided himself on keeping the lines open. It was for this reason, he said, that he remained at the White House no matter how discouraging the assignment became. "There were many months when nobody would see me. But I felt that it would be even more difficult for somebody else to give it a try. They were more likely to return *my* phone calls, simply because they knew what I looked like."

Semple drove himself hard in the White House job, often growing so absorbed in his duties that he became woefully absent-minded. (On a later Presidential trip to California, for instance, he woke up one morning in his hotel room, packed his suitcase, placed it outside the door, and heard the baggage handler pick it up; it was only as he was about to go out for breakfast that he realized he had packed his shoes. He had to spend the day padding around in his stocking feet.) He was one of three or four men in the White House press corps who went beyond the briefings and press conferences to cultivate sources on the staff, study the White House hierarchy, and dig out original "inside" stories. But by

time of the 1972 campaign, he was growing increasingly bored and frustrated. With the election at stake, his best sources were drying up. "When you're reduced to the status, as we were toward the end, of listening to Nixon's speeches and listening to Ronald L. Ziegler once a day, then you're reduced to guesswork," he said later. "And that is not work for a grown man."

Of course, John Osborne's work sometimes consisted largely of guesswork, and it was consistently the most informative writing on the White House. But Semple was playing by the rules of *The New York Times,* and they did not allow for guesswork. Nor did he push Ziegler especially hard for more information. That wasn't Semple's style. Semple did not want to demean the dignity of the *Times* by getting into any open fights with the Administration. Ziegler usually treated him cordially, and Semple did not seem to know, or want to know, about the ways in which Ziegler abused reporters from lesser papers. Semple resigned himself to writing pieces which did little more than report what Nixon said, and much of his reporting in the fall of 1972 lacked guts. At the end of the year, he left the White House and became a deputy national editor in New York. Many of his colleagues guessed that he was being groomed to be chief of the Washington Bureau in four or five years time.

Yet people who knew Semple sometimes felt that for all of his complaisance and willingness to play by the rules, he anguished over his failure to confront the Nixon people in the White House. Among his closest friends were some of the toughest Washington journalists—Tom Wicker, Peter Lisagor, and John Osborne—and he often talked to them about the problems of covering the Administration. Semple went out of his way to do things which seemed almost to be acts of contrition. For instance, he pulled the few strings he had in the White House to try to get credentials for Hunter Thompson of *Rolling Stone.* Semple knew Thompson slightly from the days when they both worked on the

National Observer, and he liked Thompson's wildly satirical writing. He seemed to enjoy using his influence to put Thompson on the same plane with Ron Ziegler.

WHEN THE PRESS PLANE LANDED IN OAKLAND, the weather was gloomy and overcast. The White House operatives and the Secret Service immediately herded the whole pack of journalists into a tiny area which had been formed by stretching yellow plastic ropes around red, white and blue oil drums. The band was playing "Yankee Doodle Dandy" and the crowd, drummed up by the Nixon advance team, was pressing against the airport fence. I looked around and suddenly spotted Hunter Thompson heading for the press enclosure in his springy lope, looking only moderately bizarre in his blue pants, white jacket, red-and-white shirt, and light blue aviator's sunglasses. I introduced him to a Secret Service man, who got him his credentials. Meanwhile, Air Force One had landed and taxied to within fifty yards of the press. The door swung open and Nixon stepped out on the ramp, grimacing and waving. "Go get 'em Dick," Thompson yelled. "Throw the Bomb!" The whine of the plane's engines drowned him out, but he got a few funny looks from immediate neighbors. "Fifty years more!" he yelled. "Thousand-year Reich!"

Then Nixon headed for his panzer-limousine and the press headed for the buses, with the women in curlers screaming "Dan, Dan!" at Dan Rather, who acknowledged the screams with a curt nod and little shooting motion of the index finger, reminiscent of Elvis Presley. They carted all the reporters to a newly finished terminus of San Francisco's BART system, where Nixon was sighted for a moment, on the other side of a glass partition, shaking hands with six subway functionaries. Then to a San Francisco Hotel to eat a buffet lunch in the pressroom and hear Nixon's speech piped in over loudspeakers. Most of the men filed, it being early afternoon, typing furiously and then holding up a page and shouting "Western!" for the plane's resident Western Union man to pick it up.

Next the reporters flew to Los Angeles, where they saw the President emerge from the plane again. The press was bused to the Century Plaza Hotel, where the Nixon people had set up a press headquarters in a little pseudo-Spanish meeting room that had a tiled fountain in its center. Standing outside the pressroom in the late afternoon, Hunter Thompson told Bob Semple how appalling it was to observe the White House press, even for a few hours. "They're like slugs on a snail farm," he said, taking a nervous puff on his cigarette holder. "Jesus, Ziegler treats them like garbagemen and they just take it."

Semple was beginning to reply when Ziegler himself rounded a corner and Thompson went over to ask him a question. McGovern had stupidly charged that Nixon was soon going to introduce a right-to-work law and put an end to collective bargaining—which even McGovern must have known was ridiculous. Thompson asked Ziegler, talking very fast, "Uh, will there be any comment from you people on McGovern's charge that Nixon is backing a right-to-work law?"

Ziegler didn't even stop to look at him. "No!" he said, but it was more of a popgun explosion than a word. Thompson was stunned by this display of rudeness.

"Does he ever talk like that to you?" he asked Semple.

"Yes," said Semple, and mumbled something about how the job was making him crazy. "Excuse me," he said, "I have to get a martini."

That night, there was a large antiwar demonstration outside the Century Plaza. Many of the reporters watched the milling, chanting throng from the hotel balconies, which gave the demonstration a gladiatorial air. A few reporters, Jim Doyle among them, went out to have a closer look at the demonstration. As he stood outside the hotel, watching the protesters wave signs and beat wooden sticks against an iron railing, he said, "I used to think this was power. But these people have no power."

By 9:30, most of the reporters had returned to the press headquarters in the Granada Room to watch another thousand-dollar-a-plate dinner on the same Sony monitors which had been set up in New York the night before. The dinner was taking place just upstairs. This time the featured guest was Bob Hope, in his pathetic court-jester-to-the-GOP incarnation.

"McGovern's running out of money," piped Hope. "Yesterday, he mugged an Avon lady!" You could divide the pressroom into two types—those who laughed and those who didn't. Cassie Mackin sat there stone-faced, taking notes and furiously chain-smoking small cigars. David Broder looked somber and angry. Germond slumped in his chair, half-asleep, his head in one hand. Bob Pierpoint patted a dour John Osborne on the shoulder, rolled his eyes, and said, "You inspired?"

"McGovern had a hundred-dollar-a-plate dinner the other night," said Hope, "and they stole the plates." Over in another corner of the Granada Room a bunch of reporters were jiggling with laughter over Hope's routine. Bill Theis, a white-haired mesomorph from the Hearst papers found it very funny, as did some other men from Midwestern papers. But no one found it as killingly funny as George Embrey of the Columbus *Dispatch*.

George Embrey loved the President. Nixon had a habit, whenever he got into his helicopter at the airport, of going to the window for a moment and waving at the crowd. George Embrey was the only member of the press who would always wave back. "Goodbye," he would cry softly as the helicopter started to take Nixon away, "Goodbye!" Embrey was a blank-faced, clean-cut man who wore white shirts, striped ties, neat suits, well-shined shoes; he spent a great deal of time at the National Press Club bar, soliciting votes to become the club's secretary. He liked pool assignments, and once blew up at Ziegler for not letting him follow Nixon out the kitchen exit of a hotel. "My job is to stay with him *at all times!*" said Embrey. What he really wanted, many of his colleagues thought, was to become a Secret Service man.

He liked to hang out with other ultraconservative reporters, like the man from the Dallas *Morning News.* Sitting together on the bus, they chatted happily about how much they loathed George McGovern. On one trip Embrey expressed shock that McGovern had used the phrase "Kiss my ass." Embrey said that he had washed his son's mouth out with soap for using that kind of language—someone ought to do the same for George McGovern.

Embrey adored Nixon, but he was not considered the foremost shill in the White House. That distinction was generally conceded to Frank van der Linden of the Nashville *Banner.* Van der Linden was a short, redheaded man with the thin lips and rimless glasses of a mean little principal of a very backward high school. The Administration fed Van der Linden an "exclusive interview" whenever it sensed that the right wing was about to blow. In December 1971, when some of the White House aides were beginning to worry that John Ashbrook's insurgent candidacy might steal the right from Nixon, a White House aide named Harry Dent summoned Van der Linden. Harry Dent, a former factotum to Strom Thurmond, did little chores for President Nixon like rescuing Southern textile firms which were about to lose defense contracts just because they refused to hire Negroes. Frank van der Linden had written a book based on the premise that Nixon was a great leader because he was a super-hawk. "In private, he is tougher than Spiro Agnew," Van der Linden said approvingly in his book. One of Harry Dent's jobs was to keep Van der Linden happy by reinforcing the impression that Nixon would nuke anybody in the world for the sake of peace. So on December 24, 1971, Van der Linden wrote this in the *Banner:*

Washington—President Nixon is moving to quell a revolt in the right wing of the Republican party by urging the mutineers to have faith in his devotion to his aim of "keeping America No. 1."

"That's what I hear him say more than anything else—'I'm not going to let the United States ever be less than No. 1,'" said Harry Dent, his chief political technician in the White House.

And so on. Frank van der Linden also liked the Vice President, even though Agnew wasn't as tough as Nixon. When Agnew went on his trip to Greece, Van der Linden led the pack of shills and conservative columnists who accompanied him. In one of his first dispatches, Van der Linden described Agnew as a "consummate diplomat," which set the general tone of the reporting. Walter Mears was also along on the trip, and he felt the odd man out. One day on the plane, Agnew announced that the U.S. would keep sending aid to Greece, no matter what Congress wanted to do. After the party landed, Mears went to his hotel room and filed the story. Later he found out that Van der Linden and the rest of the reporters had agreed to "embargo" the story until the Agnew people put out a full text of Agnew's remarks. They always insisted on handouts, because they didn't like to have to take notes; the Agnew people always obliged.

When Mears came down to breakfast at the little hotel in Crete the following morning, he found he had unwittingly broken an embargo. "Van der Linden starts leaping all over me and screaming, waving his arms and raising hell," Mears later recalled. Van der Linden and his cronies got so ugly that Mears finally called New York and told the AP to hold the story for a day. But even then, Van der Linden wouldn't lay off him. He kept bitching and whining at regular intervals throughout the day about how Mears had tried to betray the group. Finally, at Knossos, standing right in front of the Labyrinth, Van der Linden started in again. Mears decided to shove him into the Labyrinth. But just as Mears was about to deliver the blow, Spiro Agnew appeared around a corner, surrounded by Secret Service men, waving, smiling, and yelling hello. Thus was Frank van der Linden saved from meeting the Minotaur.

THE NEXT MORNING IN LOS ANGELES, Nixon made a final speech to a group of cancer scientists amidst the tacky splendors of the Biltmore Hotel. Then most of the reporters flew home to Washington with Nixon, but Cassie Mackin stayed behind. She was completing her two-week tour of duty with the Nixon campaign and was therefore expected to do an overview piece. She had been thinking about it for several days, and she knew precisely what she wanted to say. She shot her "stand-ups" at the Biltmore immediately after Nixon's speech and went to the local NBC affiliate station to edit the piece and feed it to New York. At the time the piece went on the air, she was boarding a plane to fly back to Washington, so she did not find out until late the next morning that she had just filed the most controversial piece of the year. Cassie Mackin was the first, if not the only, member of the press to point out that the emperor had no clothes.

She opened her report by observing that "the Nixon campaign is, for the most part, a series of speeches before closed audiences, invited guests only." Then she moved into the heart of the matter. She said: "On defense spending and welfare reform, the two most controversial issues in this campaign . . . the two issues that are almost haunting George McGovern, there is a serious question of whether President Nixon is setting up straw men by leaving the very strong impression that McGovern is making certain proposals which in fact he is not."

She showed a film clip of Nixon saying: "There are some who believe that we should make cuts in our defense budget . . . that it doesn't really make any difference whether the United States had the second strongest

Navy, the second strongest Army, the second strongest Air Force in the world."

Then Mackin said: "The President obviously meant McGovern's proposed defense budget, but his criticism never specified how the McGovern plan would weaken the country. On welfare, the President accuses McGovern of wanting to give those on welfare more than those who work, which is not true. On tax reform, the President says McGovern is calling for 'confiscation of wealth,' which is not true."

Mackin concluded: "When all is said and done, it's like Mr. Nixon says, he is the President and it is the power of the Presidency that makes it possible to stay above the campaign and answer only the questions of his choice."

Before the Nightly News was off the air, Herb Klein was on the phone to NBC, demanding corrections. The next morning, Reuven Frank, the president of NBC News, looked at Mackin's script and could not find anything to correct. Nevertheless, as Mackin was about to leave her home for the White House, which was her assignment for the day, she got a phone call from NBC telling her to come to the office instead. That was the first she heard about the White House protests, and she had to spend the day compiling background material from Nixon and McGovern speeches to substantiate her report. She sent the material to New York and heard nothing more about the matter. Rumors circulated in Washington all week to the effect that NBC was getting ready to fire her, but the rumors were apparently generated by alarmists in the McGovern office.

The extraordinary thing about her piece was that it was virtually unique. Nobody else who reported on the trip said in simple declarative sentences that Nixon had made demonstrably false accusations about three of McGovern's programs. Bob Semple said that you couldn't do it—it was against the rules. But Mackin did it, without even thinking about the consequences. Even months later, she did not like to talk about the piece, because she felt that it put her in the position of defending an action that was natural and obvious, an action that required no defense.

The reason that the piece packed such a wallop was that it was so simple and direct. There were no lengthy film clips to *prove* that McGovern didn't believe in confiscation of wealth. There were no complicated references to "observers" or "experts" who would vouch for McGovern. Mackin was confident of her own honesty and intelligence, and she simply expected people to believe her when she said that Nixon was wrong. This was a revolutionary belief; hers was one of the few reports on the White House during the fall that did not automatically assume a need for dozens of built-in defenses against an anticipated assault from the Administration. Perhaps it was no coincidence that it was a woman who went for Nixon's jugular. Mackin was an outsider. She had neither the opportunity nor the desire to travel with the all-male pack; therefore, she was not infected with the pack's chronic defensiveness and defeatism. Like Helen Thomas and Sarah McClendon, she could still call a spade a spade.

OTHER PEOPLE ON THE TRIP wrote tough pieces about the absurd isolation of the President and the lack of access to even his most junior advisers. David Broder wrote the toughest. In fact, it was clear that Broder had seen things in San Francisco and Los Angeles that touched off his obsession with the fragility of institutions. Broder took one look around and sensed that Nixon was trying to kill off that most sacred of institutions, the Presidential election. He wrote:

In every way possible, the Nixon entourage seems to be systematically stifling the kind of dialogue that has in the past been thought to be the heart of the Presidential campaign. That is the source of McGovern's unhappiness, but it's a problem the press must address—directly, even at the risk of being thought partisan.

An election is supposed to be the time a politician—even a President—submits himself to the jury of the American voters. As a lawyer, Richard Nixon knows that if he were as highhanded with a jury as he's being in this campaign, he'd risk being cited for contempt of court.

The press of the country ought to be calling Mr. Nixon on this—not for George McGovern's sake, but for the sake of its own tattered reputation and for the public which it presumes to serve.

The editors of the country and the television news chiefs ought to tell Mr. Nixon in plain terms, that before they spend another nickel to send their reporters and camera crews around the country with him, they want a system set up in which journalists can be journalists again, and a President campaigns as a candidate, not a touring emperor.

With that, Broder retired from the campaign trail for the rest of the year. "You shouldn't write that kind of a piece and then come back as an 'objective reporter' immediately thereafter," he said. So he left the day-to-day work to his chastened White House colleagues, who actually seemed to like the piece—since they were always momentarily braced by any show of balls—and he went off with Haynes Johnson to take the pulse of the electorate.

I WENT ON ONLY ONE MORE "TRIP OF THE PRESIDENT" (as it said on the hexagonal press tag that hung around my neck). This was in late October, an excursion to Westchester and Nassau counties, fat suburbs to the north and east, respectively, of New York City. Nixon was going to motorcade through Westchester County and then fly to Nassau for a big rally. Since it was only a day trip, it afforded small papers a chance to see the campaign on the cheap. Enough reporters came to fill seven press buses. In honor of the motorcade, the Nixon people revived the custom of piping in a running pool report over the PA system of the buses—a technique which they had pioneered during the 1968 campaign.

"It was a big leap forward in press bus technology," recalled Stuart Loory. "You no longer had to rely on the pool-after-the-fact. You had the pooler up there broadcasting, so you could sit back there in the press bus and know what was happening a mile ahead. This guy became known as the Z-pooler, Z for Ziegler, because he rode in Ziegler's car."

In more innocent times, they used to let anybody be Z-pooler. Loory once had the job when Nixon went to Manila. "Having seen a lot of manufactured demonstrations, by what we used to call Rent-a-Crowd in Moscow," said Loory, "I noticed that the Manila demonstration had all the signs of being manufactured, as if John Ehrlichman had been there with the balloons beforehand. And I reported it that way over the microphone. My colleagues loved it." Ziegler had been sitting next to Loory in the car, connected by earphone to almost every other aide on the White House staff. "Ziegler was on a different channel, and he was getting feedbacks on what I was saying, or else he was getting heat from Haldeman, I don't know. They were embarrassed. They wanted to cut me off but they couldn't. So they started pointing out positive things for me to report. I would attribute that stuff to Ziegler. I was having fun. I was really enjoying it. That was the last time they let me have that job."

After the Loory fiasco, the White House began to refine the technique of Z-pooling, and by October 1972, they had found the ideal Z-pooler—Forrest Boyd of Mutual Broadcasting. Boyd was such a congenial type that you could hardly tell he was a reporter. In fact, Boyd was one of the very few journalists whom Nixon sometimes invited to a state dinner. Boyd was up there with Ziegler on this cold, gusty October afternoon. First came a limousine containing Nelson and Happy Rockefeller, then came the 500,000-dollar tank carrying Pat and Dick Nixon, then a Secret Service car, then a pool car, then five open pickup trucks containing rheumy-eyed, shivering, mutinous network camera crews, then the seven press buses full of reporters guzzling soda and beer and listening to the squawk of the PA system. Though Forrest Boyd identified himself quite shamelessly at the outset of the running commentary, almost everyone on the buses assumed that he was a White House flack. Even Bruce Biossat, a syndicated columnist for the Newspaper Enterprise Association who later wrote an amusing column about the commentary, labored under this false impression.

At the outset, Boyd established himself as a master of euphemism. "The President is waving to people along the street . . ." he said. "A few are holding signs giving a message."

A "sign giving a message" meant a pro-McGovern sign. There were an astounding number of them that day, considering that Westchester was supposed to be solid Nixon country. The messages included: "Re-elect the Dike Bomber," and "Robots for Nixon, People for McGovern." In fact, the anti-Nixon turnout was so striking that Rowley Evans, sitting in one of the buses, became visibly alarmed. The hundreds of McGovern signs did not quite jibe with the Nixon landslide that he and Novak were confidently predicting.

"Rowley was really sweating," one reporter later said to another. "I mean, he just *shat*."

"That's funny," said the other reporter, "Rowley usually goes back to his room to get nervous."

"Yeah," said the first reporter, "it's hard to get him nervous in public."

FORREST BOYD MANAGED TO IGNORE all the anti-Nixon signs and plowed on in his Kurt Gowdy voice.

"There's a lot of noise here," he said in Mamaroneck. "Some favorable, some unfavorable, but of course the favorable are outshouting the others by a considerable margin . . . The President has signed a football apparently belonging to the Mamaroneck Midgets. The President is going back to the limousine, I'm going to see if I can get back there too! . . . This crowd is really terrific! It's almost impossible to get through here!

"We're an hour and fifteen minutes behind schedule. The most we've ever been behind before was forty-five minutes, *so this may be an historic first*. We're trying to make up time, but it's impossible. The crowds have just been too big, bigger than expected. Ron Ziegler is very apologetic."

The reporters on the bus found this all very funny, but they listened carefully for the crowd count.

"We have an estimate here from Captain Keefe of the New York State Police, who will be keeping us posted. Up to the last town the estimate is that 312,000 people have seen the President today. Hold it. We just got a new figure on Larchmont. The chief there says it was 80,000 not 50,000. Make the cumulative total 342,000."

Len Garment and Bill Safire, two White House aides who were on one of the buses, kept promoting Captain Keefe every time the estimate went up. *"Captain Keefe!"* Safire would say. "I'd say that makes him *Lieutenant Governor* Keefe!" Later that day Ziegler told Semple, "Listen, that's an honest estimate. This Captain Keefe makes an honest estimate." There was a pause while the implication sank in. "Of course," Ziegler added, "all our estimates are honest."

Just a few weeks before, Ziegler had assured the press that at least 700,000 people had come out to see Nixon in Atlanta. Maybe more. Many reporters printed the figure, or something approaching it. Only Jim Perry of the *National Observer* bothered to check it out. He phoned the Atlanta Public Works Department and found out that each city block was about 400 feet long. He generously estimated that 400 people a block, 5 rows deep, both sides of the street, for 15 blocks, had seen Richard Nixon. That made 60,000 people. Then he threw in another 15,000 people to cover the side streets between the blocks. "So," he wrote, "in an act of charity I'm willing to say that 75,000 people turned out to welcome Richard Nixon to Atlanta."

Yet the other reporters on the bus, especially the wire-service men, still took the White House estimates seriously. The word going around the buses that afternoon was that you could trust Captain Keefe; he was an honest estimator. The pack was yapping at full cry.

The motorcade ended in Tarrytown, where the press had dinner at the Hilton Inn. George Embrey was glowing with enthusiasm. "What impressed me," Embrey told a crony from a Buffalo paper over the roast beef, "was that he got his best reception in that *working-class* section of New Rochelle. I'll tell you one thing," he went on, looking straight into his friend's eyes. "There was no busing-in today. Absolutely nobody was bused in."

After supper, the press flew in Air Force helicopters to Uniondale, Long Island. The choppers were dark and noisy and it was impossible to work inside them, so the reporters simply sat there, with their backs to the walls, and tried to turn around to look out the portholes. They disembarked in a vast parking lot outside a gigantic white whale of an auditorium called the Nassau Coliseum. Thus far, it had been a normal Nixon trip—meaningless, boring, predictable, slightly grotesque, and hardly worth the $87.50 transportation charge.* Suddenly, inside the Coliseum, it turned ugly.

No sooner had the President arrived on the platform in the middle of the Coliseum floor and started to speak, than a small group in the third balcony began to jeer. The rally had been tightly screened; admission was by

---

* There is a common misconception that the candidates picked up the tab for the travel expenses of the press. Bus rides, it is true, were usually gratis. But for plane trips, the candidates' staffs normally billed each of the news organizations on board for 150 per cent of first class fare. The reporters paid their own hotel bills and were then reimbursed by their organizations.

ticket only and the local GOP organizations had handed out the tickets. Somehow, a few dozen hecklers had got tickets, and now they were way up in the gallery behind Nixon, small figures in the blue fluorescent haze, shouting: "Stop the war!"

They had only been chanting for about a minute when a coalition of cops, men in trench coats, and ordinary spectators began beating them up. They clobbered the hecklers with a merciless series of roundhouse rights, then stomped and kicked the ones who fell down, and finally dragged them off. At the sight of the protesters getting their bones broken, the crowd of 16,000 gave off a sustained, sickening Nuremberg roar.

Nixon turned around, looked up, and turned back with a broad grin on his face. Maybe, as some reporters speculated later, it was a grin of nervousness, but it was Nixon's only immediate comment on the brutality. Later in his speech, Nixon had only praise for the cops in the auditorium. "I have seen tonight the blue uniforms of the police," he said. "Give them the backing and respect they deserve." He also declared that his Administration had ended "the age of permissiveness."

Other hecklers continued to jeer at Nixon from the floor. Some were ejected by guards, to great cheers from the crowd. Others were shoved and punched by Nixon sympathizers directly in front of the podium where Nixon was speaking.

The brutality at the rally was the only strikingly newsworthy story of the day. It was a natural lead. Yet many of the reporters shrugged it off. It was as if the barrage of propaganda to which they had been subjected all day had numbed their ability to register horror. Only a few reporters, so far as I know, led with the incidents at the Nassau rally. Many newspapers failed even to mention it the next day.

If you were up at 7:05 in the morning the next day, you saw it on the CBS morning news; and you saw it on NBC if you happened to be watching at 8:15. It didn't make the evening news on any of the networks. If you read the city edition or the late city edition of *The New York Times*, you saw no mention of it. It finally appeared deep in the story in the very last edition, which few people see. Bob Semple said he had phoned in an insert to Frank Lynn's story about the day. He had dictated it to a tape recorder at the *Times*, but nobody checked the tape until much later that night.

If you read the Washington *Post*, you saw no reference to the incident. Carroll Kilpatrick, the *Post*'s veteran White House man,* didn't want to talk about it when I first asked him. Later he relented. "I phoned in an insert from the Coliseum," he said, "but it must have gotten lost on the way downstairs to the printer. Things like that happen every day. Listen, I hate to think how often things like that happen."

A young reporter for a large metropolitan daily was so appalled by what he had witnessed that he phoned in a passionately indignant story suggesting similarities between the Administration and the Third Reich. His paper killed it (and ran a milder account in a late edition). The original version of the story was too one-sided, said the editor. It made Nixon sound too much like Hitler. The Jewish readers would get upset.

One of the very few reporters who managed to lead with the incident and also managed to get it in his paper intact was Curtis Wilkie. His P.M. story in the Wilmington *Evening Journal* began:

A handful of hecklers who managed to infiltrate a Republican rally, coupled with strongarm tactics by police and

---

* At the beginning of Nixon's first term, the *Post* assigned three reporters to the White House. Two of them, Don Oberdorfer and Ken Clawson, were "inside men." They were assigned to get to know the White House staff and write investigative stories about the Administration. Kilpatrick, meanwhile, was the "outside man," the reporter who covered the briefings and served as the *Post*'s ambassador to the White House. He was, in effect, a tougher version of Jack Horner. When Clawson defected to the Administration and Oberdorfer went to the Tokyo Bureau in early 1972, Kilpatrick was left to cover the beat alone. As a result, the *Post*'s coverage was accurate and voluminous, but at the same time superficial.

GOP vigilantes, turned President Nixon's personal appearance in suburban New York from a gala event into a battleground last night.

Despite carefully laid plans by the White House, the Long Island campaign swing by the President was climaxed by an evening reminiscent of disruptions that once followed Gov. George Wallace.

Having spent most of his life in the Mississippi Delta, Wilkie knew a Wallace rally when he saw one.

Just after the rally ended, Don Fulsom of UPI radio sat down at the press table in the cinder-block lobby of the Coliseum and batted out his lead. "Though admission was by ticket only," it read in part, "a number of anti-Nixon demonstrators had infiltrated the audience, touching off several disruptions and even a few fist fights."

Suddenly Fulsom heard a familiar voice over his right shoulder. "You've got an obsession with this 'admission-by-ticket-only' business, don't you?" said Ron Ziegler. Then Ziegler read the rest of the copy, patted Fulsom on the back, and walked away.

A lot of people were aware that Big Brother was watching that night. Nobody wanted to get that ominous pat on the back.

CHAPTER XII

Agnew's Campaign

IF THE Nixon People's willingness to have me along on Presidential trips remained a mystery, it came as no surprise when the Agnew people banned me from the Vice President's plane. They went about this in a typically spiteful way: they lied to me for five weeks before declaring me anathema. A secretary from Random House, a courteous lady with a redoubtable telephone voice, phoned the Vice President's office twice a week. Each time she was told that the plane was full. Mr. Crouse was fourteenth on the waiting list and there might be some room next week. Keep trying. Once she even got through to Agnew's press secretary, Victor Gold; he gave her the same excuse.

After this charade had gone on for five weeks, I asked Bob Semple to intercede. Semple contacted Jim Wooten, who was covering Agnew for the *Times*. Wooten examined the plane's records and discovered that the plane had never been filled to capacity. Then Wooten con-

fronted Victor Gold and asked him why I was being
kept off the plane.

"I don't want the press to be inhibited," Gold shouted, for he always spoke as if he were giving orders in a
hurricane. "I want the press to cover the campaign! I
don't want the press to worry about being covered while
they cover the campaign!"

Here was the number one running dog of the World
Champion Press Baiter, claiming that he wished to protect the press. Whether or not Vic Gold was blind to this
glaring irony, the incredible fact remained that he was
probably totally sincere in his solicitude for the reporters. No one doubted that he would throw himself on a
live hand-grenade to protect his boss. Many suspected
that he might sacrifice one or two fingers for the sake of
his charges, the press.

If Victor Gold had been a character in a Broadway
play, he would have been played by Martin Gabel. He
was a short man on a short fuse, with a high forehead, a
drill instructor's bearing, and eyes sufficiently full of fire
to suggest that smoke would momentarily shoot out his
nostrils. He was the most unshakable kind of fanatic—a
convert. In his University of Alabama law school days,
he had roomed with the man who went on to head the
Washington office of the ACLU. He had been a liberal
Democrat in the Deep South, but the racism of the Fol-
soms and Wallaces gradually drove him away from the
Democratic party into the arms of the Republicans. By
1964, he was working as assistant press secretary to
Barry Goldwater.

At the end of the 1972 campaign, the reporters on
the Agnew press plane gave Gold a strait jacket as a
going-away present. That was because Gold tended to
fly into quasi-psychotic rages at the slightest provoca-
tion. Every reporter who traveled with Agnew had at
least a dozen Vic Gold stories. Vic screaming horrible
threats at cars in the path of the press bus. Vic terroriz-
ing press-bus drivers who fell behind the motorcade. Vic
becoming so deranged he distractedly pounded the as-

sistant press secretary over the head with a rolled-up newspaper. Vic in Provo, Utah, sitting in the pool car, furious at the bus drivers behind him:

"Those goddam motherfucking cocksuckers! Those shitheads! Christ, why can't those fuckers learn to stay in line!" said Gold. Then he glanced at the apple-cheeked Republican volunteer who was sitting at the wheel of the car.

"Say, are you a Mormon?" Gold asked him.

"Yes, I am," the young man said softly.

Gold looked guilt-stricken. "Oh, I'm sorry," he said. "That's the way we Christians talk."

Gold also liked to wallow in paranoia. On the last day of the campaign, the McGovern and Agnew planes landed simultaneously in the same corner of the Phila-delphia airport. While McGovern sped off to a street rally, Agnew went into town to address the Fraternal Order of Police. After the speech, Wooten rode back out to the airport in a convertible with Gold. A suave, good-looking man in his middle thirties and a bit of a bon vivant, Wooten thoroughly enjoyed the ride; it was a beautiful fall day, warm enough to drive with the top down. But Gold, as usual, looked as if he had just drunk hemlock.

"What's the matter, Vic?" asked Wooten.

"It's those McGovern people," said Gold. "You never can tell about those people. There must be some reason why they came in at the same time we did. They're gon-na start something at the airport. They're gonna make some kind of trouble, I just know it."

"Oh, come on, Vic," said Wooten. "They're no more anxious to start anything than you are. That's just ridic-ulous."

"That's easy for you to say," said Gold. "You're not the press secretary. But I am, and I'm a good one and that's why I worry about these things."

Wooten just laughed at Gold, as countless other re-porters laughed at him whenever he ranted, cursed, shook his fist, or worked himself up into a right-wing heaven of paranoia. But they also respected Gold for being a stickler for perfection. He made sure that everyone had a room, that everyone knew where the phones were, that the baggage never got lost, and that the Western Union man was never more than a few feet away.

"Vic is a guy who's got all the moves about protecting his candidate Ziegler has, except he's got a little shame, which comes from having some respect for the guy he works for and from wanting to get some respect from the press guys," said Jules Witcover. "And I think that makes him better than Ziegler, who has a basic contempt for us. Vic cares about what people think of him, so he'll go that extra mile."

Gold was the architect of the major innovation in Agnew's 1972 campaigning—the "all-media conference." When Agnew began stumping in the middle of September, his primary mission was to explode the notion that the Administration was inaccessible and isolated. So for the first week of campaigning, Agnew gave the press tons of access. "You want access?" the Agnew people seemed to be saying. "We'll give you so much access you'll wish you never asked." They held three or four press conferences in the first two days on the road. Except they weren't press conferences. The reporters looked at their schedules on the first day and found something called an "all-media conference." They went to Gold and asked him to define the difference between a press conference and an all-media conference. After a long go-round, the difference finally emerged. At a press conference, the Vice President stood. At an all-media conference, *the Vice President sat down.* That was a big joke on the plane for the first week. But the all-media conference was actually a clever device, invented by a connoisseur of TV logistics.

At an all-media conference, Agnew did indeed sit down, with a water pitcher on a little table at his side and a light blue backdrop behind him. The addition of these few props meant the local TV newsmen could shoot the press conference as if it were an exclusive in-

terview in their own studios. Even though a hundred reporters might be present, the TV men could zoom in on
the enthroned Veep and capture a feeling of intimacy.
That way, Agnew didn't have to chase around to three
or four local TV stations in every city. The all-media
format made the TV men happy. No matter that they
didn't have an exclusive interview; they got what *appeared* to be an exclusive interview.

"It was just a little thing," said Jules Witcover, "but it
underlined how much the Agnew people thought about
these things. They realized that by accommodating the
press, they could have the press do things their way.
They saw that one of our big weaknesses is our desire
for convenience."

Convenience was the order of the week. Agnew gave
the press that treasured gift, the easy hook. In his meetings with reporters he was sufficiently cool and low-key
that they could go off and happily file portraits on the
New Agnew. It was an obvious, inevitable and comfortable story, and nearly everybody on board was pleased
to write it. Of course, there were a few brief flashes of
the old Agnew, such as when the Veep opined that
someone had "set up" the Watergate break-in to embar-
rass the GOP, or when he mistakenly announced that
the FBI had undertaken to investigate the grain deal.
The *Times'* Ned Kenworthy, back in Washington, found
out that Agnew had asked Caspar Weinberger what to
say if reporters questioned him about the grain affair
and Weinberger had said, jokingly, "Tell 'em that the
FBI is investigating." So Agnew had gone out and told
them just that. When the story broke, however, Agnew
simply issued a brief and dignified denial.

Vic Gold punished the *Times,* but quietly, by making
the Veep available for exclusive interviews with *Newsweek* and the Washington *Post.* Jim Wooten, who had
requested an interview in August, reminded Vic from
time to time and Vic nervously assured him, "We're
working on it, Jim, we're working on it." But somehow,
Agnew never did find a moment for the *Times.*

A year or two before, Vic might have summoned Wooten and squalled at him for ten minutes, impugning Wooten's patriotism. But the new style was all cordiality. There was a groggy truce between Agnew and the reporters. Agnew seemed actually to enjoy sauntering back to the pool section of his plane and getting to know the reporters. One day during the first week, Gold announced on the press plane that the Vice President was going to give a party for the reporters that night. Then he ran around collaring everyone individually, warning them that the conversation at the party was off the record. That night, the party was held in the Mark Twain Room of the Louisville Ramada Inn, a small function room with two well-stocked bars. Agnew arrived early, was handed a Scotch and soda, and stood alone for a while. An awkward silence ensued.

Bob Greene, a 25-year-old columnist for the Chicago *Sun-Times,* describes what happened next in his book *Running*:

Finally Victor Gold started nudging people in the direction of Agnew, and introductions were made and hands were shaken. The staff people stood next to the walls, not knowing exactly what their function was. . . .

Here were all these famous reporters, the same ones who sit in press buses and bars and call Agnew everything from neanderthal to buffoon, and what did they say now that they had him to themselves?

"What do you think the Redskins' chances are this year, Mr. Vice-President?"

"Do you have tickets to the Colts games this year, Mr. Vice-President?"

"Did you get to see any of the Olympics on television, Mr. Vice-President?"

What happened was the same thing that happens when any American males get together and feel vaguely unfamiliar and uncomfortable with one another and need something to fill the air. They turned to sports, a virile, healthy middle ground where no one can get into any trouble.

"When I came out for that press conference in St. Louis,

I had a good line that I was going to use, but I forgot," Agnew said. "I was going to say 'Gentlemen, there is one subject I would like to declare out of bounds for the press conference. I will not discuss the subject of Colts-Cardinals football.' But I forgot to say it."

The people at the party laughed and laughed. This was just how the gawkers at some GOP $100-a-plate private reception must act when they get close to the Vice-President.

To some reporters who were there, the party seemed a curious kind of release. Most of the men on the plane had spent weeks or even years disliking and distrusting Agnew, and the energy lost in hating him had depleted them. Now, the momentary lifting of antagonism came as a relief. But not for everyone. Wooten spent most of the time drinking by himself in a corner of the room. He could not put his finger on what troubled him, but he was vaguely uneasy at the sight of his colleagues making cocktail party talk with Agnew. It was just somehow unseemly, and Wooten did not wish to take part in it. About two thirds of the way through the party, Vic came up to Wooten, took him by the arm, and said, "Come on, I want you to meet the Vice President."

Wooten gently disengaged his arm and said, "No, Victor, I don't want to meet him." Gold was taken aback. "I'll meet him sometime," said Wooten, "but not at a party. I just don't want to."

"The Vice President's very interested in you," said Gold.

"Bullshit, Victor," said Wooten. "He doesn't even know me. I haven't written more than two or three stories about him."

"Oh, but he knows you," said Vic. "He's *interested* in you."

"Victor," Wooten said firmly, "I am here to *cover* the Vice President, not to be his buddy."

Gold was crestfallen. He walked off, his shoulders sagging. The next day he told Agnew about the conversation, and when a pool reporter asked the Vice President how he thought the press was doing this year, Agnew replied that he thought the press was doing fine, that he enjoyed getting to know the reporters better, but that he understood that there was one who had no desire to meet him for fear of injuring his objectivity. And, said Agnew, perhaps the reporter was right.

Wooten was merely saluting the reality that no reporter was truly going to get to know Agnew. Why play the game? In spite of all the press conferences, press parties (three in all), and interviews, no one was going to lay a glove on the Veep. On the first day of campaigning, a bunch of veteran reporters surrounded Agnew whenever he came down the ramp of the plane. They threw questions at him and tried to eavesdrop on the conversations he had with dignitaries who had come to meet him. Such was the procedure followed with George McGovern. But Gold was appalled. He couldn't believe his eyes. By the third stop, the reporters found themselves being ushered into a little corral on the airfield when Agnew landed. At a rally, the Secret Service told them that they would not be allowed to cross a certain crack in the sidewalk. At later rallies, the Secret Service laid down red masking tape as the line of demarcation. When the reporters—notably Jules Witcover—complained, Gold grew indignant. Didn't they understand? This was the Vice President of the United States!

"You make your moves, and you have a little fun, and you let 'em know you're there," Witcover said later. "But it doesn't amount to a row of beans. Because they have control of the operation. They have the extra layer of the Secret Service, they have the aura of authority— the aura of the Vice Presidency and the Presidency. That is a positive tool in their hands. It's an intimidating kind of thing on a day-to-day basis. It's fine to say 'Why don't you guys get in there every day?' But the Agnew people know it's the human element in there—you don't continue to dog it day after day after day. You realize it's not doing any good so you don't spin your wheels. The masking tape didn't bother me that much, because you could just step over it. What bothered me was the mentality that went into doing that."

After the first week and a half, the all-media conferences petered out and the campaign settled into a dull hum of one or two speeches a day in which Agnew praised the local Republican candidates, boosted the Administration, and gently lamented McGovern's errors. Agnew spent most afternoons in his hotel room. When he was not being an ogre, it became clear, Agnew was a bore. A few papers like the Los Angeles *Times*, had resolved to cover Agnew constantly on the theory that he *was* the Nixon campaign, that if Nixon was going to send out any message, Agnew would be the delivery boy.

But no message came. A mild depression descended on the press. A routine developed. The press plane sprouted decorations—posters and Halloween paraphernalia. Lou Cannon of the *Post* periodically wrote satirical news stories, signing them Irving Doppelganger of the Transylvania News Service. Once a week, Wooten composed something called the Barry Goldwater Memorial Intelligence Test. One day Joe Alsop appeared. He rode on Agnew's own plane, not the press plane. Agnew went back and talked with him for a half hour, with Alsop handing out advice in his phony Oxford accent. After Agnew returned to his private quarters in the front of the plane, Vic Gold went back. "How was it?" he asked Alsop.

"It was wonderful, Vic," said Alsop. "Really, really wonderful."

Few of the regulars thought the campaign was so wonderful. Wooten later said that he had felt angry from first to last—there was no way to make the Nixon/Agnew outfit talk about the issues. His purpose was not to see Nixon defeated and McGovern elected —he claimed not to "give a shit" about that—but he did want to help make the election more of a real plebiscite. Other reporters shared his vague feelings of frustration. I doubt whether any of them appreciated the real problem, which was that Agnew's significance in 1972 stemmed entirely from his actions in the past: in 1970 and 1971, he had poisoned the well against the press. Robert Semple pointed this out at the bottom of a story he wrote in the middle of October:

"Do you know why we're not uptight about the press and the espionage business?" one White House aide—not Mr. Ziegler—asked rhetorically the other day. "Because we believe that the public believes that the Eastern press is what Agnew said it was—elitist, anti-Nixon, and ultimately pro-McGovern."

The irony is that Mr. Agnew himself has adopted a low profile and is saying little about the press. But his allies in the White House freely admit that the seeds of suspicion he sowed in times past are bearing fruit today.

Was this a planned strategy? If so, who had planned it? Nobody bothered to ask these questions. Reporters, especially campaign reporters, had no mandate to explore the past; recent history was just so much stale news. The story lay in the present. Agnew's people knew this fact of journalism, and exploited it by feeding the reporters a new Agnew and thus diverting all attention from the past. "I don't think that we put in nearly as much thought to covering a campaign as they put in to how we're going to cover a campaign," said one reporter, quite correctly.

Yet some of the coverage was interesting, especially Jim Wooten's. Before being assigned to the Agnew campaign, Wooten had spent six years and gone through seven typewriters covering George Wallace. He had followed Wallace in 1968, 1970, 1972, all through the South and into Northern cities; he had gone everywhere with Wallace, in fact, except to Laurel, Maryland. On May 16, 1972, the first event on Wallace's schedule had been a dinner at 5:30 in Glen Birney. Wooten had a late breakfast with his wife and did some work on a piece suggested by Johnny Apple about the unusually heavy security that surrounded Wallace. He phoned the Wallace Headquarters in Montgomery, Alabama, to make sure that no events had been added to the schedule. No, they assured him, the first event was still the dinner. (Later, Wooten would kick himself for not having known better than to rely on the Wallace staff. The Wallace campaign was a badly disorganized affair, run by total incompetents, and the Wallace people were always making changes in the schedule at the last moment, such as the addition of the shopping center rally at Laurel.)

Wooten drove out to the Atlanta airport and caught a 1:30 plane to Washington. Just as the plane was touching down at National Airport, at 3:00 o'clock, Arthur Bremer pulled out a cheap revolver and emptied it into Wallace. Wooten found out about the shooting five minutes later from the girl at the Avis counter. He felt, he later said, "an almost indescribable sickness in my soul." He had attended every Wallace rally for six years but missed the one that counted most. He dashed for his rented car and headed for Maryland. When he reached the hospital, he found that four men from the *Times'* Washington Bureau already had the story well in hand, and he soon became convinced that his absence had not gravely damaged the *Times'* coverage. But months later he still felt slightly sick whenever he thought about that day. No one on the Agnew plane was more conscientious about sticking with the candidate than Jim Wooten.

In some ways, the experience of covering Wallace had prepared Wooten well for the Agnew assignment. He had learned to live with ease and confidence inside enemy camps. He and Wallace disliked each other intensely, but they got along. Wooten refused to be bullied. (When Wallace, during an interview, began talking about "niggers," Wooten said, "Governor, you don't have to say 'nigger'; you don't have to impress me.") And Wooten refused to be unfair to Wallace. He realized from the start that Wallace only thrived on attacks from the Eastern press, using them to his own political advantage. Now Wooten applied the same principles to the Agnew campaign.

He treated Agnew with scrupulous fairness, taking pains to mention that Agnew had given a well-researched speech or received an enthusiastic reception at a particular rally. But Wooten also pointed out Agnew's inconsistencies and exaggerations with an exemplary directness. When Agnew lashed out at a group of antiwar hecklers in San Diego, comparing them to Nazi Brown Shirts, Wooten reminded his readers that Agnew had blasted McGovern for comparing Nixon's policies to those of Hitler. He also devoted four paragraphs to describing how a spectator punched a heckler in the nose, and how plain-clothes-men then dragged the heckler away but ignored the assailant. It was just the sort of description that the Nixon Nassau rally had cried out for.

Wooten's best story, however, was an impressionistic description of a day in Palm Springs, a story that did more to explain the Agnew appeal than any analysis or survey. Wooten had risen around five one morning, to drive out to the edge of town and watch a desert sunrise, which he had never seen before. Coming back, he stopped for breakfast in a diner with a name he found irresistible, the Cozy Cafe. After a half-hour of eavesdropping, Wooten finally tuned in on the conversation on which he based his piece. The article began: "At the Cozy Cafe, early this morning, some of the fellows were drinking their first coffee of the day from thick, chipped mugs and bemoaning the fact that they weren't rich."

Wooten quoted some conversation among three working men:

" 'All the man here wants is to live like Sinatra, right?'

"Howard nodded. 'Yeah,' he said, 'or maybe like Spiro.'

"Lou scoffed, semiseriously. 'Come on, Howie,' he said. 'You've got to dream bigger than that. I mean, Agnew don't have no money—no real money, if you know what I mean. Hell, he's just staying out at Frank's place. He's just a guest.'

"Howard glanced at his watch, picked up his change and pushed his chair away from the table. 'Maybe so, Lou,' he said as he stood up. 'But he's there, ain't he. Anytime he wants, he's there.' "

Later in the article, Wooten described a golf game that included Agnew, Sinatra, Bob Hope, and Jack Benny. It was a perfect understated portrait of square decadence. Then he flashed back to the Cozy Cafe for his tag:

" 'Oh, yeah,' said Jimmie. 'Yeah, I'd settle for Agnew's life, I guess.'

" 'Me too,' said Lou, 'As long as I could stay at Frank's place.' "

Wooten had worked on the article for almost eight hours, rewriting it three or four times, and he took great pride in the fact that the article had "said something without actually saying it." Which was the trick of getting controversial pieces past the copy desk at the *Times*.

Although Wooten didn't know it, he could have found similar attitudes much closer than the Cozy Cafe. Just up the aisle on the press plane was a member of the press corps, a good and sincere man, who later showed me his personal journal of the Agnew trip. Here, in part, is the entry for October 31:

When we got back, I was tired so I laid down and took a rest. Actually, I went sound asleep. The phone rang about 11:30. I had been asleep for an hour and a half. It was Pete Malatesta, Agnew's personal aide. He said, "Come on down to the Granada Bar, we're having a little party." I walked in and joined the group which included Pete, his brother Tom, Dr. Bill Voss, Roy Goodearle and Frank Sinatra. We chatted and drank and then Frank, Pete, Tom and his girl friend and I went to a private club called the "Candy

Store" where we were Frank's guests. Then we were joined by a guy named Jilly, who owns a place in N.Y. and is a close Sinatra friend and by Keely Smith who had just finished her opening show at the Century Plaza.

The place was filled with Hollywood stars and I'm afraid I was a little goggle-eyed by it all. Sinatra is an easy guy to talk with. He's genuinely interesting, and is interested in people. He was relaxed and very friendly at the hotel bar where people didn't recognize him and he could be alone with friends. He was on edge at the Candy Store as would-be starlets, etc., came by to glad-hand or smile at him or otherwise annoy him. He's a guy who obviously enjoys his privacy and his friends.

When we left, he drove his own Chevrolet (FAS-1) home, after telling Pete, "Only six more days until the greatest ever. We're gonna win, baby, we're gonna win big, B-I-G."

Pete, Tom, his girl friend and I went back to Pete's penthouse suite next to the Vice President's, had a nightcap amid almost unbelievable opulence, and I went down to my room, to bed. it was 4:00 A.M. What a day! What a night! It was worth a little lost sleep.

PART THREE

COVERING McGOVERN'S CAMPAIGN

CHAPTER XIV
Chafing at the Rules

JOURNALISM IS probably the slowest-moving, most tradition-bound profession in America. It refuses to budge until it is shoved into the future by some irresistible external force. The few innovations which appeared in the coverage of the 1972 election year had all come about in response to pressures from outside the profession. It was mainly the inescapable influence of Teddy White's books, for instance, that forced the news organizations to attempt more stories on the inner workings of the campaign organizations. The success of Joe McGinniss' *Selling of the President* embarrassed them into examining the candidates' use of media. The repercussions of the Chicago Convention persuaded them to give more space to the mood of the country.

And the process continued. Six months after the election, the Watergate scandal broke open in the courts, and the Washington *Post* found itself magnificently vindicated. Suddenly dozens of editors and reporters from all over the country began calling for more investigative journalism in covering politics and government. The triumphant example of Bernstein and Woodward gave promise of prodding American political journalism into a new era; perhaps, in elections-to-come, reporters would be instructed to investigate candidates instead of merely quoting them.

Even during the campaign year, some of the younger reporters had felt that the changes in political journalism were too few and too superficial, that a full journalistic revolution was called for. Brit Hume, a young assistant of Jack Anderson's who had helped uncover the ITT scandal, was disgusted with the coverage of the campaign. "You think anyone's interested in all these polls, or the gruel served up by the guys riding around in the press plane?" he demanded. "Hell, no. It's just a waste of time. All those reporters care about is 'Who's gonna run, who's gonna win?' And that just isn't enough. The press has a greater responsibility than to do a bunch of goddam handicapping stories.

"They ought to do one big story on each candidate's overall strategy and then bag it. Let the AP cover the candidates and play that stuff on page 7, page 8. Maybe have your best reporter go out and write a highly opinionated story about each guy, and then put him to work on something useful, like the money."

Hume thought that the real story was the money. Here, in 1972, with the new law that obliged contributors to make public their gifts, was a unique opportunity to follow the big corporate rats as they stole out of their holes to deposit a large bag of cash at the door of some candidate and—almost invariably—ask for some favor in return.

"They ought to just swarm over that money stuff," said Hume. "Check out every lead. Get pictures of these guys covering their faces with their hands. Quote all the reasons their secretaries give for them not answering your phone calls.

"Like we did a story on this McDonald's Hamburger

king who put up all this money for Nixon because there's a bill pending which they're all hot for which will lower the minimum wage for youth. Which is gonna be great for McDonald's. This guy gave Nixon a thousand dollars in '68 and 149,000 dollars in '72. And we think we figured out how he came to be 149 times happier with Nixon.

"There are a lot of stories like that, and the public just loves to read about that stuff. Just loves it. Shit, that's what Jack does, and he has the single most popular column in America. They ought to have that stuff all over the front page in an election year.

"Those guys on the plane," said Hume, "claim that they're trying to be objective. They shouldn't try to be objective, they should try to be honest. And they're *not* being honest. Their so-called objectivity is just a guise for superficiality. They report what one candidate said, then they go and report what the other candidate said with equal credibility. They never get around to find out if the guy is telling the truth. They just pass the speeches along without trying to confirm the substance of what the candidates are saying. What they pass off as objectivity is just a mindless kind of neutrality."

Strangely enough, some of the men on the campaign trail might have agreed with Brit Hume. There was a strain of frustration infecting the campaign reporters that nobody could remember having seen in other election years—at least not in such virulent form. Some of the better minds on the plane had begun to feel caged in by the old formulas of classic objective journalism, which dictated that each story had to make some neat point; had to start with a hard news lead based on some phony event that the candidate's staff had staged; had to begin with the five w's; had to impose some *meaning*, however superficial or spurious, on the often insignificant, or mysterious, or downright absurd events of the day. Yet if the candidate spouted fulsome bullshit all day, the formula made it hard for a reporter to say so directly—he would have to pretend that "informed sources" had said so, or actually find someone in the crowd or the opposition who would say so.

A reporter was not allowed to make even the simplest judgments; nor was he expected to verify the candidates' claims. The classic example came not from a national election, but from the contest for the presidency of the United Mine Workers Union between Tony Boyle and Joseph Yablonski. In that contest, all of the charges made by Yablonski were probably true; at the same time, a resourceful reporter could have shown that many of Boyle's accusations were lies. Yablonski was an honest reformer; Boyle was a corrupt executive interested only in perpetuating his own rule. But the press insisted on reporting the election as a dispute between two warring factions in the union; using the time-honored techniques of objective journalism, they gave equal weight to each man's charges. It was objective coverage, but it wasn't fair. When a gang of hired thugs murdered Yablonski and his family one night, the press suddenly began to hint that the election might have been a contest between forces of good and evil.

ONE OCTOBER EVENING when the McGovern plane had dumped us in Pittsburgh in the course of what was becoming an increasingly haphazard campaign, I had a couple of beers with Jim Doyle at the Hilton. We talked about the fact that many political reporters were beginning to yearn for new freedoms—freedom from the pack, from the routine of the campaign plane, and from the restraints of formula writing. Doyle was a shortish man in his mid-thirties, a dapper dresser who wore a beret and French lunettes on his round, ruddy face. He came from a large Catholic family, and like Marty Nolan, he had grown up among hardhats and conservatives in lower-middle-class Dorchester, but had somehow emerged as a committed liberal.

An outspoken man, he didn't mind revealing his

doubts about the practice of journalism. Doyle thought that the campaign reporters, especially the national political men, ought to be on a much looser rein.

"I think a guy ought to be able to say something like 'I'm gonna go into Macon County, Georgia, because I remember that Macon County is more liberal than the rest of the state, and I just want to go in and see if there's a McGovern organization and what they're doing,' " said Doyle.

"It's tough deciding what story to pick, because you don't want to waste your time. But once you go in there, I say that the formulas ought to go out the window. What you ought to do is follow your instincts, follow your training, and then sit down and write as if you were writing a letter to Jules Witcover. Write a letter saying, 'This is why I came here, this is what I found out'—and then, if you don't know what it means, I think you ought to say that. I mean, we never write stories in which we say, 'I don't know what this means but let me tell you about it.' We always say, 'The reason I'm here is because this is the crucial race in the Midwest and it could decide the future of the Senate.'

"And when we write it, we think, 'That's bullshit. The one up the hill is just the same.'

"Right now, the big cliché is that this election's going to decide whether the New Deal coalition dissolves. Well, it may not decide that at all. It may be that the New Deal coalition started evolving the day it was formed and is going to keep on evolving until no one recognizes it, but it's never gonna dissolve. So to write in those terms just doesn't make sense. We don't do enough of saying, 'We don't know what this means, but it's out there and it's interesting.'

"Look," said Doyle, "if a reporter knew that he had to say 'I thought such-and-such'—if he couldn't hide behind this phony business of 'informed sources' and 'veteran observers'—he'd be goddam careful what he put his name on. He'd be much more worried about being fair and about writing what he really thought."

Doyle was slouching in an armchair by the picture window of his bedroom, dead tired from a week on the road. Later that night there would be a McGovern telethon and Democratic party dinner to cover. He took a gulp of beer and looked out the window at the sun setting on the river.

"A lot of people," he said, "look at this coverage as if it were some kind of a cross-country race—you gotta get two paragraphs in when he stops at Indianapolis and two more when he stops at Newark. If you do it that way, without making any meaning out of it, it *is* going to come out like some crazy disjointed trip across the country.

"The problem is, if you try to write every day, you get caught up in sheer exhaustion. It's as simple as that. You do it by rote, because that's all you've got the energy for. It's the lack of sleep, the keeping up with deadlines, the disorientation from all this flying around—your mind just goes blank after a while. When it comes time to write the story, all you can do is just kind of a level job of stumbling through the day's events.

"I don't think I know how to cover a campaign. I feel a little bit more confident about it this year. What has to happen is, you have to develop faith in your own judgment. Then you've got to develop confidence that your editors will accept your judgment. If you think an editor is back there second-guessing you, then your judgment starts to get watered down and you start to rely on formulas. My impression is that a lot of the guys are getting second-guessed. But you've got to know that the paper's going to back you up—that your by-line's on the piece and that everybody knows it's all yours and hasn't been tampered with, so you're stuck with it and it has to be good.

"The other thing is that I find it hard not to write, because I'm compulsive. A lot of these guys are. It's a very hard thing to do—to say, it's not worth it today, so I won't file. You always say, 'But Jesus, Bill Greider's gonna write today and he'll be on page one and the edi-

rs will think that Greider found a good thing to write
oday for the *Post* and Doyle didn't write anything for
ur paper.' You always worry about that. But the fact is
at we all write too much and we all write with too lit-
le in the piece, with too little to say. So I'm trying to
rite only when I've got something to say that goes be-
ond the average story."

A good many of these powerful men began to feel impotent toward the middle of the campaign. The longer
hey were on the trail, the more exhausted they became;
and fatigue made them slaves of the formula, since they
ost all will to fight either the desk or their own misgivings. It was fair to argue that the press would become
both more interesting and less powerful if given more license. Much of their power stemmed from the fact that
they often acted as a pack. Given a chance to ditch the
formula, the reporters would produce more complex and
ambiguous descriptions of the campaign, and their stories would not sound so similar. If every story took the
form of a letter and began, "Damned if I knew what's
happening here, but I have a few guesses," there would
be a cacophony of rival voices instead of the usual re-
sounding chorus.

Some of this was already happening. Jim Perry, for
instance, wrote weekly pieces for the *National Observer*
that approached the letter format. Each week he examined one topic, such as the implications of the Muskie
"crying incident" in New Hampshire or the nature of
Spiro Agnew's campaign, and he was original, discursive, and amusing without being partisan. Bill Greider of
the *Post*, who covered McGovern throughout the summer and fall, developed an uncanny knack for filling his
articles with feeling while still remaining within the
bounds of conventional journalism. The *Times* allowed
some of its reporters to write an occasional "news analysis"—and James Naughton learned to make excellent
use of this device. (Jules Witcover, on the other hand,
ried to insert some analysis into his dispatches and
found that his paper, the Los Angeles *Times*, was not

interested.) Even the wire-service men succeeded in pushing back some of their traditional restraints; the top wire-service men like Mears and Gerstel were allowed to do some cautious analysis.

There were a few reporters who were able to finesse the formula. The best example was Dan Rather, the White House correspondent for CBS. Rather often adhered to the "informed sources" or "the White House announced today" formulas, but he was famous in the trade for the times when he by-passed these formulas and "winged it" on a story. Rather would go with an item even if he didn't have it completely nailed down with verifiable facts. If a rumor sounded solid to him, if he believed it in his gut or had gotten it from a man who struck him as honest, he would let it rip. The other White House reporters hated Rather for this. They knew exactly why he got away with it: being handsome as a cowboy, Rather was a star on CBS News, and that gave him the clout he needed. They could quote all his lapses from fact, like the three times he had Ellsworth Bunker resigning, the two occasions on which he announced that J. Edgar Hoover would step down, or the time he incorrectly predicted that Nixon was about to veto an education bill. But these were all relatively trivial errors. The important thing was that Rather was making a balls-out effort to deal with a White House staff which refused to release any meaningful information.

IN A BEHEMOTH DEMOCRACY, the mass circulation papers would always want to have straight reporters deliver up the political news, and these reporters would always be caught between the demands of objectivity, on the one hand, and the freakish stranger-than-fiction reality of the campaign plane on the other. Of course, there remained the radical solution of simply chucking all pretense of objectivity, and writing from a totally personal frame of reference. This luxury was given only to a few. There were the literary people sent by magazines to cover the Conventions—Germaine Greer, Kurt Vonnegut, and Norman Mailer. "For them," Renata Adler wrote in *The New Yorker,* "the reporter's basic question— what is the story and what the point—was resolved autobiographically: story and point were whatever happened to impinge on the author's sensibility." There was Bob Greene, the twenty-five-year-old whiz kid of the Chicago *Sun-Times,* who was dispatched, as a representative of the youth culture, to write his own daily impressions of the Conventions and the fall campaign. There was Ron Rosenbaum, a red-bearded young writer from New York, who did several excellent impressionistic campaign pieces for *The Village Voice.* But the nonobjective journalist who created the greatest sensation, and the only one who covered the campaign full-time from January through November, was Hunter S. Thompson of *Rolling Stone.*

Rolling Stones? Is that the fan magazine of the rock group? Nobody on the campaign trial had ever heard of the magazine back in January of 1972, and it was not an easy publication to define in one or two sentences. The *Time* magazine of the Counter Culture? Well, not exactly. An underground rag? Well, it was too slick, expensive and apolitical really to claim underground status. It was really a music magazine, a hip *Variety,* that made extensive and literate sorties into all kinds of other phenomena—the drug scene, the movie scene, the literary scene, and now . . . national politics. *Rolling Stone*'s young founder and editor saw himself as the Charles Foster Kane of the seventies; it was his dream that *Rolling Stone* would muster the gigantic, newly enfranchised Youth Vote and throw it to the best man. Things did not exactly shape up that way, but fortunately the editor had the wit to hire Hunter Thompson as political correspondent.

At the time Thompson had two main credentials. First, he had written a book about the Hell's Angels, based on having lived and ridden with them for almost two years. Although the Angels had beaten Thompson up at the end of his stay, and his book was more critical than sympathetic, still it was clear in many passages that he identified with the Angels; he had the heroic aura of the veteran war correspondent about him, from having lived among the savages and survived. Secondly, he had received national publicity when he ran as the Freak Power Candidate for Sheriff of Aspen, Colorado, on a platform that called for free mescaline for anybody who wanted it; ripping up the streets and resodding them with grass; and harassing all the corporate "greedheads" and real estate developers who were ruining the beauty of the valley.

Thompson seemed just the man to establish a truly "adversary" relationship with the Presidential candidates. In December 1971, he was dispatched to Washington to open a *Rolling Stone* office and to turn his violent, satirical, epithet-studded style on the men in the Democratic primaries. I also worked for *Rolling Stone,* and they sent me out to write the serious backup pieces, keep Thompson out of trouble, and carry the bail bond money.

It was interesting to watch Thompson and the other reporters get to know each other. Thompson was a tall, lean thirty-five-year-old who wore sneakers, Miami sport-shirts, a motley hunting jacket, and bat-wing blue-tinted sunglasses. He looked more like a Sierra Club back-packing nut than a hippie, but there was no confusing him with the rest of the reporters, all of whom wore suits and ties.

And Hunter wanted no part of them, at least not at first. His memories of the press corps from the 1968 campaign, which he had covered for an aborted book, were all unpleasant. He told me that they had been a bunch of swine, a collection of suspicious reactionary old hacks who cared only about protecting their leads and were hopelessly out of touch with anything interesting that was happening in the country. He had met only one decent person the whole time—Bill Cardoso, who edited the Boston *Globe* Sunday magazine. Cardoso had spotted him as the author of *Hell's Angels* on the Nixon press bus in New Hampshire and offered him a joint. "Don't worry," Cardoso had said, "these fuckers are all so square they won't know what you're doing." He had been right.

For his first outing in 1972—a ride around the New Hampshire hills in the airport limousine that then served as the McGovern press bus—Thompson had come equipped with two sixpacks of ale and a fifth of Wild Turkey. He had smiled with satisfaction when the other reporters turned down his offers to share the booze, and when James J. Kilpatrick, the conservative columnist, moved uneasily to the front of the limo. At every stop he would turn to me and suggest loudly, "Let's go to the men's room and eat some acid" or "Maybe there'll be enough time here for us to shoot up." He talked in gruff bursts, like a squawkbox in a squad car. Toward the end of the ride, he began grumbling that he needed "Sex, Dope, and Violence."

But nothing happened. Nobody threw him off the bus. The press corps was no longer so shockable. As the campaign went on, Thompson began to find kindred spirits without even looking for them. There were usually a few young reporters around with whom he could roll a joint or share a tab of MDA—not to mention the young staffers on the McGovern campaign. Even some of the representatives of the nation's great newspapers had taken to smoking dope.

But what baffled Thompson was that some of the straightest men on the bus soon began to accept him and to read his articles. The first sign that Hunter had caught on with the straight press was when they began searching newsstands all over the country or phoning their home offices to get them a copy of his lengthy chronicle of the Florida primary. Thompson had loaned his press card to a freak, who had run amuck aboard Muskie's whistle-stop train, insulting reporters and heckling the candidate when he tried to speak at the final stop in Miami. Many of the reporters, seeing only the badge on the freak's lapel, had taken him for Hunter S. Thompson of *Rolling Stone*. In the article, Thompson explained the mistake but revelled in its consequences. The piece was a big hit with the press corps, and they soon began to read him regularly. Thompson's best lines were quoted in *Newsweek*. "Ed Muskie talked like a farmer with terminal cancer trying to borrow on next year's crop." Hubert Humphrey was a "treacherous, gutless old wardheeler who should be put in a goddam bottle and sent out with the Japanese current."

Chris Lydon—a *New York Times* reporter who was only thirty-three but dressed like an Exeter headmaster and wore a James Reston Memorial Bow Tie—admired Thompson and went so far as to quote him in a Sunday *Week in Review* piece to the effect that Humphrey was campaigning "like a rat in heat." However Lydon worried for weeks afterward about having used the quote; his wife told him she thought it was "unfair." Wherever the campaign went, local reporters would come up looking for Hunter, wanting to see what he looked like and to congratulate him. "After the revolution, we'll all write like Hunter," a local TV man in Los Angeles confided to me. "We'll stop writing all this Mickey Mouse shit."

Not many people in the press corps went that far in their admiration. But reading Thompson obviously gave them a vicarious, Mittyesque thrill. Thompson had the freedom to describe the campaign as he actually experienced it: the crummy hotels, the tedium of the press bus, the calculated lies of the press secretaries, the agony of writing about the campaign when it seemed dull and meaningless, the hopeless fatigue. When other reporters went home, their wives asked them, "What was it really like?" Thompson's wife knew from reading his pieces. Thompson was free to write the unmentionable —that the campaign was essentially meaningless, that some of the candidates were shams and liars, that the process was unjust and anachronistic. There were times when the other reporters ached to say the same things, but the rules would never allow it. I remember Lydon standing around the Silver Spring hospital in his tweed outfit after George Wallace had been shot, saying with his usual earnestness that "Hunter Thompson should be here to record this for history," as if only Hunter possessed the license and proper style to capture the grotesqueness of the scene.

Of course, there were no journalists aboard who actually agreed with Thompson's basic premise that the "only possible good that can come of this wretched campaign is the ever-increasing likelihood that it will cause the Democratic Party to self-destruct." Even the New York lefty journalists like Pete Hamill, Jimmy Breslin, and Jack Newfield were fond of the party. In the late spring of '72, Hamill had even engineered a meeting between his friend Meade Esposito, the Democratic Boss of Brooklyn, and George McGovern. Hamill, Esposito, and McGovern had breakfasted in the Senate dining room, and Esposito agreed to back McGovern. Later, during the New York primary, Hamill, Breslin, and Newfield had met with McGovern and chewed him out for the condescending way in which his people were treating the New York regular Democrats. Breslin, using language McGovern had never heard in South Dakota, advised the Senator to get out and meet the real Democrats by campaigning at firehouses, police headquarters, and party clubhouses.

But Thompson detested the regulars. This hatred, he explained in print, stemmed from the fact that Larry O'Brien had promised him the governorship of American Samoa in 1968, and then reneged. Thompson claimed to be nursing a desire for revenge, waiting for O'Brien to send the Democrats into a hopeless battle that would "destroy the party by plunging it into a state of financial and ideological bankruptcy from which it would never recover. Wonderful, I thought. I won't even have to *do* anything. Just watch, and write it all down."

But Thompson's real reason for loathing the party was that he felt it excluded outsiders, like himself. There was a touch of Genêt in Thompson. As a kid, he had

grown up in the stifling small-town atmosphere of Louisville, Kentucky, where his father was an insurance man
whose only diversion consisted of going out to the track
at five every morning to clock the horses. Thompson rebelled and found other means of amusement—mainly
knocking off liquor stores and gas stations. The authori-
ties never nailed him for theft, but they managed to put
him in jail for thirty days on a phony rape charge.
Thompson was just short of eighteen and the whole experience scared the hell out of him. He decided to swear
off stealing and channel his criminal energies into writing. He wrote to provoke, shock, protest, and annoy.

His favorite pastime was hoaxing people, and he was
forever springing outlandish rumors on the McGovern
people, just to see if they would bite. His greatest
triumph came one night late in the campaign at a New
York restaurant called Elaine's, a favorite of the literary
set. Thompson walked in and spotted a group of Mc-
Govern heavies at one of the tables. He ran over to
them, banged his fist on the table and started yelling that
Tom Eagleton was in the back room, having a nervous
breakdown. "He's jumping up and down, screaming that
McGovern is a sellout and a fraud." The McGovern
staffers were on their feet and heading for the back
room before they realized that they had been pranked.

This sort of joke was also a staple of Thompson's
writing. In a column on the Wisconsin primary, he
claimed to have discovered that Muskie was taking an
obscure Brazilian drug called Ibogaine, which accounted
for the Senator's zombie-like performances on the
stump. Many readers, including several journalists, believed this. So in subsequent articles, Hunter telegraphed
his punches by writing, "My God, why do I write crazy
stuff like this?" at the end of each hoax.

In any case, these hoaxes symptomized Thompson's
antisocial tendencies and his steady identification with
outcasts like the Hell's Angels, blacks, women, Chicanos, freaks, and people below the poverty line. He was

looking for a candidate who would really represent these people and fight the greedheads. George McGovern might do it, he thought, but even before the New Hampshire election, his instincts warned him that there was a serious flaw in McGovern. "When the big whistle blows, he's still a party man," wrote Thompson late in March. But McGovern's first primary victories made a convert of Thompson. McGovern looked like a gutsy crusader for many of the causes that Thompson embraced. His enthusiasm for McGovern peaked around the time of the Wisconsin primary, in April, and he began to become more and more intrigued by the machinery of the campaign, getting to know the staff more closely than any other reporter on the road. He even built up a working relationship with McGovern, and McGovern paid Thompson the supreme compliment of reading his articles and telling him that they were "brilliant."

But by the time of the California primary, in June, Thompson began to smell the fat cats latching onto the campaign, and to sense that McGovern would sell much to get the nomination. By midsummer, Thompson had become wholly appalled at McGovern's effort to woo the old party regulars like Richard Daley and Lyndon Johnson. "McGovern could have won this time if only he'd followed the strategy his own man, Fred Dutton, laid down in his book [*Changing Sources of Power: American Politics in the 1970's*]—tapping the new forces in the land," said Thompson. "Dutton understood that it's only at times like these—when you come in with a wild card—that you can play on your own terms. They started that way. But McGovern—or somebody around him—lost his nerve. And I'm going to find out who."

Throughout the fall, Thompson searched for the "villain" of the campaign, the adviser who was counseling McGovern to sell out. He never found the villain, though he haunted the Washington McGovern Headquarters for several weeks, systematically stalking his prey. His last election piece conceded failure and ended with a painful outcry:

This may be the year when we finally come face to face with ourselves; finally just lay back and say it—that we are really just a nation of 220 million used car salesmen with all the money we need to buy guns, and no qualms about killing anybody else in the world who tries to make us uncomfortable.

The tragedy of all this is that George McGovern, for all his imprecise talk about 'new politics' and 'honesty in government,' is really one of the few men who've run for President of the United States in this century who really understands what a fantastic monument to all the best instincts of the human race this country might have been, if we could have kept it out of the hands of greedy little hustlers like Richard Nixon.

McGovern made some stupid mistakes, but in context they seem almost frivolous compared to the things Richard Nixon does every day of his life, on purpose, as a matter of policy and a perfect expression of everything he stands for.

Jesus! Where will it all end? How low do you have to stoop in this country to be President?

This was without a doubt the most passionate piece of writing that the campaign produced, and more than a few men on the plane probably agreed with it and would have liked to have written it themselves. But they were also keenly aware that you could not sway millions of Middle Americans by sneering at used car dealers. Thompson had the luxury of a limited audience. He could say what he liked because he was talking to his own people. No matter how much the other reporters envied Thompson's freedom, they also resented him for not having to play by the rules. For when Marty Nolan sat down to write a column, even one that was thoroughly leftish, he reminded himself to write for the "milkman in Dorchester." When Dan Rather went before the camera, he remembered to address the construction worker in El Paso. And who was Thompson speaking to? A Chicano welfare lawyer, or perhaps a very hip college student. He did not have to learn the very dangerous skill of balancing honesty with tact. The others did.

The straight reporters who worked for news organizations with vast audiences had been taught since their cub days that their first duty was to protect their own credibility and the credibility of their employers. It was for just this purpose that the rules of objectivity had been created. If a reporter wished to retain the trust of his readers, then he had to write about politics from a totally impartial point of view. Most of the reporters covering the campaign hewed closely to the rules of objectivity not only for the sake of advancing themselves in the profession, but also out of a genuine belief that the objective approach produced fair and honest coverage.

As the fall campaign progressed, however, it began to dawn on many of the McGovern reporters that the rules of objectivity were no longer doing the job. The trouble was the staggering inequality between the coverage of the two campaigns. Given their new mandate to explore "inside" stories, the McGovern reporters were having a field day with the wide-open McGovern campaign. Meanwhile, the White House reporters were failing to get across the obstacle course that the White House had set up; indeed, they were not even trying.*

There was nothing in the rules of objectivity to rectify such a situation. Only the national political reporters had the leeway to write about both campaigns; among them, only Broder expressed real outrage over Nixon's invisibility, and he declared himself *hors de combat* im-

---

* Which is not to say that the McGovern reporters were more courageous than the White House crew. It is perfectly possible that if the men covering McGovern had had the White House assignment instead, they would have failed just as miserably. In fact, a number of the McGovern reporters, including Adam Clymer of the Baltimore *Sun* and Dean Fischer of *Time,* moved to the White House beat after the election. Their presence did not noticeably change the quality of White House reporting.

mediately thereafter. As for the McGovern campaign reporters, they were trapped on the plane and they could do little but file their stories and anguish over the imbalance in the coverage.

CHAPTER XV

The Black Hills

SINCE RICHARD NIXON was declining nearly all invitations to share the pleasure of his company with the electorate, the only real Presidential campaign belonged to George McGovern. McGovern's campaign did not officially begin until the second week in August, but soon after the Democratic Convention adjourned, in mid-July, McGovern retreated to his home state of South Dakota for two weeks of rest and strategy-planning. Good Senator that he was, he had been persuaded to take his working vacation in the picturesque Black Hills in hopes that the tag-along press might boost South Dakota's flagging tourist industry.

McGovern installed himself and a skeleton staff in comfortable cabins hard by Sylvan Lake, in a wooded area at the top of a hill. The press was parked eight miles down the hill in metropolitan Custer, S.D., a tourist paradise that contained antique shops and Indian souvenir stores—everything but the requisite snake ranch. The reporters were billeted in the Hi Ho Motel, a modern, Holiday Inn-type establishment which was nevertheless overwhelmed by the arrival of thirty-odd national reporters. It was the kind of a place where the desk clerk kept asking for autographs and the chambermaid walked on air for two weeks because she had made Harry Reasoner's bed. There were no phones in the rooms, a fact which disturbed some of the reporters. But the McGovern staff pulled a bed out of one of the suites, hooked up twenty phones and a defective Telex machine, which received but could not transmit messages, put a big table in the center, and called it a pressroom.

Once a day, McGovern's press secretary, Dick Dougherty, pulled into the parking lot outside the pressroom and stood in the hot sunshine, dressed in a denim jacket, telling the press what McGovern had eaten for lunch and how many sets he had played with the tennis pro he had imported from Washington. The relaxed routine was perfect for a group of people who were still recovering from the sleepless madness of the Convention. The reporters played tennis, canoed, took long drives to inspect the scenery, or simply sat around the Hi Ho's swimming pool ogling the Secret Service lady in her bikini. There was a birthday party for McGovern, reminiscent of Muskie's birthday night but tamer. The staff somehow conjured up a White House-shaped birthday cake, and Jim Naughton talked Dick Stout into coming out of retirement to do another stand-up routine. "The Senator went to Mt. Rushmore for a measurement," said Stout. "The sculptor will be instructed to comb the rocks forward on the head." McGovern smiled wanly.

During the first week in Custer, a new nucleus of "regulars" emerged, and they remained the central figures in the McGovern press corps for the rest of the campaign. Besides Naughton and Stout, there were Doug Kneeland, Adam Clymer, and Bill Greider.

Doug Kneeland was a *New York Times*man who had given up a good desk job in New York for a chance to move to the San Francisco Bureau, where he could produce the kind of human interest stories he most enjoyed writing. He was an energetic man who spoke in a sharp, pinched Maine accent; he had long, shaggy black-and-grey peppered hair, which he was constantly pushing out of his pouchy face. In July, he and Naughton were assigned to cover the McGovern campaign as a team; Kneeland would write one day, Naughton the next. At first, many of the other reporters scoffed at this system. It was a typical example of the *Times'* extravagance, they said, to assign two full-time reporters to the campaign when every other paper got along with one. But toward the end of the campaign, when everyone began to crumble from exhaustion, the reporters admitted that there was some wisdom in having two men on the plane.

Adam Clymer, a priggish, pear-shaped reporter for the Baltimore *Sun,* joined the McGovern party in the late spring. A shy man, he communicated most easily by griping. He bitched incessantly about everything—the food, the accommodations, the staff, the press operation, and the campaign in general—but he obviously reveled in all of the rituals of the campaign. A president of the Harvard *Crimson* during the fifties, he had since distinguished himself on the *Sun* with his reporting on India, Moscow, and the Department of Justice. Despite his proven journalistic competence, he remained moody and insecure; more than anyone else in the press corps, he seemed to derive his whole identity from being a campaign reporter. He seemed to love the dozens of ways in which the campaign made the press feel *important;* they had special phones set up for them at every stop, they had entrée to backstage areas, they were men apart. This was his first Presidential campaign, and he clearly longed to be a member of the Inner Circle, to receive the approval of his peers. To this end, he took great pains in writing satirical pool reports for his fellow reporters. After a while, he was accepted as a "character" and a wit.

The most extraordinary reporter on the McGovern campaign was Bill Greider of the Washington *Post.*

Greider grew up in a little town outside Cincinnati, went to Princeton in the same class as Johnny Apple, tried to make it as a playwright in New York City, and ended up writing for a small paper in Wheaton, Illinois. "In a town that small," he said, "you really learn in a hurry that if you're gonna kick somebody, you'd better kick him fairly. Because if you don't, he's gonna be leaning over your desk the next day, hollering at you and canceling all his advertising." From Wheaton, he went to Louisville and then to the *Post,* where he gained attention for his superb coverage of the Calley trial. The editors at the *Post* talked him into covering McGovern almost against his will, for he liked neither the high pressure nor the pack quality of campaign reporting. "My real vision, which I sometimes lay on the editors to their horror," he said, "is to find some backwater college and teach journalism there and get a farm and fuck the whole business." After doing a few campaign pieces in the spring, Greider joined McGovern full-time in the Black Hills.

Greider was a tall man with a long, sad, big-eared Lincolnesque face and the rumpled appearance of a man in a Matthew Brady photograph; he always looked as if he lived in the age before dry cleaning. His black Corfam shoes were permanently scuffed, his herringbone suit had lost its shape long ago, his collar was always open, his tie undone, his receding brown hair falling down around his ears; once he walked around for an entire day with a splotch of catsup on his shirt front.

Unlike his fellow reporters, Greider did not constantly, nervously check his watch. He didn't have a watch. Every night during the fall campaign he would leave a wake-up call with the hotel operator and every morning he would awaken with the first light, groggily thinking: *Those bastards, they forgot to phone me. It's ten o'clock and the buses are gone and they fucked me.* Then he would lie in bed stewing about it, wondering whether he should phone the hotel operator and find out what time it was. This phenomenon helped explain the fact that he always looked tired. But he never bought a watch.

Greider was restless with conventional journalistic formulas. His model reporters were the correspondents of the Civil War. "Have you ever read any of the reporting from the Civil War?" he asked one day. "It would blow your mind! Great stuff. Very partisan, most of it, as you might expect in that situation, but they had none of the mechanical crutches that we're given. The editors would just put some guy on a train and say go on down and find out where the army is and tell us about it. And these guys were essentially writing letters back which might be two or three weeks old by the time they got in print."

Many of Greider's articles read like letters. They described the temper of the campaign, reflected the shifts in mood, articulated the doubt and ambiguity that the press and staff often felt in judging the day-to-day events. "Who knows what the public at large is deriving from all this?" Greider wrote at one point in the fall. "Does the candidate seem more human, more tuned to their bread-and-butter hopes and fears? Or does he seem more frantic and weak?" With the possible exception of Wooten, no reporter on either side of the campaign was as comfortable with ambiguity as Greider.

He was the master of the "soft" lead, backing into his stories with a vignette or a piece of "color" rather than pegging them on the latest press release or most recent speech by McGovern. In September, for instance, he began an article:

In the cool nights that end summer, visual bedlam follows the man through the noise of the crowds, a wild careening of glaring lights and darkness, pushing past a web of shadowy faces.

Then, suddenly, all of the light is on McGovern, standing at a rostrum alone, beneficiary of the spotlight and prisoner, too.

The *Post* encouraged this approach, although the editors sometimes kidded Greider about it. Greider would phone the national desk from some distant pressroom to say that he was about to file his piece via Western Union, and the man on the desk would say, "Okay, Bill, just so you don't have any substance in your lead." Of course, his stories were full of substance, but they also contained a deep compassion for McGovern; Greider saw McGovern as a complex, interesting man, not as a dull-witted fumbler, and this view helped to enliven his pieces.

He took great care with his writing. When he had to write a conventional spot story, he never worried; he could come in late and "blow it out." But he sweated out the longer meaning-of-the-campaign stories. While working on a longer story he would stop drinking and grow tense. When he finally finished it, he would float around in a kind of mystic high for a day.

WHEN Greider, Stout, Kneeland, Clymer, Bruce Morton, David Schoumacher, John Dancy and all the other reporters arrived in the Black Hills, they expected no deep insights into George McGovern or into the workings of his campaign. They had no idea that within a few days, the Eagleton affair would bring out one of McGovern's greatest problems: he did not understand how he would look in print, just as a neophyte actor is not prepared for the effect that his performance will have when projected on a screen. "He never got a focus on how his actions as a candidate translated to the people out there," Greider said later, and that turned out to be as good an epitaph as any. The classic example was the way in which McGovern handled the press during the Eagleton mess.

The Eagleton story took the reporters by surprise, and they were so deeply settled into the tempo of boondoggle that it took them nearly a day to get revved up. On Tuesday, July 25, Eagleton was scheduled to drop into Custer on his way to the West Coast and hold a cere-

monial press conference with McGovern. They would
pose together for photographers and express mutual admiration. The prospect of such a press conference did
not excite the reporters, but late Tuesday morning they
dutifully drove up the hill in their rented cars and assembled in the little pine-paneled recreation cabin adjacent to the Sylvan Lake Lodge. They stood around chatting idly and waiting for the candidates. A few of them
declared their intention of leaving the next day; nothing
was happening and the tedium was getting on their
nerves. Noon came, and still no sign of Eagleton. The
TV men grew slightly annoyed; they had helicopters
waiting in a nearby field to take the film to Rapid City,
and it was getting precariously late.

Then Tom Eagleton arrived, was introduced by
McGovern, and announced that he had been hospital-
ized three times for "nervous exhaustion and fatigue."
The reporters asked him embarrassed questions. Eagleton admitted that he had twice received electroshock
therapy. Then McGovern said he would discourage any
talk of dumping Eagleton.

Given the surroundings, these disclosures did not
seem terribly momentous. Some tourists who had snuck
in were milling around the back of the room. A sultry
breeze was blowing through the screen door. A dog tied
to a tree outside was barking. When the press conference was over, Harry Reasoner bet someone that Eagleton would be off the ticket within the week. Not many
people agreed with him. Eagleton had seen a shrink, so
what? It would blow over. The only drama of the day
consisted of watching John Dancy and David Schoumacher dash out of the room to do their hasty stand-ups
and throw the film at the chopper pilots.

That night, however, the Western Union Telex in the
Hi Ho pressroom began to erupt. Since the pressroom
Telex was the only such machine for miles around, it re-
ceived all telegrams addressed to Senator George Mc-
Govern. So the reporters were able to take an instant
reading of the public reaction simply by sitting around

the clattering Telex and reading each wire as it appeared. The telegrams overwhelmingly damned Eagleton. "Listen to this one," a reporter would say. "DO YOU WANT NUT FOR VICE PRESIDENT. DROP EAGLETON." McGovern's two young press aides, Carol Friedenberg and Polly Hackett, would look at their nails and pretend not to hear.

*　　　*　　　*

EARLIER THAT DAY, just after the press conference, Carl Leubsdorf had seen Tom Ottenad of the St. Louis *Post-Dispatch* going into McGovern's cabin for a chat with the Senator. Ottenad was about to join Eagleton in California, and since he represented the biggest paper in Eagleton's home state, McGovern had granted him an interview. When Ottenad and McGovern came out of the cabin and drove off, Leubsdorf followed them to their destination, which turned out to be the tennis courts. Leubsdorf walked over to McGovern and asked whether he could ride back from the courts with him. McGovern said yes. That was his first mistake. But it was typical of McGovern. "You know how he was," Leubsdorf later told me. "If he saw a reporter he knew, and the reporter asked him a question, he'd go right ahead and answer it."

While McGovern played tennis, Leubsdorf sped down the hill to get his tape recorder at the Hi Ho. He found that it was in use. Gregg Herrington, the young AP backup man, was playing a cassette of the press conference for a group of reporters in the pressroom. Leubsdorf couldn't announce that he was about to grab McGovern for an exclusive interview, so he made up a little story in the best *Front Page* tradition. He said that he needed the tape recorder back so that the McGovern people at Sylvan Lake could make a transcript of the press conference. Then he drove back up the hill to meet McGovern.

During the ride from the tennis courts to McGovern's cabin, which took place in a violent hailstorm, Leubsdorf asked the Senator what he thought the public reaction to the Eagleton disclosures was going to be. "We'll have to wait and see," said McGovern. So Leubsdorf wrote a "roundup" piece for the next day's afternoon papers, saying that McGovern was keeping Eagleton and was going to "wait and see" about the public reaction.

The next morning, when word of Leubsdorf's story hit Custer, two groups of people immediately freaked out. First, the press blew up at Dougherty. As usual, Adam Clymer screamed the loudest. "This place is becoming a jungle," he said. The others chorused him. They wanted no more exclusives. Either everybody saw McGovern or nobody saw him.

Meanwhile, some people on McGovern's staff—it has never been determined which people—became very upset over Leubsdorf's story. They thought it implied that McGovern was wavering in his support of Tom Eagleton. Leubsdorf claimed that the story did not imply this at all, that it merely reported McGovern's flat statement that he was going to "wait and see" the public's reaction. Nevertheless, late on Wednesday morning, Dougherty telephoned Carol Friedenberg in the pressroom and dictated a statement from McGovern. She typed it and taped it to the door of the pressroom. It summarized the Leubsdorf story, called it "utterly untrue," and then said that George McGovern was "1,000 percent for Tom Eagleton." No one has ever determined whether the statement was written by McGovern or whether some staffer wrote it and McGovern merely approved it. McGovern never said the words in person in front of a press conference, and it later seemed odd that he should have made such a statement at a time when newspaper editorials and party opinion were damning Eagleton and when McGovern clearly *was* wavering in his support of his running mate. Perhaps somebody on

the staff panicked in the face of a press mutiny and decided to placate the angry reporters with a perfect nug-
get of a quote.

Soon after the "1,000 percent" statement appeared
on the door of the pressroom, Carl Leubsdorf underlined certain sentences and wrote in the margin, "Not
correct. AP story did not say that." By that time, however, the debate over whether the AP story had really
portrayed McGovern as backing away from Eagleton
was entirely academic. What mattered was that Mc-
Govern had furnished the reporters with a perfect spot
story—before evening every reporter in the Hi Ho had
seen the statement and filed on it. And in trying to deny
a relatively harmless wire story, McGovern had branded
himself with one of those little catch-phrases that voters
never forget. Richard Nixon, with his hard-won knowledge of the media, would doubtless have known better
than to stand 1,000 percent behind *anything* in the middle of a hot public controversy. But McGovern apparently did not.

What made McGovern's statement doubly incredible
was that two days later, on Friday, he decided to dump
Eagleton. And he chose to use the press to send Eagleton the bad news. McGovern's first step was to try to
plant a not-for-attribution story with Jules Witcover to
the effect that Eagleton was going to get the ax; Mc-
Govern evidently hoped that Eagleton would read the
story in the Los Angeles *Times,* take the hint, and resign
from the ticket.

On Friday afternoon, Dick Stout of *Newsweek* and
Dean Fischer of *Time* were sitting in the pressroom
when one of the telephones rang. Carol Friedenberg, a
young red-headed press aide answered the phone, said
"Yes, Senator, I'll see if I can find him," and ran out of
the room. A minute later, Jules Witcover dashed into
the room, out of breath, and picked up the phone.

"Yeah, Senator . . . I'm fine," said Witcover. "Sure
. . . When? . . . six? Sure, Senator . . . goodbye."

When Witcover hung up, Stout went over to him and

asked, "What are you going to do, Jules? Why are you going up to see the Senator? And six o'clock on what day?"

"Oh, uh, today," Witcover said nonchalantly.

"Well, *why?*" asked Stout.

"I don't know really," said Witcover. "He just wants to talk. Has something to do with the last chapter in my Agnew book. We've talked about it before."

"Well, what's the last chapter? I don't remember it," said Stout, who hadn't read the book.

"Well," Witcover hesitated. "It's about the importance of the whole process of selecting the Vice President."

Stout and Fischer immediately set up an appointment to see Witcover after the interview. It was deadline night for both of them; neither wanted the other to get a newsbeat. "I'm not going to let you out of my sight," Fischer said to Stout, a little apologetically. That evening they ate together at the Sylvan Lake Lodge. It was the beginning of a strange, symbiotic friendship. The two had close to nothing in common. Fischer, a tall blond, who with his horn-rimmed glasses bore a slight resemblance to the actor Michael Caine, was a silent man who occasionally flashed the tight, cryptic smile of a hatchet murderer; he seemed the complete opposite of the voluble Stout. But their jobs were sufficiently similar to make them professional twins. Without saying anything, each knew all about the other's work life. They often ate together and rode together on the bus, and every Saturday, when no more copy could be filed, they compared notes.

They were not alone at the lodge that night. Dougherty had tipped Doug Kneeland and some of the other reporters that the Senator might come out of his two-day seclusion to have a buffalo steak in the Lakota Room. Bill Greider was there, too. Having just finished an article based on the fact that McGovern had stopped seeing the press, Greider had a premonition that McGovern would show up and ruin the piece. Adam Clymer was

back at the Hi Ho waiting to cook a trout dinner for
Kneeland and Greider, who had forgotten all about the
date.

McGovern did dine in the Lakota Room that night.
He sat at one table with his family, while the press sat at
various other tables around the room. An organist
played big hits of the forties. Everybody devoured buffalo steaks under a mural depicting "The Legend of the
White Buffalo."

When McGovern finished his meal, he walked over
and sat down with Greider, Bill Eaton of the Chicago
Daily News, and a UPI man. Greider thought: "Well,
gee, this is decent enough, the guy is just trying to do a
little farewell number and make a little social chatter,
and to let bygones be bygones." The reporters at the table were itching to broach the Eagleton matter, but no
one wanted to spoil McGovern's evening. Then Mc-
Govern suddenly brought up the subject himself. He
started talking about how a decision would have to be
made, and it would be up to Eagleton to withdraw if
public opinion ran against him. And McGovern's tone
of voice implied that Eagleton was dead. "It slowly
dawned on us," Greider remembers, "that we were the
ones who were being used."

McGovern excused himself. "The reporters," Greider
wrote later, "discussed briefly among themselves the
question of whether it was proper to quote a casual dinner conversation. Very briefly. Then they took out note-
pads and began trying to reconstruct what McGovern
had said. Ever so casually, they slipped off to the lobby
telephones, no point arousing all those other reporters."

Meanwhile, McGovern went over to Stout and Fischer. They were joined by Doug Kneeland and Bob Boyd
of Knight. McGovern repeated his observations on Eagleton, and Stout surreptitiously recorded it all on a tape
recorder he was holding in his lap. When McGovern
left, the Stout-Fischer group gathered around the tape
recorder to try to pick out a few words from the overwhelming organ music. Then they looked around and

realized that they weren't the only ones with the story. Kneeland headed for a phone. The only two in the lobby were being used, so he raced down the hill to the Hi Ho. On the way down he passed Clymer, who was steaming up to the lodge to find out what he had missed.

Later that night, Fischer and Stout cornered Witcover in the pressroom. He showed them the unattributed story he had just finished. "It was learned," the story said, that McGovern was going to dump Eagleton. Stout and Fischer knew exactly where Witcover had learned it, and they phoned the news to their home offices.

NOT THAT IT REALLY MATTERED what they phoned in —their files made up only a small part of their magazines' coverage of the Eagleton affair. *Newsweek*'s Washington Bureau chief, Mel Elfin, an old friend of Eagleton's, flew to California and interviewed him. Eagleton gave Elfin a lengthy, totally self-serving autobiographical monologue, to which *Newsweek* devoted most of its space. Since *Newsweek* had obtained an interview from Eagleton, *Time* had to get one too. It was equally self-serving. Both magazines appeared on the day Eagleton resigned, July 31, but they helped to pump the public flow of sympathy for him.* The newsmagazines served as Eagleton's best forum for self-beatification, but not his sole forum. The newspapers gave Eagleton loads of straight coverage, thus allowing him to play the victim and to establish mental health as a red herring issue. The real issue, as *The New York Times,* the Washington *Post* and the Los Angeles *Times* pointed out in editorials, was the difficulty Eagleton had experienced in telling the truth. Eagleton's great victory over both McGovern and the press consisted in the agility with

---

* This sympathy had actually begun four days before, when Jack Anderson claimed to have "located photostats of half a dozen arrests for drunken and reckless driving." When Anderson failed to produce the photostats, Eagleton promptly became a victim of slander in the public eye and his stock soared.

which he appropriated the hard news columns for his own designs—namely, to portray himself as a martyr for the cause of psychotherapy, a totally cured man who was wrongly suspected of being dangerously sick.

Long after Eagleton was dropped from the ticket, several reporters kept trying to clear up the mysteries of the Eagleton affair. They tried unsuccessfully to reconstruct the phone conversation, held during the Democratic Convention, in which Mankiewicz had asked Eagleton about his possible disabilities. They tried in vain to pry loose Eagleton's medical records, which were locked in a safe in St. Louis. Bill Greider attempted to follow up a rumor that had Eagleton's doctors telling McGovern on the phone: Eagleton is a very sick man but he doesn't know it, so you can't tell him. But Greider never was able to substantiate this rumor. No reporter effectively counteracted Eagleton's stunning week of self-promotion by writing a clean, fact-studded profile of the opportunistic, overambitious hack that Tom Eagleton was.

In any case, McGovern did himself no good that night at Sylvan Lake. He succeeded only in making himself look like a sneak, a man who was trying to get the press to do his dirty work for him. He was hopelessly naïve to believe that Witcover's story would remain unattributed for more than a couple of hours among such a confined, rivalrous group or that the press would not write about his awkward efforts to slip a big story into an after-dinner chat. Richard Nixon would not have made these mistakes; the least that could be said for Nixon was that he had painfully learned how the press worked. He would have known that while you might hope to plant a story with one reporter at a time, you could not play such a cozy, informal under-the-table game with an entire pack of reporters.

The evening also revealed a new, disturbing side of McGovern, a side which some of the reporters had sensed but none had witnessed. Greider's "news analysis" in the *Post* of July 31 described it well:

"The South Dakota senator has always insisted that he is, above all, a pragmatic politican and his handling of the Eagleton crisis confirms this description. Beneath the exterior of the earnest and open man, there is a cautious tactician, more calculating than either his hardboiled critics or his starry-eyed admirers have admitted." Greider went on to describe McGovern's table hopping in the Lakota Room and then wrote: "What McGovern did was either very slick or very clumsy. The people who watched still are not sure which."

Jim Naughton, who had spent the week back in Washington, was more severe. "In the Democratic primaries," wrote Naughton, "Senator McGovern managed to convey the impression that he was somehow not a politican in the customary sense—that he was more open, more accessible, more attuned to the issues and more idealistic than other candidates. But his reaction to Mr. Eagleton's disclosure may have seriously impaired that image."

CHAPTER XVI

Calling It
from 30,000 Feet

It is an unwritten law of current political journalism that conservative Republican Presidential candidates usually receive gentler treatment from the press than do liberal Democrats. Since most reporters are moderate or liberal Democrats themselves, they try to offset their natural biases by going out of their way to be fair to conservatives. No candidate ever had a more considerate press corps than Barry Goldwater in 1964, and four years later the campaign press gave every possible break to Richard Nixon. Reporters sense a social barrier between themselves and most conservative candidates; their relations are formal and meticulously polite. But reporters tend to loosen up around liberal candidates and campaign staffs; since they share the same ideology, they can joke with the staffers, even needle them, without being branded the "enemy." If a reporter has been trained in the traditional, "objective" school of journalism, this ideological and social closeness to the candidate and staff makes him feel guilty; he begins to compensate; the more he likes and agrees with the candidate *personally,* the harder he judges him *professionally.* Like a coach sizing up his own son in spring tryouts, the reporter becomes doubly severe.

Most of the reporters who covered George McGovern in the fall campaign preferred him to Richard Nixon and ended up voting for him (if they voted at all). For just this reason, they were careful to be tough on him as *reporters.* The best example is Jim Naughton. In early October, Naughton went home for a couple of days. One of the things he did was go to the Registrar's Office in Fairfax, Virginia, and apply for an absentee ballot. To his surprise, he was allowed to fill out the ballot on the spot; after a minute or two of meditation, he voted for George McGovern and Sargent Shriver.

Naughton returned to the McGovern campaign almost immediately. Two days later, at a press conference in Chicago, McGovern accused the local Republicans of bribing Spanish-American voters to stay away from the polls in November. The reporters pressed McGovern for details, but he failed to provide any evidence to back his charges. Just as the press conference was about to end, Naughton raised his hand and asked a final question.

"Senator," said Naughton, "you've made a fairly serious charge about Republican involvement in this nefarious activity, but you haven't given us any details and you haven't told us where details can be obtained. As a student of history, how do you distinguish what you are doing from what Joseph McCarthy used to do?"

There were groans and startled glances from Naughton's fellow reporters while McGovern fumbled for an answer. To Naughton, the question seemed perfectly fair. But later, he had qualms about the *tone* of the question. "In looking back on it," he said, "I wonder whether I would have been as cutting, as direct, and as vicious in my question if I had not voted for McGovern a couple of days before. I think I may have been tougher on McGovern after that."

When the press conference ended, Dick Dougherty

was furious at Naughton. "That's the last time I ever get *you* recognized after the time has expired," the press secretary said. Naughton believed that Dougherty "never forgave" him for having asked the Joe McCarthy question. But by that time, Dougherty was already fed up with the press in general.

Dougherty had been a fine journalist himself (New York Bureau chief for the Los Angeles *Times*), a vice-commissioner in the New York Police Department (public relations division), and the author of four good novels. He looked like a dapper Irish detective, with steely grey hair curling back from his forehead and a cigarette constantly hanging from his lips. He spoke in a growl, which grew more pronounced when he referred to the press. On one occasion he threatened to punch several reporters in the nose. Another time, he warned a group of reporters that they were writing their own obituaries by "sucking up to the moral runts in the White House." He was convinced that the campaign reporters were portraying George McGovern as a "sneaky bumbler" when they knew all the while that McGovern was really a sincere, honest, capable man.

"I would guess that 90 percent of the news people who covered McGovern voted for him,"* Dougherty wrote in *Newsweek* after the election. He continued:

Why, if that was their ultimate judgment of him, could they not pass that judgment on to the public? Hard news wouldn't let them. It wouldn't have been objective reporting. You can write about a candidate who is being sneaky and bumbling: that's objective reporting. But you can't write about a candidate who is being kind and forgiving: that's editorializing. Curiously limited objectivity, isn't it?

---

* Naughton later estimated that 95 percent of the reporters on the plane voted for McGovern. "But I suspect that many of them felt as I did—that they weren't exactly eager to do it," he said. "Most of us have not been terribly fond of Nixon. At the same time, McGovern did not seem to demonstrate in his campaign an overwhelming capacity for administrative ability, and the Presidency *is* an administrative job, after all."

Dougherty went on to endorse advocacy reporting: only if the reporters let their feelings show could they give a true picture of a candidate. The reporters who read Dougherty's piece when it came out two months after the election enjoyed the prose style but did not take the content seriously.

DURING THE CAMPAIGN, Dougherty had not been highly regarded as a press secretary, for he was seldom around when the reporters needed him. Unlike Ronald Ziegler, he was not interested in running a perfect public relations operation; he had been too good a journalist to stomach easily the prospect of becoming a great flack. During the summer, he gradually promoted himself to the position of personal adviser to the candidate. Whenever the reporters saw a shot of McGovern on the evening news, Dougherty would be right at his side, and a great chorus of jeers would go up from the reporters.

One night in early September, on a long, hot bus ride from New York City to Waterbury, Connecticut, Jules Witcover began talking about Dougherty. Witcover was sitting in the back of the bus with Tom Oliphant, a skinny, bespectacled twenty-six-year-old reporter from the Boston *Globe* who was known affectionately as "The Kid."

"Dougherty said with a straight face that this was less bother for us than riding out to La Guardia and flying up to Connecticut," said Witcover.

"Yeah," said Norm Kempster, a UPI man sitting across the aisle, "but Dougherty's making a big sacrifice and flying up with McGovern in a chartered plane!"

"Have you ever seen Dougherty on a press bus?" asked Oliphant.

"Not lately," said Witcover. "You know what we ought to do? We oughta give Dougherty a tour of the bus." Witcover enthusiastically sketched out a scenario. First, they would muster all the reporters outside some hotel one morning. Then they would introduce Dougherty as if he were a total stranger—"You've seen him on TV, here he is in person!" Finally, they would give Dougherty a floor plan of the bus, show him where each person sat and how the reporters worked. Witcover and Oliphant decided to leave the execution of this plan to Jim Naughton, who was building a quiet but solid reputation as the most efficient prankster on the bus. Naughton never carried out the scheme, but he did author a memorandum to Dougherty, which was signed by all the regulars on the bus. The memo suggested, among other things, "that the presence of the press secretary on press buses and at access points would be of more benefit to us than the knowledge that he is supervising crowd control." The reporters didn't want a great writer for a press secretary; they wanted a Vic Gold, a fussbudget who always knew where to find the phones and the pool cars.

Later on the bus ride to Waterbury, Gordon Weil came aboard and tried to hold a briefing. Weil, the Senator's personal aide and the alleged author of the thousand-dollar-a-head welfare proposal, was an officious man with curly black hair, goggle-type glasses, and close to no sense of humor. Early in the fall, Weil had thrown a well-pubicized tantrum because he had been confined to the Washington headquarters when he wanted to be traveling with the Senator. After Weil calmed down, they let him come on the plane. The night Weil joined the campaign, Naughton organized a demonstration in his honor. When Weil got off the elevator in the Minneapolis hotel, he saw the whole press corps lined up in the corridor, waving hand-made posters with slogans like "Gordon Bugs Everybody" and "Where's My $1,000, Gordon?." They were also singing a song (lyrics by James Naughton) that went in part: "You were number one/ When this all began/ And now . . . you're . . . shit."

Now, on this sultry September evening, Weil decided to brief the press on an economic statement of McGovern's which had been handed out earlier in the day. In New York City, he boarded the first of the two press buses which were going to Waterbury and started to speak over the PA system. Stout, Greider and some other reporters were playing bridge on an upended garbage can in the aisle, and they found Weil's spiel pointless and annoying. So they stopped the bus and made Weil get off. The second bus picked him up. He stood in the dimly lit front section and asked: "Do you want a briefing?" One AP man put up his hand.

"What?" said Witcover.

"An economic briefing," Oliphant explained. "Shit, of course we want it, with all the fudge in that release."

"How does McGovern's plan differ from Nixon's Phase II, Gordon?" asked Norm Kempster of the UPI. "In a practical way, I mean."

"Real action," said Weil. "There would be real action."

Kempster gave a skeptical nod, Oliphant laughed, and Witcover said, "Right!"

Weil kept talking about the statement and said, "Food prices are not a dominant factor in inflation."

"Grind that up in your hamburger, Gordon," somebody yelled.

"Boy," said Oliphant, "I've heard bullshit before but this takes the cake. I can't believe Gordon checked this out with anybody in the campaign before giving this briefing. We deserve to have a press conference on this."

"I don't understand what he's proposing," said Kempster, "but it sounds the same as Nixon's plan to me."

And so the briefing broke down in confusion. This was not entirely typical of the briefings in the McGovern campaign; Dougherty and Mankiewicz often briefed the press with humor and smooth professionalism. But the point was that such a scene would never have taken place on a White House press bus. No one would have dared throw Ron Ziegler off a press bus or treat him with such patent contempt. The White House press operation was manipulative, frustrating, and sometimes downright evil; but it was always professional. From

Nixon on down, the people in the White House knew the art of feeding news to the press at a proper digestible rate, doling out just the right amount at the right time. The McGovern people never mastered this technique. McGovern's press secretary was never around. There never seemed to be enough filing time. Reporters who had to write in the afternoon kept getting assigned to afternoon pools.

Frank Mankiewicz constantly complained that the reporters never wrote about the issues. They wrote about staff problems and Democratic county chairmen who refused to support McGovern, he said, but never about McGovern's ideas on health care and pollution. Mankiewicz claimed to have answered 10,000 questions in the course of the campaign, only seven of them about a real issue. This was a valid point, but the reporters had a valid problem: they were swamped with prepared texts, *but McGovern did not deliver many of these speeches.* On a typical day, the press would receive a statement on anti-trust policy and another on veterans, both of them provocative treatises by McGovern's most eloquent speech writers. But then McGovern would scrap both statements in favor of a new blast at the Administration over the Watergate affair, and the reporters would have to devote all of their space to the Watergate speech. This frustrated the good reporters, but there was nothing they could do about it. The Nixon people would have carefully scheduled the statements so that each one received maximum coverage.

Dick Dougherty claimed that McGovern "conducted the most open campaign for President in history." Here a distinction must be made. It is one thing for a candidate to see the press frequently and answer their questions honestly, which McGovern tried to do, thereby providing an admirable contrast to the reclusive Nixon. However, it is another thing for a campaign staff to talk openly about its problems, feuds, and discontents. That is the political equivalent of indecent exposure, and the McGovern staffers indulged in it with a relish that bordered on wantonness. While the Nixon people, by keeping their mouths tightly shut, managed to keep the lid on the largest political scandal in American history, the McGovern people, by blabbing, succeeded in making their campaign look hopelessly disorganized and irresponsible.

One could not blame the reporters for writing that Lawrence O'Brien and Gordon Weil were threatening to quit—that was just the sort of Teddy White stuff that their editors were demanding. Nor could one blame them for finding George McGovern highly unprofessional; he could not even make his own advisers stop preening their wounded egos in public. And so a certain disrespect grew up among the press corps. They disdained McGovern not only because he seemed a likely loser—although that had something to do with their attitude—but also because he displayed a lack of professionalism. "From the beginning of the fall campaign, when we flew off from Washington on September 3," said Dick Stout, "nobody ever dealt with McGovern with much respect, as though he might be the next President. It wasn't that loose with Goldwater in the fall of 1964; he was a loser too, but they showed him more respect."

AND YET, FOR ALL THEIR IRREVERENCE, the campaign reporters on McGovern's plane remained curiously reluctant to write him off as a loser. Perhaps this attitude stemmed from a desire to be fair, to offset the pollsters and national editors who seemed so certain of McGovern's defeat, who seemed almost to be setting up a self-fulfilling prophecy. (Late in September, Greider returned to the *Post* for a day and told his editors he thought McGovern might have a chance. "They looked at me as if I had been smoking something," he said.) Then too, the reporters were as isolated as a bunch of submariners, trapped in the world of the press plane, seeing the enthusiastic crowds at the rallies and living with the intermittently manic McGovern staffers. This isolation nourished their atavistic urge to be with the winner, to write the upset story of the century. They kept talking of the election of 1948, of how the campaign reporters with Truman had been blind to the meaning of all those cheering crowds . . .

The first journalist to suggest in print that McGovern had a chance was Mary McGrory, the Washington *Star*'s liberal political columnist. Like several other reporters on the plane. Mary McGrory was a renegade from the conservatism of Boston's parochial schools. She had a plain Irish face, a regal manner, a mighty ego, and a taste for oversized earrings in the shape of coral clusters and alpha-helixes. She was fifty-five, but looked ten years younger. She had risen to prominence covering the ascension of John Kennedy, and had become his close friend in the process; indeed some of the amateur psychologists in the press corps claimed that she had fallen in love with Kennedy, and had transferred these feelings to every new hero of the Left since his death. Certainly she had written passionately about Eugene McCarthy in 1968, and now she was a deep believer in George McGovern. In California, just before one of the Humphrey-McGovern debates, I mentioned to her my feeling that McGovern might lose the primary. She gave me a scorching look. "Oh ye of little faith," she said.

At times, she could be more imperious than Joseph Alsop. On one of the last nights of the campaign, as everyone trooped off the planes onto the tarmac of the Little Rock airport, only Mary McGrory noticed the small crowd at the fence. "Frank, Frank," she shouted, running after Mankiewicz. "Make him go over there! Christ, it's one-to-one and it won't take a moment." So McGovern went to the fence and drank in the adoration of the blacks and college kids who had been waiting for hours to see him. She watched them reaching for his hands and glowed with happiness.

Besides being a believer, she was a first-rate reporter. Her columns were full of facts and incidents that appeared nowhere else, the fruits of her hard digging. She slaved over her prose, which was invariably bright and witty. The men on the plane, who were not necessarily friends of the feminist movement, automatically treated her as an equal. The last man to treat her as an inferior had been James Reston, who offered to give her a job in the Washington Bureau of the *Times* on the condition that she work part-time on the switchboard—her reply was probably still burning in his ears.

ON OCTOBER 22, McGRORY WROTE A COLUMN WHICH BEGAN: "Detroit—Here in Michigan, they have failed to get the word about the Nixon landslide. They're talking victory—not big, not easy—but victory for George McGovern." She had been impressed both by the United Auto Workers' drive for McGovern and by the high-powered McGovern canvassing operation. She knew the state coordinator, Carl Wagner, from the primaries, and Wagner had showed her the canvassing results for the Polish working-class town of Hamtramck:

McGovern—263
Nixon—68
Leaning to McGovern—85
Undecided—107

McGrory concluded that "something was happening in Michigan" and that if the same thing were happening in other industrial states "the mandate could be something less than the size of Mt. Rushmore in November." Privately, she went beyond this prediction; she was convinced that McGovern was going to win the election.

The day after the column appeared, Nixon made his short trip to Westchester, and I saw Mary McGrory on the White House Bus to Andrews Air Force Base. No sooner had she found a seat than she got into a long argument with Rebecca Bell of NBC, who was skeptical about the Michigan piece. "Carl Wagner is twenty-seven," I heard McGrory say. "He's too young to lie.

They've never lied to me before. Maybe they're starting now but I don't think so."

During the Westchester motorcade, McGrory sat in the back of the bus looking out the window and counting the pro-McGovern posters with mounting glee. When the bus passed five people holding up a long "Nixon in '72" sign in front of a car sales lot, she said, "Used car place, it figures." Seeing Nixon aide Bill Safire, she confidently asked him, "You don't get any bad vibes? Those registration figures don't worry you? We hear a lot of new voters have been signed up in Westchester County. We don't know whether they're ours or yours."

But in the next two weeks, McGrory began to worry about her Michigan column. "I've taken more grief for that article than for almost anything I've ever written," she said. Traveling briefly with Agnew in Michigan she met Senate Republican whip Bob Griffin who told her, "You're all wrong." She began to talk about it obsessively with her friends on the McGovern plane. During the last week, she phoned the *Star* from an airport pressroom in Corpus Christi, making monster faces throughout the conversation. "At the *Star*," she said when she hung up, "they called a Hamtramck source who told them I was completely wrong. And they told me so, they made it very clear how they felt. If McGovern loses, I'm moving to Ottawa. I mean, I really went out on a limb and it could be very bad."

THE SAME WEEK MARY MCGRORY VISITED DETROIT, Adam Clymer went to Freemont, Ohio, for a couple of days to sample popular opinion. He returned to the campaign plane with good news for McGovern. Knocking on doors, Clymer found sixteen people for Nixon and only two for McGovern. But polling on the street, where people were anonymous, he found sixteen for Nixon and twelve for McGovern. Clymer concluded that people were scared to tell pollsters that they intended to vote for an unpopular candidate, especially when they were at home, where they could be easily identified. This was the same theory that McGovern's own pollster, Pat Caddell, was pushing at the time, and not everybody bought it. "Hell," Dick Stout said later, "The Goldwater people tried that kind of reasoning in '64. But there was Clymer passing this off as great evidence that McGovern was really surging. He just *wanted* McGovern to win."

During the last week of October, Jim Naughton also began to feel optimistic for McGovern. Returning from a rally outside Detroit one night, he leaned across the aisle of the press bus and in confidential tones told Stout, "He's gonna win."

"Who's gonna win?" said Stout.

"McGovern."

"You got facts to back this up, you got any evidence?" demanded Stout. "Or are you just saying this from the elbows?"

"Oh, it's just from the elbows," Naughton said quickly.

"Well, you want to bet on it?" asked Stout.

"Well," said Naughton, "if you put it that way, no."

Naughton kept going hot and cold about McGovern. During the first week of October, he thought McGovern might win; during the second week, no; during the third week, it was barely possible. There were so many entrails to read—the crowd response, McGovern's mood, the polls, the testimony of the staff, and the reaction of Naughton's wife. Naughton considered his wife an accurate barometer of the mood of the Republic. At first, she had been ready to vote for Nixon, so angry was she at the dumping of Eagleton; then she was going to vote for no one; finally she had decided to vote for McGovern because of the Watergate scandal. So Naughton thought that the Watergate affair might be sinking in at last, and he also thought the fact that McGovern had received nearly a million dollars in contributions in one day signaled a turnabout in the campaign. He had, in fact, bet someone in the *Times'* Washington Bureau that McGovern would come within five points of Nixon. And Doug Kneeland placed a bet putting McGovern within two points of the President.

During the last weeks of the campaign, Naughton wanted to write a piece about the signs pointing to a possible McGovern victory, but he was loath to make any solid predictions. If McGovern lost, Naughton would look like a fool. His problem was finally solved when the *Times'* Anthony Lewis appeared on the campaign plane with the page proofs of a book by Arthur Tobier called *How McGovern Won the Presidency and Why the Polls Were Wrong.* That gave Naughton the hook he needed. He struggled over the piece for nearly six hours one night, searching for the right tone. In the end he settled on whimsy. "Walt Disney built an empire out of fantasy and in it, at a campaign rally in the Disneyland Hotel here yesterday, Senator George McGovern predicted that he would win the Presidency on Nov. 7," Naughton wrote in the *Times* of October 29. He went on to treat the book and other pieces of evidence in McGovern's behalf as freak exhibits which were nevertheless worthy of interest.

Adam Clymer never committed himself in print, either, and Mary McGrory survived the election without dire consequences to her career. But the fact that these people thought that McGovern had a chance to win showed the folly of trying to call an election from 30,000 feet in the air. "Those guys thought that at the very least it was going to be close," a seasoned national political reporter said later. "So they misread the whole fucking thing from beginning to end. The interesting thing is that Dick Cooper, at least, was hurt by it." Dick Cooper, one of the regulars on the McGovern plane, was a blond, taciturn, pipe-smoking reporter from the Los Angeles *Times'* Chicago Bureau.

"They put Cooper on the plane at the very beginning and left him there until the very end," the national political man continued. "And apparently Cooper said in staff conferences, 'This guy's doing all right, he's got a shot.' So after the election, Jules Witcover quits and they're looking for a national political reporter. So what do they do? They hire the Supreme Court reporter from *Newsweek* and claim that he's got a national reputation as a political reporter. Which is absurd. I mean, the guy is smart but he doesn't have any reputation for covering politics. And they bring Cooper to Washington, but they don't give him the national political job. They put out the word that Cooper showed some very bad judgment during the campaign. Well, I know what they're talking about. They're talking about Cooper saying that Mc-Govern had a shot. What the fuck! They put him in a steel capsule for three months and then bring him out and say, 'Whaddya think?' Of course he thinks Mc-Govern has a shot. It's just a lousy system, that's all."

CHAPTER XVII

The Last Days

THE REPORTERS attached to George McGovern had a very limited usefulness as political observers, by and large, for what they knew best was not the American electorate but the tiny community of the press plane, a totally abnormal world that combined the incestuousness of a New England hamlet with the giddiness of a mid-ocean gala and the physical rigors of the Long March.

There were two press planes, actually—the Dakota Queen II (named for the B–24 McGovern had piloted during World War II) and the Zoo Plane (etymology uncertain.)* Both were United Airlines 727's with all the "tourist" seats replaced by "first class" armchairs. The Dakota Queen II carried the Senator (who usually

---

* Since Presidential campaigns first took flight, the second (or third) plane has always been known as the Zoo Plane. Apparently, this name derives from the large numbers of TV technicians who ride the second plane and who are considered slightly less than human by the print journalists.

remained in his curtained-off working space at the front of the plane), the major staffers (who had an office complete with telephones, typewriters and mimeograph machines in the rear of the plane) and the journalistic heavies—the network correspondents, the man on duty for each of the wires, the reporters from the big dailies, newsmagazines and chains, and *both* of the *New York Times*men. Many days, they spent five or six hours in the air.

The atmosphere aboard the Dakota Queen II was informal but businesslike. The reporters with deadlines looming banged away at their portables; the others milled in the aisles, talking shop with each other and the staff, drinking, and sifting through the latest barrel of rumors. Every so often, McGovern wandered back to the press section, and the reporters piled up around him like ants on a crumb; small talk was made, pleasantries exchanged, nothing momentous emerged. After Mc-Govern left, the reporters who had been at the fringes of the group hopped from seat to seat, trying to piece together the conversation. Sometimes, on long, mellow night flights, some of the reporters sang hymns or danced to a tape recorder in the rear compartment, but usually the Dakota Queen II remained staid.

The Zoo Plane carried the lesser staffers, the backup men from the networks and wires, the reporters from small papers, the cameramen and technicians, the bulk of the Secret Service and the occasional *persona non grata* like Bob Novak or Joe Alsop.

("Put him on the Zoo," Mankiewicz snapped one night upon learning of Alsop's imminent arrival. "I don't want to see him on the Senator's plane, I don't want him anywhere near there."

"Why not?" asked Polly Hackett, the press aide.

"Because I'm liable to punch him in the nose, that's why," said Mankiewicz.)

A whole status system grew up around the two planes. The heavies—the men at the top of the pecking order—had permanent seats on the Dakota Queen II;

therefore, these seats became symbols of journalistic glory. To sit with *The New York Times* and the Washington *Post* meant that you had arrived. To be banished to the Zoo Plane meant social disgrace. Reporters *begged* Polly Hackett not to send them to the Zoo Plane. A man like Adam Clymer would rather have traveled by dogsled. But more and more heavies showed up as the campaign progressed, so a number of reporters were bumped from the Dakota Queen II. Some took it badly and worried so incessantly about missing something on the No. 1 plane that they were unable to concentrate on their work. What made this all the more absurd was the fact that the Zoo Plane was ten times as much fun as the Dakota Queen II; the difference between the Senator's plane and the Zoo was the difference between Lent and Mardi Gras.

The Zoo Plane had the look and air of the poorest but wildest frat house on a Southern campus. There were posters and campaign totems everywhere—a cardboard skeleton labeled "Ms. Boney Maroney," a dandruff ad onto which had been pasted a picture of George McGovern with confetti in his hair, a Roosevelt and Garner poster, Polaroid snapshots of all the regulars, orange and black streamers for Halloween and, taped to the sides of the overhead racks, keys from hotels in every other city in America. Seven hundred fourteen keys, all of which were mass mailed at the end of the trip.

The excitement of riding the Zoo Plane sprang from the fact that all rules had been totally suspended. As the plane took off on the first flight of the morning, half the reporters crowded into the galleys, mixing themselves Bloody Marys from the endless supplies of free booze. The cameramen were up front, letting loose spools of film, apples, oranges—anything that would careen wildly down the aisle of a plane that was climbing at 45 degrees. Meanwhile, as the FASTEN SEAT BELT signs still flashed their warning, other reporters worked their way up the aisle to fetch their own breakfasts and make more drinks. A Bach organ toccata swelled from the speakers in the front of the plane. The Rolling Stones blared from the rear. The stewardesses had long since given up trying to control the situation. They were just happy to be along for the ride. Three of them were McGovern supporters. The fourth, slightly more old-fashioned, had a thing for Secret Service men and entertained no less than eighteen of them before the campaign ended.

You could do anything you wanted on the Zoo Plane; it was like smashing china at Tivoli. The network technicians were the most uncontrollably manic people on the plane, and with good reason—they were making upwards of $1,500 a week. They had constant wars with aerosol cans that shot long, sticky filaments of plastic. And it was the TV technicians who held one of the crew one night while a drunken lady journalist stripped him down to his boxer shorts which were badly ripped in the rear. The rest of the crew locked the wretched man out of the cockpit until just before landing.

There were drugs on the plane, too, pot, hash, MDA, cocaine. And those who indulged in such stimulants swore that there was no greater thrill than standing in the cockpit as the plane came in for a landing, listening to the crackle of the radio, surrounded by green and orange dials, watching the bright blue lights of the runway rush up at the window as the powerful engines cut back. Then a United Airlines liaison man who called himself the Hippy Dippy Weatherman would launch into his jive weather report over the PA system: "Hey, baby, it's seventy-one degrees down here in L.A.—that's *sixty-nine* plus two!" Every night, the pilots played to an overflow crowd in the cockpit.

THE PLANE ALWAYS TAXIED to a carefully staked-out corner of the runway. After each flight, the campaign began anew. The arrivals were strangely like reunions. The Zoo Plane always landed first, and the TV crews stampeded for the taildoor, rushed out and set up their cameras. Then the Dakota Queen II landed, slowly rolled up beside the Zoo, and let down its rear door so that the reporters could disembark. There were greetings, new stories, fresh rumors, a curious delight at seeing these familiar faces in a new city.

Everyone would crowd around the front ramp of the plane in the drizzle, or sleet, or darkness, to await McGovern. Gordon Weil would rush down the ramp first, carrying the Senator's attaché case. After a pause, McGovern would appear at the top of the ramp with Eleanor, wave, make a statement and submit to questions while all the reporters held their Sonys above their heads to catch his words. Finally, Dougherty would cut off the questions: "That's it, that's enough. The Senator is late." Everyone would dash for the buses, which were waiting in a row. Then the motorcade would start off, with motorcycles roaring and police sirens screaming, and the buses would slice through the traffic of some great city; nobody would admit it, but it was more fun than riding a fire engine. There was all the noise, speed, pomp, and license that only a Presidential candidate could generate, and it was these things that gave the press the energy to survive the eighteen-hour days.

As the campaign unfolded, loose pairings emerged. Stout and Fischer. Naughton and Kneeland. Witcover and Mears. Adam Clymer and Bruce Morton, both Harvard men, both affecting disenchantment with the campaign. Morton claimed that he intended to vote for Benjamin Spock. At rallies, they stood together at the edge of the crowd taking shots at McGovern's performance. Frank Reynolds of ABC, on the other hand, found a friend in George McGovern, for they had similar problems with their teenage sons.

Other, romantic, pairings formed. These casual affairs produced at least three cases of the clap and one lawsuit—a stewardess, finding out on the last day of the campaign that her paramour was married, sued him for "illegal acts committed over the state of Iowa." The few serious affairs produced frustration. The men were invariably married,* if not to a woman then to the paper. There were inevitable arguments. *He* wanted them to go to *his* room, in case he got a call-back. *She* insisted on going to *her* room, in case *her* editor called. Eventually they would settle the quarrel, arrive at the room, and then he would suddenly remember he had to get the "overnight," the last handout of the day. He would run off to get it, find something he had to file, and return two hours later, barely able to keep his eyes open.

"My God," one of the veterans said of campaign romances, "all those tired men. It must be dreadful for the women."

THE CAMPAIGN LURCHED ALONG in ten-day cycles. Every week and a half, just as everyone on the plane was coming down with the flu and beginning to go crazy with boredom from listening to the standard speech, McGovern would return to Washington for a day. Most of the men would troop off to see their wives with mingled feelings of guilt, dread, and longing. "There's no way to win," said one of them. "Even if you're not screwing around, she thinks you're screwing around." At the very least, their wives were jealous of the freedom, the excitement, the sheer fun of the campaign. The men often felt badly about their neglected wives, or guilty because they had not thought to buy anything for the kids and so were forced to take them hotel soap for the third time; and the kids were growing disenchanted with Camay from the Sherman House. Some of the reporters were hopelessly torn between their professional duties and situations that cried out for them to be with their families; one man's wife had suffered a miscarriage, another's daughter was dying of an incurable disease, and a third had a mentally disturbed son. And the campaign served

* Which gave rise to the West-of-the-Potomac-Rule: "Nothing that happens West of the Potomac is ever talked about East of the Potomac." The penalty for violating this rule, I was repeatedly warned, is lynching.

as a kind of Foreign Legion for more than one man who wanted to escape from a shaky marriage or forget about a broken home.

Even the men with solid marriages suffered. Jim Doyle, for instance, believed that you couldn't survive the demands of the campaign if you didn't have a healthy family life to replenish your wasted spirits. One Saturday night, he tried to skip a rally in Spokane in order to get back to his family a few hours sooner. The *Star* told him he couldn't afford to miss the rally; something might happen to McGovern. He flew back with everyone else on the red-eye flight, getting home at 6 A.M. He woke his wife and they agreed that he would get up at 9 A.M. "But my daughters didn't wake me until ten," he said, "because I was out on my ass. Then they gave me a pitch about Was the job *that* important to me that I was never home? And I told them, 'Well, we have to eat, I have to make a living.' But they knew that was bullshit. And I realized that my wife had put the girls up to it as a joke, but I also knew that they were all really pissed at me and jealous of my time, and I didn't blame them for being pissed."

Doyle had breakfast with his wife and daughters, and they chatted and laughed all morning. Being a family of football fans, they watched the football game at one o'clock. At two o'clock, Doyle left to rejoin George McGovern, who was starting off on another ten-day swing.

IF YOU STAYED AWAY FROM THE CAMPAIGN for any period of time and then came on again, the first thing that struck you was the shocking physical deterioration of the press corps. During the summer, the reporters had looked fairly healthy. Now their skin was pasty and greenish, they had ugly dark pouches under their glazed eyes, and their bodies had become bloated with the regimen of nonstop drinking and five or six starchy airplane meals every day. Toward the end, they began to suffer from a fiendish combination of fatigue and anxiety. They had arrived at the last two weeks, when the public finally wanted to read about the campaign—front-page play every day!—and they were so tired that it nearly killed them to pound out a decent piece.

The reporters were trying desperately to write well, but it sometimes took them five minutes to think of the answer to a simple question. At filing time, everyone would suddenly become jittery and manic—smoking, crumpling papers, biting fingernails, shouting into phones, cruising on the last dregs of nervous energy— and then they would lapse back into catatonia. To do a decent job, they often had to stay up all night to finish a long piece, and there was no way to catch up on sleep. They were coming down to the wire—they had to save a few volts of energy to grind out long pre- and post-election articles. Yet all they could feel was numbness. McGovern, too, was pushing himself to the limits of his strength, pulling out all the stops on Vietnam and the Watergate affair, but through the haze of exhaustion all of his speeches sounded like one long echo of the same speech. The men had to force themselves to listen for new themes, new accusations.

During the last week, the press bus looked like a Black Maria sent out to round up winos; half the reporters were passed out with their mouths wide open and their notebooks fallen in their laps. When they were awake, they often wandered like zombies. On one of the last days of the campaign, Jules Witcover walked from the Biltmore Hotel to a rally in midtown Manhattan and had to be repeatedly stopped from sleepwalking into traffic against the red light. Bill Greider, perhaps the most exhausted man on the plane, had a strange habit of placing his arms by his sides, as if wearing an imaginary strait jacket, and walking around in circles. Toward the end, the only thing that stimulated Greider's adrenal glands was martial music, and he recorded the high school bands at every rally. Later, when he needed a shot of energy in the pressroom, he would turn up his

Sony all the way and bang away at his Olivetti as "Onward Christian Soldiers" or "Happy Days" blasted out of the speaker.

* * *

THE EXHAUSTON OF THE FINAL WEEK drew the press together in a strange, almost mystic bond. It was as if the massed weight of fatigue had dragged everyone down into the same dream, where all emotions were electric but somehow inappropriate, and nobody could quite remember why all these people were flying all over America. The scheduling grew increasingly surreal—nobody could explain the long trips to Waco or Corpus Christi or Little Rock, deep in the hostile South. Why not Guam? Toward the end, an eerie serenity descended on McGovern, and he began to act like a man who was not only about to be elected, but beatified as well. Had he actually deluded himself into thinking he would win, or had he merely made his peace with defeat? The reporters couldn't figure him out, but their natural cynicism gradually turned into a kind of sentimental admiration. They liked him, and as his defeat became more and more certain, they felt it was safe to show their affection. They also began to realize how much they liked the way of life, the womblike protection of the plane, and how sorry they would be to leave it. They were tired, cross, and so overworked that they could not stand another second of the campaign, and yet they wanted it to go on forever.

The last week formally began with the anniversary party which the press gave for the McGoverns late on Halloween night in a function room on the top floor of the Biltmore in New York. As usual, Dick Stout was emcee. The reporters seemed a very close crew that night, bound together by their appreciation of Stout's arcane jokes, most of which were based on incidents from the campaign. Like the reporters at the long-forgotten Muskie party, these people wanted badly to laugh; their laughter was shrill and almost hysterical, as if this were the last party before the end of some golden era.

Stout introduced Jim Naughton, Adam Clymer and David Murray of the Chicago *Sun-Times*. They huddled around the podium at the front of the room and read imaginary leads which they claimed had been set in type "for possible use next Tuesday night." All the leads dealt with a McGovern victory.

Joe Alsop: 'The end of Western civilization, as we know it . . . Now only Nguyen Van Thieu stands as the representative of the Free World."

Tom Wicker: "There is grey in Ted Kennedy's hair now, and the sap is freezing in the maples around Hyannis . . ."

William S. White: "Finally, the all-out support of Lyndon B. Johnson . . ."

R. W. Apple, Jr.: "As I predicted two years and three months ago . . ."

David Broder: "The clue to the McGovern victory lies in conversations one housewife had in O'Leary, Ohio . . ."

Evans and Novak: "Despite the revelations of Thomas Eagleton, the American people decided in a secret meeting on Tuesday . . ."

Finally, Pye Chamberlyne, the UPI radio man, presented the couple with a Tiffany silver bowl, for which everyone on the two planes had chipped in. It was inscribed with the words McGovern had called out to the crew of his shot-up bomber in World War II: "Resume your stations. We're bringing her home." As everyone was happily applauding and the Senator was offering good-humored thanks, Dick Dougherty looked at the bowl and growled: "Whaddya want him to do, bleed in it?"

Dougherty had sported a nice, mordant humor early in the campaign. Escorting McGovern out of a Safeway, he turned to the manager and said loudly, "If there's any breakage, just charge it to the networks." But by the last week, he and almost everybody else on the staff had grown tetchy as mad dogs. Their blowups were the talk of the press plane. Frank Mankiewicz and Gordon Weil dressed down John Dancy for broadcasting a report that McGovern had pulled as large a crowd in New York "as more traditional Democrats had in the past." Why was Dancy labeling McGovern an untraditional Democrat, they demanded in a paranoid frenzy. Was he out to get them? Then Pye Chamberlyne put out a story saying that McGovern probably could not capture the twelve states he needed to win the election. He had got his information from McGovern staffers. But Mankiewicz gave him a severe tongue-lashing, telling him that the piece was inaccurate and that there was no excuse for broadcasting a story that could ruin them five days before the election.

Then Stout's story hit the stands. Two weeks before the election, Stout had taken a day off, locked himself in a Milwaukee hotel room, and started preparing his final overview piece on the McGovern campaign. He lay in bed, surrounded by all his notebooks, all of McGovern's speeches, and the 350 pages of copy he had filed on McGovern since the California primary. As he sifted through the stacks of pages he had written, it struck him that "really, there wasn't very much there." There were passages from policy statements, descriptions of the candidate's activities, notations of changes in theme; but Stout felt that he had missed the real story, which had been the grass-roots organization of the campaign. He remembered that four years earlier, writing his book on Eugene McCarthy, he had found that only ten percent of his *Newsweek* files were useful. Nonetheless, he wrote all night and sent off his impressions of McGovern to Peter Goldman, *Newsweek*'s flashiest writer, who was responsible for putting the piece into its final form.

Stout's impressions were almost entirely negative, a fact which surprised almost everybody on the plane when the piece came out. Stout was always grumbling about McGovern, but everyone assumed that he was simply exercising his bizarre sense of humor. "My wife just sent another check to McGovern," Stout would say, "but she's not really a Communist. She's just one of these liberals who hasn't thought it all out." All the reporters made fun of McGovern, but most of them secretly wanted to see him beat Richard Nixon. But Stout did not think that McGovern would make a good President. He did not even like McGovern as a candidate. "McGovern had an attitude of righteous convenience that rubbed me the wrong way," Stout declared after the election. "He demanded higher moral standards for everybody but himself. He would always be 1,000 percent for everybody but then, in a different situation, he would backtrack. He just annoyed me."*

This attitude, embellished by Goldman's elegant prose, came through in the *Newsweek* wrap-up:

His eyes go flat and lifeless on television. His voice struggles for passion and sounds like grace at a Rotary lunch. His mandatory candidate's tan, in these last sunless hours before Election Day, is fading toward vellum. . . . He is, in a sense, the preacher's boy from Mitchell, S.D., come home in the end to the politics of rectitude. . . . But now, with his polls still stubbornly low and his own good-guy reputation tarnished by events, he has returned more and more to the old moral absolutes—and to the harshest rhetoric of any campaign in memory. What he offers is not so much a campaign as a calling—a vocation for virtue that he finds secure in himself and wanting in Richard Nixon. . . . But there are risks to the politics of rectitude. To charge that the war is racist or genocidal is to impute

---

* Stout also had a growing aversion to losers. "I can't *stand* losers any more!" he said after the election. "I've never covered a winner! Not one! I covered Percy when he ran for Governor and lost. I covered Goldwater, McCarthy, Muskie and then McGovern. I think there's absolutely nothing noble about losing! You find a good loser —he's still a loser."

In January, Stout volunteered to cover Agnew full time for *Newsweek*. "At the same time, I said, 'I don't want to cover any more losers.' And the editors said, 'Well, we're putting *you* on Agnew because we want him to lose.' "

guilt not only to the President but to the nation; to argue that the society is unjust is to demand further changes of a people grown weary of change. The failure of George McGovern's evangelism, if that is the final outcome next week, may not be that his manner is too cool but that what he is trying to tell America is too hot.

Although the piece came out on Halloween, nobody mentioned it until November 2. Then, just after the Dakota Queen II took off from Cincinnati for Battle Creek, Michigan, George McGovern walked back to where Stout was sitting, leaned over, and inquired good-humoredly whether Stout had been responsible for the piece or whether *Newsweek*'s editors had written most of it. Stout replied that most of the ideas had been his and that he had agreed with and okayed the final version. The smile vanished from McGovern's face. He nodded and began to walk away.

"Why did you ask, Senator?" said Stout.

"Well," said McGovern in his monotone, "I thought it was just a bunch of shit."

A few minutes later, Mankiewicz came down the aisle and said, "Dick, you'll be getting an awful lot of flack from the staff over that story in *Newsweek*."

"Why?" said Stout, affecting innocence.

Mankiewicz said that it was the worst piece of political journalism he had ever seen, that it was intended to hurt rather than inform.

"Would you please be specific," said Stout, getting angry. "What was intended to hurt?"

"The whole thing!" said Mankiewicz. He went on to say that *Newsweek* had knocked McGovern from the beginning. "Up in New Hampshire," he said, "they thought so little of us that they sent us that après-ski reporter, that second-string art critic, Liz Peer." Soon after Mankiewicz finished his attack, Dick Dougherty came by and added that the piece was "small-minded, mean-spirited and vindictive." Stout later observed, with some bitterness, that Dougherty, the self-appointed champion of personal, advocacy journalism, did not admire the technique when it was turned against McGovern.

When the plane landed George McGovern got off and told a heckler at the airport fence to kiss his ass. On the long bus ride from the airport to the TV taping at Jackson, Michigan, Stout sat next to Fred Dutton and told him about McGovern's bunch-of-shit remark. Dutton, once a key aide, had long since grown disenchanted with the campaign and was now on the plane only so the reporters could not write that he had abandoned ship.

"Oh, my God," groaned Dutton. "The man doesn't know what he's doing. You don't go tell a guy he's written shit. All you do is say, 'That's the way it goes,' and then you quietly freeze the fucker out."

That was the clean, professional, Zieglerian way to do it, and it was doubtless the most efficient method from the candidate's point of view. But there was something close and personal about the McGovern people's relationship with the press that didn't admit that kind of tactic. Mankiewicz and Dougherty were both former journalists, and they kept expecting their brothers to give McGovern the benefit of the doubt, even to help him. Like Richard Nixon, they assumed that the press had a liberal bias. They could never understand why a reporter would report McGovern's flaws, and thus give comfort to Nixon; after all, Nixon was the press's natural enemy. So Mankiewicz and Dougherty felt baffled and betrayed whenever a reporter slammed George McGovern, and they reacted from the gut. But their angry outbursts were never as effective as the icy, calculated disdain of the Nixon men. The reporters simply resented the McGovern staffers for blowing up, laughed at them behind their backs, and dismissed them as "unprofessional."

That night, at a hotel bar in Grand Rapids, Stout stayed up late drinking with Mankiewicz, Bill Greider, Hunter Thompson, the *Times* duo, and a couple of other reporters. That was standard procedure in the McGovern campaign. The staff and the press got along well most of the time; they ate and drank together.

Hunter Thompson, who had arrived late that night, suddenly brought up the *Newsweek* article. He said he found it shallow and malicious. Which set off Mankiewicz again. Stout protested that he thought the article had been fair. The other reporters at the table studiously ignored the argument. They liked Stout, but they didn't agree with his article. Finally Stout excused himself, looking hurt and dismayed. He did not appear on the plane the next day. When he returned, he explained that he had remained in Grand Rapids to finish an article. But he acted shy around the plane for the last few days of the campaign.

ON SUNDAY, NOVEMBER 5, Johnny Apple predicted on the front page of the *Times* that George McGovern was going to lose forty-eight states, with the outcome "in serious doubt" only in Massachusetts and Wisconsin. The next morning in a pressroom on the top floor of the Bellevue Stratford in Philadelphia, Jim Naughton passed around a floridly worded challenge; for five dollars a shot, the reporters were invited to bet Apple that McGovern would take more than two states. Everybody signed up. Stout later claimed that he had signed under duress. "Word would have gotten back to the staff if I hadn't signed, and all my entrée would have been shut off," he said. "When they passed me the sheet to sign, I had to ask somebody what state McGovern was supposed to win besides Massachusetts." Naughton telexed the wager to Apple, who replied that so many separate bets would complicate his bookkeeping. So Clymer and Naughton threw in fifty apiece and bet Apple an even hundred.

By that time, Naughton and Clymer had no hopes of a McGovern victory; they merely thought that McGovern might pick up more than two states. There was one among the press, however, who did not so easily give up hope. He represented a mass-circulation Fleet Street daily, for whose quality he made no great claims.

"It is considered a serious paper," he said, "by its readers. I choose my words carefully." A gregarious chap with a crazy, brown-toothed grin, he was known to take a drink; in fact, his full account of the campaign, had he written it, would have closely resembled *The Lost Weekend*. Somehow he never missed a bus or plane. At the last second some good Samaritan would always pull him away from the hotel bar, waving madly at some new-found American friend and shouting farewells: "Listen, it's been really great . . . Yes . . . yes . . . I've got your address . . . We *must* send Christmas cards."

As Naughton and Clymer were passing around their wager in Philadelphia, this refugee from Fleet Street was buttonholing reporters and telling them the good news. "Listen, we're all going to be writing the story of the century tomorrow night. Just remember there was one Englishman who said so. And buy me a drink when he wins." ,

From Philadelphia, the planes flew to Wichita, Kansas, for a brief and pathetically small airport rally that was broken off by a sudden, violent prairie squall. Then a long flight to Long Beach, California, for a larger, floodlit airport rally. At Long Beach, Candice Bergen, who was working for McGovern, walked into the makeshift pressroom where everybody was phoning in stories. She looked around and announced: "You all suck."

Finally the planes took off into the California night for the last flight of the campaign, the return to Sioux Falls. The mood aboard the Dakota Queen II was quiet and somber. The day had ravaged everyone's emotions. At a street corner rally in Philadelphia that morning, George McGovern had hoarsely spoken his favorite words from Isaiah: "They that wait upon the Lord shall renew their strength. They shall mount up with wings as eagles, they shall run and not be weary; they shall walk and not faint." A number of reporters had bitten their lips to keep from crying. For George McGovern grew stronger and calmer as his staffers grew more desolate, and the reporters could not help being awed by his incredible serenity.

In the last forty-eight hours of the campaign, many of the reporters worked on strange ghostly pieces describing McGovern's victory, to be set in type in advance so that the newspapers would not be completely unprepared if McGovern should do the impossible. Some of the reporters discovered their true feelings about McGovern in writing these pieces. Jim Doyle found that he had only dire predictions for a McGovern Presidency; the stock market, he wrote, would go down, the transition period would be the ugliest in American history, and McGovern would immediately face a pile of crises for which he was hopelessly unprepared. However, Doug Kneeland's "Man in the News" analysis was an admiring portrait which began:

Sioux Falls, S.D. Nov. 7—As it turned out, George Stanley McGovern, the preacher's son from Avon and Mitchell, really was "right from the start."

He kept saying he would win, serenely, earnestly, convincingly. And as the days in his plodding 22-month old campaign for the Presidency dwindled down to the final few, when his closest advisers showed by their eyes, if not by their words, that they thought all was lost, almost everyone on the McGovern trail believed that he believed.

Kneeland knew that this fairy tale would never run in the paper, so he allowed it to be passed around on the flight to Sioux Falls. It set off a massive flow of tears. The press aides cried, the baggage handlers sobbed, and the speech writers got lumps in their throats. From then on, the plane was like a flying cortege.

When the plane finally landed in Sioux Falls, at 1:30 in the morning, there was a high school band playing and a crowd that had waited since 9:30 to see Mc-Govern. He spoke briefly. More staffers broke down as they listened to him thank his fellow South Dakotans for their "love and devotion." It was 37 degrees. Greider stood shivering at the front of the crowd with a flimsy United Airlines blanket pulled around his shoulders for warmth. Other reporters came up to him, raised their hands, and said "How!" When the speech was over, Greider walked slowly to the bus and sat down in the front. Earlier in the evening, at Long Beach, he had been in a sarcastic mood. "McGovern said that voting was a sacrament," he had said. "You know what comes after the sacrament? The cross and nails, boy!" He had tried to write an article on the plane, but was too tired to finish it. Now he sat in the cold bus, grey with fatigue, his eyes watering.

"Anything exciting happen on the Zoo?" he asked after a long silence. "You get laid?"

"Nothing happened."

Greider was silent. He started fiddling with the buttons of his Sony, trying to find a certain passage on the tape. Finally he located it and pushed the play button. "The Battle Hymn of the Republic" came squawking out of the speaker as we had just heard it played by the Sioux Falls High School Band. Greider closed his eyes and soaked it in. When it was over, he flicked off the Sony and sat in silence for the rest of the ride, looking as if he had just lost his best friend.

THE NEXT MORNING, half of the press slept while the other half rose at 8:30 to take the hour-long bus ride to Mitchell, McGovern's hometown, and watch the Senator vote. After handing his ballot to a grey-haired lady in the basement of a parish hall, McGovern went to shake the hands of the citizens who had gathered along Mitchell's main street. Adam Clymer and several other reporters bought cowboy hats. Dean Fischer spotted

Gordon Weil and asked him, "What did McGovern have for breakfast?"

"Danish, milk," said Weil.

"Juice?"

"No, I didn't see any juice."

Not for nothing was Fischer a golden boy at *Time*.

AT LUNCH, Bill Greider, Doug Kneeland, and several other regulars agreed that McGovern could not lose by much more than ten points. By seven o'clock, they knew that they were wrong. The reporters got the news from the three televisions set up at the front of the pressroom in the Sioux Falls Holiday Inn. It was like every other pressroom of the campaign—long rectangular tables loaded down with office typewriters and telephones. The reporters walked around with hands in pockets, fetching beers from a large cooler, and helping themselves to coldcuts. Nobody could feel any emotion. Mary McGrory sat at a typewriter, calm, smiling, but still obsessed with her Hamtramck story; she kept asking whether anyone had heard the returns from Michigan.

The Englishman who had expected to write the story of the century stared into his beer bottle. "Don't talk to me," he said. "I don't want to think about it."

Everyone commented on the general numbness. "It's like a bad homecoming, where nothing happens," said Tom Oliphant. "You drink about eighty drinks and you can't get drunk and all you get is bad breath."

"It's like jumping into a cold pool of water so that your balls shrivel up," said Stout, who was wandering around in rumpled blue pants and a blue shirt. Later in the evening, he put it another way. "For two years," he said, "I circled the country looking for it. I looked for it in Hackensack, New Jersey, but did not find it there. I did not find it in Logan, West Virginia, nor even in Kennebunkport, Maine. But I finally found it in a little Holiday Inn in Sioux Falls, South Dakota."

"Found what?"

Stout cupped his hands and looked at them as if he were holding the object of his search.

"The perfect pile of shit," he said.

Greider was pacing the room, looking ineffably sad. He had stayed up all night finishing the piece he started in Long Beach. He had slept for most of the day. The rest had done him little good. He was neat on the surface, having shaved and combed his hair, but the dark rings remained under his eyes. He was talking, almost reminiscing, about how much he liked John Holum, one of McGovern's aides. "Holum was going to the Pentagon, you know, as a Deputy Secretary of Defense," he said. "Just think about it. The generals would come to the White House to see George, and George would say, 'That's all right, gentlemen, I'd like you to see Mr. Holum at the Pentagon.' And Holum would listen to the generals and nod in that quiet way of his and say, 'No.' And then he would write down a number on a piece of paper and say, 'That's what you get.'

"Now it's just sodden," said Greider. "Now nothing will happen in this country for another four years. And that's very bad."

Some of the reporters had started to file, but without much enthusiasm. There was little demand for news out of Sious Falls. Greider and I put on our coats and started to walk the four blocks to a dingy auditorium called the Coliseum to watch McGovern concede. As we walked past pizza parlors and third-class hotels, Greider mused about what would happen when he phoned the *Post.*

"I'll call the desk and say, 'Do you want anything on the speech?' and they'll say, 'No, we got it from the networks.'

"Then I'll say, 'Do you want to know how it feels?' And they'll say, 'Naw, that's all right.'

"And I'll say, 'Well, how about a piece on the disillusioned McGovern kids?' And they'll say, 'Naw, we don't need it.'"

I LOST GREIDER at the Coliseum but ran into him later back at the pressroom. He was shouting at the TV sets. Richard Nixon was on all three networks, addressing the nation from the Lincoln Sitting Room in the White House. "Peace with honor!" Greider yelled. "Right on, Abe! You tell 'em." There were whistles and catcalls from the other reporters.

Turning to me, Greider shook his head and said, "You remember what I said they'd say on the desk? Exactly what happened. Almost word for word. They said, 'Well, how are things going out there?' but you knew it was one of those questions where they didn't really mean it."

Adam Clymer was still showing off the cowboy hat he had bought that morning. "Big-time Washington correspondents need hats for their press cards!" he said for the fifteenth time.

Meanwhile, Jim Naughton was walking back from the Coliseum with Carol Friedenberg, the press aide. They spotted a despondent bunch of kids coming down the street, stopping every twenty feet or so to chant: "Awwwwwwwwww, *shit!*" Naughton and Friedenberg took up the chant themselves. They found it made them feel better.

NOBODY WANTED TO STAY in Sioux Falls any longer than necessary. The planes were ready to take off from the town's tiny airport by midmorning of November 8. The Dakota Queen II was full of men who were trying to figure out what had happened; they were going to have to write articles explaining how George McGovern had got buried by a landslide. All the reporters were trying to trace the roots of the disaster, testing theories on each other. It was the Eagleton thing. No, the trouble started back in California when Humphrey cut him up. Well, actually it was more that the press had started to examine him seriously just as he started to make terrible mistakes. They were all searching for a key incident that symbolized the whole campaign. One reporter would try out an incident on a colleague and then say, "That sums it up, doesn't it." The phrase spread through the plane like an epidemic of hiccups.

George McGovern and his wife came aboard at the last moment, entering through the tail section. The reporters stood up and gave him a warm ovation. McGovern slowly began to move up the aisle. He gave each reporter a smile and a good, firm handshake.

"Hello, Bill. Hello, Doug."

"Congratulations, Senator," said Kneeland. "You made a great speech last night."

Some of the reporters exchanged glances. They could not believe McGovern's composure, and they were deeply moved by his personal farewells. He let his distraction show only once, when he asked David Murray, "You flying with us all the way back to Washington?" Murray's only alternative would have been to bail out.

After takeoff, Frank Mankiewicz came back with the telegram that Richard Nixon had sent McGovern. The Nixongram was very short. "You and Mrs. McGovern have our very best wishes for a well deserved rest after what I know must have been a very strenuous and tiring campaign," it read.

Mankiewicz smiled and dragged on a Kool. "It's worded with the felicity that has characterized the Administration," he told a bunch of reporters who had gathered around him. "It's a perfect example of gracelessness without pressure. Nixon does better for a losing manager in a playoff."

The reporters and staffers had begun to mill around in the aisles. I was sitting next to Stout when a staffer wandered by and began to make a long, lachrymose farewell speech

"Don't do the funeral bit, Bill," Stout said gently. The staffer nodded, shook hands, and moved on to do the funeral bit elsewhere.

Then Doug Kneeland came by, and I immediately braced for an argument. For the last week and a half,

Kneeland had been needling me about an article I had written about the campaign press for *Rolling Stone*. The article was full of cheap shots, he said; it was a snide hatchet job which imputed all kinds of low motives to men who were actually decent, honest and hard working. I tried to argue with him, but he always brought up the same old litany of accusations, and one evening the debate had exploded into a shouting match in the middle of the press bus. After that, I carefully avoided Kneeland, which was not easy to do in a crowded campaign plane. Now here he was again, but mellowed, like everyone else on the plane, and seeking to instruct rather than provoke. Wearing a wilted turtleneck, his face sagging with fatigue, he looked as if he had spent a very bad night.

"You think these guys don't care," Kneeland started in. "You think they're here because of ambition or personal selfishness or something like that. What you don't see is that they want to change things. They're idealists, romantics."

"I'm not sure that's why I do this," said Stout, staring into the Bloody Mary he was nursing. "I just wanted to see life. This was the best way I could do it with my limitations."

Kneeland acknowledged Stout's dissenting voice and then began to fill in his portrait of the reporter as romantic. Reporters were the kind of guys who cried at movies, he said. He himself had shed tears over animal books as a child and had even wept at *Love Story*. The reporters might not give a damn about the Democratic Party, but they cared about the people on the campaign who had devoted themselves to McGovern, like Polly Hackett and Carol Friedenberg.

"I cried on Monday," Stout admitted. "Sitting in that goddam bus in Philadelphia, watching those girls go through their little duties even though they knew the thing was a disaster, knew it was falling apart. Well, I didn't exactly cry, but I did feel my eyes brimming."

"A lot of guys were torn up last night," said Kneeland. "Naughton was torn up. They'd all worked so goddam hard trying to be fair, doing a lot of things they didn't want to do. I had to write that 'Man in the News' piece in case McGovern won. You think I wanted to do that?

"Every two-bit columnist from every two-bit paper that was on this plane for two days took a cheap shot at McGovern," Kneeland continued. "They'd come on and write a funny story about how the campaign was fucked up. Well, I could have written funny stories, too. I got goddam sick of doing those little daily pieces. It's a helluva lot more fun to be amusing, but I didn't let myself do it and neither did most of the other guys.

"You see, we're idealists," Kneeland went on in his vinegar New England accent. "McGovern invited us to be harsh on McGovern so we were. He invited us to hold him up to his own standards, and we've held him up to them and then some."

What irked Kneeland more than anything was that no one had held Richard Nixon up to the same standards. Taking comfort from the belief that they were merely following the "rules of objectivity," the White House correspondents had failed to make Nixon account for the actions of his Administration. Meanwhile, the McGovern reporters had adhered to the same rules of objectivity out of a genuine conviction that they must remain "fair"; they had refused to use advocacy journalism in McGovern's behalf. "We played the game by street-fighting rules," said Kneeland. "You don't kick a guy in the nuts or stick your finger in his eye, even if it means you lose. And the White House people know you won't. They knew that we played by the rules and they took advantage of that. But what can we do? We can't help playing fair, that's just the way we are."

Kneeland would have gone on, but just then George McGovern's voice came on the PA system. McGovern said that he wanted to express his "very great affection and appreciation."

"There are moments we're never going to forget,"

McGovern continued, "and I promise never to say to anyone on this plane what I said to that friend along the fence in Battle Creek, Michigan. In fact, what we extend to all of you is the kiss of brotherhood, and goodbye until we meet again."

"Class," said Kneeland. "That is one of the classiest men I have ever known."

A FEW MINUTES LATER, the two planes taxied up to a huge, empty Coast Guard hangar in a disused corner of National Airport. The reporters spilled out of the planes and stood on the tarmac, their hair blown about by violent gusts of wind. Suddenly everybody realized that it was all over, and their emotions flooded out. They wept, embraced, exchanged manful handshakes, cried on each other's shoulders, or simply stood in a daze. It was like an orphanage being shut down. Then George McGovern appeared at the top of the ramp and drew them together for the last time. "I don't think I lost anything yesterday except some votes we would have liked to have had," McGovern said into the forest of Sonys and notebooks. "The cause is just as bright . . ."

Then the group broke up for the last time. The reporters stood in little groups around their luggage, looking shipwrecked, waiting to be picked up by their wives. The cause was not just as bright for them. The man who had brought them together, made them the most unlikely of friends, given them common gripes and jokes, given them, in fact, everything that they held in common, had just driven off into political oblivion in a black Cadillac. It would be a good while before any of them would again discover the same irresistible combination of camaraderie, hardship, and luxury. They now had to go back to paying the dues which would earn them another campaign in 1976.

Index

ABOUT THE AUTHOR

TIMOTHY CROUSE has worked for newspapers since
he was fourteen years of age. His former employers
included the Gloucester *Daily Times,* the Boston
Herald Traveler, Boston After Dark, and *Variety.*
He graduated from Harvard in 1968 and then served
in the Peace Corps, as an English teacher in Oujda,
Morocco. He is currently a contributing editor on
Rolling Stone, in which capacity he covered his
first Presidential campaign in 1972. He lives in
Cambridge, Massachusetts.

More **BALLANTINE** books
You will enjoy!

BESTSELLERS
from

BALLANTINE BOOKS

RABBIT BOSS, Thomas Sanchez	$1.95
THE SENSUOUS COUPLE, Robert Chartham	$1.50
WHAT TURNS WOMEN ON, Robert Chartham	$1.50
THE SECRET TEAM: THE CIA AND ITS ALLIES, L. Fletcher Prouty	$1.95
THE ANDERSON PAPERS, Jack Anderson	$1.75
SWEET STREET, Jack Olsen	$1.50
THE TEACHINGS OF DON JUAN, Carlos Castaneda	$1.25
ENEMY AT THE GATES, William Craig	$1.95
SUPER MARRIAGE-SUPER SEX, H. Freedman	$1.50
REVOLUTIONARY SUICIDE, Huey Newton	$1.95
LONG SUMMER DAY, R. F. Delderfield	$1.50
BACK TO THE TOP OF THE WORLD, Hans Ruesch	$1.50
THE IPCRESS FILE, Len Deighton	$1.50
CITY POLICE, Jonathan Rubinstein	$1.95
POST OF HONOR, R. F. Delderfield	$1.50
THE UFO EXPERIENCE, J. Allen Hynek	$1.50

At your local bookstore, or

To order by mail, send price of book(s) plus 25¢ per order for handling to Ballantine Cash Sales, P.O. Box 505, Westminster, Maryland 21157. Please allow three weeks for delivery.

10

3760